D1521218

Effective Negotiation

EFFECTIVE NEGOTIATION

A Guide to Dialogue Management and Control

BERNARD A. RAMUNDO

QUORUM BOOKS

New York · Westport, Connecticut · London

Library of Congress Cataloging-in-Publication Data

Ramundo, Bernard A.
    Effective negotiation : a guide to dialogue management and control
/ Bernard A. Ramundo.
        p. cm.
    Includes bibliographical references and index.
    ISBN 0–89930–727–2 (alk. paper)
    1. Negotiation. I. Title.
    BF637.N4R36   1992
    302.3—dc20   91–40961

British Library Cataloguing in Publication Data is available.

Library of Congress Catalog Card Number: 91–40961
ISBN: 0–89930–727–2

First published in 1992

Quorum Books, One Madison Avenue, New York NY 10010
An imprint of Greenwood Publishing Group, Inc.

Printed in the United States of America

The paper used in this book complies with the
Permanent Paper Standard issued by the National
Information Standards Organization (Z39.48–1984).

10 9 8 7 6 5 4 3 2 1

This Guide is dedicated to my wife, Oneida, to
whom "thinking negotiation" comes naturally and
whose wizardry with the word processor made this
an enjoyable team effort.

Contents

    PRINCIPLE   129

    General   129
    Lawyering   130
    A Management Tool   132
    Decision Making   134
    Interpersonal Relations   136

6   NEGOTIATING TACTICS AND PLOYS   143

    General   143
    The Tactics and Ploys   145
    THE CLOSER   187

    SELECTED BIBLIOGRAPHY   189

    INDEX   193

Preface

In a competitive world where accommodation has become the operational rule for the pursuit and defense of interest, effective negotiation through dialogue management and control provides the best means of goal realization for individuals, organizational entities, and nation-states. To best manage and control dialogues in competitive situations, a conceptualized, how-to-do-it approach to negotiation is far more effective than others encountered in the relatively limited literature on the subject. Some of the literature describes personal techniques utilized in specific negotiating situations; others, less memoir-oriented or autobiographical in approach, analyze so-called classic negotiations to develop "rules or lessons of negotiation"; still others do little more than catalog lists of "do's" and "don'ts" with gospel-like reverence. There have even been some facetious suggestions for an ethnic approach to negotiation: "Look Irish, Dress British, Think Yiddish, and Scheme Italian!" (The preferred position is based solely on the heritage of Machiavelli.) These efforts are of little assistance to the would-be negotiator who needs an operationally oriented conceptualization and approach. Esoteric formulations and system building are not needed to convey an understanding of the basic elements and dynamics of effective negotiation.

This book is an operational guide for the effective conduct of negotiations. It suggests a single approach to dialogue management and control in all negotiating situations based upon (1) understanding of the negotiation process, (2) coherent conceptualization of that process for operational effectiveness, (3) emphasis on the "think-negotiation" or effective negotiator's mindset to complement that effectiveness, and (4) identification of prior personal experience that can be made relevant to, and utilized in, dialogue management and control. The emphasis on understanding, conceptualization, and mindset is a necessary complement to know-how; without its appreciation, there is a tendency toward mechanical, unthinking application that is unsuitable for the mind game of negotiation. Together, mindset and know-how constitute the "dynamic duo" of effective negotiation.

The purpose of this Guide is to provide a practical and simple approach to the conduct of dialogues in all competitive situations, including those not clearly or generally recognized to involve negotiation. The goal is to substitute understanding, system, and method for by-rote applications, hunch, and chance in the pursuit of interest through effective negotiation.

The Opener

This Guide dares to suggest that basic concepts and techniques can be used to manage and control all interest-oriented dialogues, whatever their form or substance. The approach is quite simple: If a dialogue has an interest dimension, it can be managed and controlled by effective negotiation.

The universal approach suggested here should be contrasted with that of commentators who classify negotiations by the subject matter involved; for example, labor negotiations, real estate negotiations, and merger negotiations. Such classification ignores the reality that *negotiation is process,* something that is separable from its substantive product. Moreover, the attempt to be helpful usually focuses more on a checklist for the product (i.e., the subject matter that should be covered) and less on how to achieve a desired result. Furthermore, the classification approach needlessly burdens the effort to understand fundamental negotiation concepts and techniques with distractions related to the substance of the particular situations.

The validity of the foregoing is not affected by the existence of special procedural rules in law or market practice for the conduct of certain negotiations (e.g., bargaining statutes for labor negotiations and bargaining protocol and practices in real estate transactions). As we will see, such rules are best treated as situational elements to be handled in the context of a universal process system.

As part of its commitment to a universal approach, this Guide makes an operationally useful distinction. The universal system of negotiation recognizes three negotiating environments (private, intraorganizational, and international), the special features of which affect the application of the system's concepts and techniques. For example, although use of the ultimatum has across-the-board applicability as a basic technique, the extent or efficacy of its use varies with the negotiating environment. In private negotiations, use of the ultimatum is frequently encountered (e.g., labor threatens a strike on a specified date unless bargaining objectives are realized; or a claimant threatens to file suit on a specified date unless a claim is satisfied); however, in the intraorganizational environment, the need to conduct organizational business in accordance with prescribed staffing procedures and deadlines reduces the effectiveness or relevance of the ultimatum. In international negotiations, the ultimatum tends to be used much less frequently. This is due to the special concern for an on-going or continuing relationship and the possible cost (negotiating or political) of disrupting the relationship by an approach approximating diktat. Thus, the would-be negotiator must learn to distinguish between the negotiating environments so that "he" can more effectively exploit their possibilities and limitations in the context of a universal system of negotiation.

I wish to cut a threshold deal concerning usage in the text of forms of the pronoun "he," which has the potential to precipitate a gender crisis.[1] I propose that (1) whenever used it be understood to include the appropriate form of "she," and (2) no one be offended by this otherwise commendable effort to reduce repetition of gender-neutral formulations. With my sensitive soul now a matter of record, I hope that the quid of a more readable text will support my quo in the deal proposed. Those wavering in their readiness to cut this deal may be further reassured by the knowledge that I am a certified admirer of Margaret Thatcher and I am most pleased to accord space to her famous dictum concerning the dynamism of women: "In politics, if you want anything said, ask a man. If you want anything done, ask a woman."[2]

Another caveat is indicated at this point. The basic concepts and techniques provided by this Guide do not guarantee success in negotiation, which is a function of many tangible and intangible factors, both personal and situational, including luck. However, awareness and understanding of these concepts and techniques (i.e., the negotiation process) can provide an advantage in negotiation that frequently permits the initiated to advance (or at least protect) his interests and make his own luck.

NOTES

1. See Jesse Birnbaum, "Defining Womyn (and Others)," *Time,* June 24, 1991, p. 51, on gender neutrality in the new Random House dictionary.

2. *Parade Magazine, Washington Post,* October 14, 1990, p. 2.

Effective
Negotiation

1

Conceptualization and "Thinking Negotiation"

Negotiation involves the pursuit (including defense) of interest with the development of interest-oriented consensus as the objective of the negotiation process. Knowledge of negotiating tactics and techniques can effectively produce the desired consensus only through an understanding of the dynamics of the negotiation process, which essentially involves crafted dialogue management and control. This understanding can best be achieved through a *conceptualization of the process,* which, in providing an operational rather than a mechanical approach, facilitates the crafting of the dialogue. In addition, understanding is enhanced when the process is broken down into negotiating environments and component phases, thereby providing vantage points from which to plan the overall negotiation strategy. The strategic perspective of a conceptualized approach assures effective utilization of tactics and ploys through their integration into the larger negotiation effort. In short, conceptualization in the sense of how-to-think-about the process is essential to effective negotiation.

The conceptualization that follows is only a suggestion; others can be equally productive. Its essential features are (1) emphasis on operational strategy as it relates to the process, and (2) reduced reliance on the mechanical application of rules, principles, techniques, suggestions, and approaches.

The understanding of process provided by conceptualization is well complemented by the "think-negotiation" mindset, which involves a special kind of sensitivity and alertness to *interest and advantage.* The mindset, reflected in a variety of well-known expressions such as "savvy," "moxie," "smarts," and "sharpness," includes (1) the *capability* to recognize interest implications and exploitable advantage in dialogues, and (2) the *discipline* to focus on them throughout the negotiation process. Initially it regards every dialogue as a potential negotiating opportunity and thereafter seeks to uncover and exploit the available advantage. The interest-oriented focus on advantage suggests distinctions between "doing well" and "doing good" and "buying right" and "buying wrong." It produces preoccupations in every situation that are reflected in questions such as "Who is being advantaged or disadvantaged? Where is the exposure? Where is the edge? What is exploitable? Where are the vulnerabilities? Which party has the burden of negotiation? How can we manage and control the dialogue to get our way? What pressures can be brought to bear?"

Lenin frequently invoked the tantalizingly adversarial questions, "Kto-Kovo?" (Who, to Whom?), in most of the difficult situations that confronted him.[1] The Amos and Andy comedy series of decades past suggested a less ominous, colloquial version: the "doer" and the "doee." One can, of course, become even more colloquial with less elegant variations of the "-er" and "-ee" theme. The point is that common to all such formulations is a sensitivity concerning where the advantage or edge lies, or who is being advantaged or disadvantaged, in a situation involving the clash or competition of interests. This concern, or "healthy suspicion," is the heart of "thinking negotiation"; it will reduce the incidence of unwittingly failing in negotiation and in other interest-oriented dialogues (such as those involved in management, decision making, and interpersonal relationships). Subsequent sections will discuss this broader applicability of negotiation concepts and techniques in the context of the universality principle, which focuses on the negotiation potential of every situation.

As an example of the application of the "think-negotiation" mindset, consider a situation where it has been proposed that the so-called Golden Rule (not further defined) be the guiding principle governing a particular relationship. Despite the general understanding that the Rule's intent is to stimulate reciprocal good behavior (i.e., "Do unto others as you would have them do unto you"), the effective negotiator should be wary that he may be accepting a loaded formulation. For example, the Rule could be interpreted to justify retaliation in the sense of "do unto others as they do unto you," thereby creating a more threatening principle for the relationship. Another possible interpretation, quite facetious but with an ominous power orientation, is that "those who have the gold, rule." The point is that the effective negotiator,[2] always "thinking negotiation," does not take anything for granted. Where there is any possibility of ambiguity that can work against his interest, he seeks clarification and certainty to set limits to his exposure. In evaluating exposure he leans toward the worst-case scenario in a situation viewed as essentially adversarial.

In this example, the effective negotiator should seek agreement on either the definition of the Golden Rule or its replacement by a substantive equivalent. In pressing for resolution of any ambiguity, the negotiator is motivated more by the veto control inherent in any "agreement" approach than by any sense of fairness to the sides in clarifying the situation. His presentation, however, would probably rely on the fairness rationale to enhance the acceptability of his proposal. His effectiveness as a negotiator is in being first and foremost interest-and-advantage-motivated in recognizing dialogue exposure and the steps required to limit it.

As it relates specifically to the negotiation process, "thinking negotiation" can be best understood in the context of the overall process, the nature of the process, and considerations involved in the conduct of the process. First, "thinking negotiation" essentially views the overall negotiation process as involving pursuit of interest through dialogue management and control in settings that rarely admit of zero-sum results. Usually the competing interests of the sides are reflected to some degree in the negotiated result. The attainable objective, therefore, is not a wipeout of the other side but the development of favorable, interest-oriented accommodation. This can best be achieved through an operational analysis of the negotiating situation and the development and implementation of a negotiating game plan (i.e., a strategy or blueprint for developing acceptable consensus). Approaches with only a tactical orientation are not effective because they tend to focus on parts of the process rather than the coherence of the overall negotiating effort.

The omnipresence of interest and the desire to have one's way tend to expand the universe of negotiation, which is even used to resolve many situations encountered daily and not considered to be formal negotiations.[3] Most interest situations have a dialogue dimension or aspect that lends itself to management or control by negotiation. To reap the benefit of negotiation, one must consider that "everything is negotiation" and "negotiation is everywhere." This approach is at the heart of "thinking negotiation"; it reflects the interest- and advantage-oriented view of every possible dialogue.

In focusing on interest and advantage, the effective negotiator attempts to influence the decisional level of the other side in order to reach a favorable conclusion. He does not limit his efforts to the formal dialogue with fully empowered representatives; rather, he utilizes every opportunity and medium to convey his message to the other side. He views the opportunities to do so, whether at or away from the negotiating table, as negotiation. In effect, his approach is more global than that of the conventional wisdom "to negotiate only with those who have authority to represent the other side." For the effective negotiator, any act or communication designed to influence the other side, whether through formal discussions or otherwise, is negotiation. In the interest of attracting academic gloss to this Guide, I will refer to the broader approach as the *globality* principle.

Furthermore, as the negotiation process involves sides pursuing their respective and usually competing interests, the interface can be expected to be adversarial in nature, although not usually in form or tone. Negoti-

ators generally strive to develop an exploitably friendly or pleasant negotiating relationship in deference to the "getting more with honey than vin-
egar" school of human relations. Experience has demonstrated that
handshakes, bear hugs, slaps on the back, and other forms of pressing the
flesh are effective "reduce-hostility" maneuvers in developing the desired
relationship. Despite outward appearances, however, the effective negotiator actually keeps the other side at arm's length and screens its actions
against the cold calculus of interest.[4]

The interest orientation of the overall negotiation process is not limited
to the divergent interests of contending sides. Intraside interests also affect the solidarity of each side's negotiating play. Clearly, this is the case
where there are multiple principals whose commitment to the posited goals
or objectives of the side may vary in accordance with differing personal
interests and needs. For example, quick settlement at a lower figure may
be more attractive to a principal who has greater immediate need for his
share of the sum proposed. This difference in interest can be identified
through probing and other discovery methods and may be exploited by
using a divide-and-conquer approach. Less obvious is the divergence of
interest inherent in the very relationship between the principal and his
agent, the negotiator. The negotiator cannot avoid being influenced by his
career stake in the outcome of the negotiation. His interest in success is
paramount. It may influence how he handles his principal's business; it
may create tension born of his desire to be the dominant force in position
formulation. Of course, this represents a sharp departure from his theoretical role as agent bound by his principal's instructions.[5] The potential
divergence in interest between the negotiator and principal borders on a
conflict of interest; it may affect the quality of representation and may be
exploitable by the other side.

The essence of "thinking negotiation" as it relates to the nature of the
process is dialogue management and control through friendly and pressured persuasion directed at inducing or inhibiting action as desired by the
persuading side. Where interest clash and competition are keen, persuasion is usually pressured by creating or molding the other side's perception of the desirability of the action proposed and by making that side
believe that its interest balance favors that action. Operational tools for
this are the orchestration, manipulation, and exploitation of actual or perceived vulnerabilities and advantages as part of the pressuring, leveraging
effort. The objective is to create apprehension and uncertainty and to control expectations as the other side is moved toward the desired result.[6] To
do this effectively, the negotiator must develop a game plan to ensure that
leverage is exerted and persuasion promoted in a cost-effective, productive manner. It is also necessary to continually probe the other side's interests and vulnerabilities and to cross-check its negotiating moves for
consistency and compatibility with the identified interest and vulnerability/

advantage pattern. The negotiator must also keep ahead of the dialogue as a means of better controlling it and building momentum in the persuading and pressuring effort. Keeping ahead may require having a bargaining chip for an "encore" should something extra be necessary to close the deal (i.e., conclude the negotiation). Closing should be viewed as an important, integral step in concluding the negotiation dialogue; provision for effecting it should be included in the negotiating game plan.

In "thinking negotiation" as it relates to the conduct of the negotiation process, the effective negotiator is sensitive to the importance of the "burden of negotiation" and how it can adversely affect the negotiating position and style of the burdened side. The side made to feel that it has the burden (i.e., that it needs the negotiated result more) will tend to be inhibited from taking substantive or procedural chances (e.g., making a very high demand or suspending the dialogue) because of the perceived threat to dialogue continuation. Thus, the effective negotiator actively works to keep the other side pressured by the burden of negotiation through appropriate perception creation and manipulation.[7] Perception concerning the location of the burden is more operationally relevant than an objective determination based upon considerations of negotiating strength or position.

Other process-related considerations of "thinking negotiation" are keyed to alertness to, and exploitation of, tacit communication and nuance; agenda-related plays; personal and positional vulnerabilities and exposure; commitment avoidance and, if unavoidable, reduction; presentational techniques; personal and positional consistency and credibility; role playing; tactics and ploys; personal rapport and the tone of the dialogue; the drafter's advantage; momentum and breakthroughs; and audience play. Moreover, the effective negotiator is preoccupied with the avoidance and reduction of negotiating or bargaining costs, substantive as well as procedural (the former produce position slippage; the latter, deterioration in the negotiating relationship). Also involved are concern for the reasonableness and viability of positions; the continuing relationship (both during and after the dialogue) of the sides and nonparties collaterally affected by the dialogue or its results, including audiences; the ethical issue in determining how far to go in pursuing interest; and the exploitation of process to pressure persuasion. Also high on the list of concerns is how best to achieve cost-effective bargaining results. For this purpose, bargaining chips should be viewed from the thrift-oriented perspective of the harried shopper who has limited resources to cover the "purchases" that have to be made.

After general consensus has been achieved, "thinking negotiation" is concerned with closing (including obtaining the last formal approval on the other—and sometimes one's own—side; that is, being able to "deliver" one's principal) and, thereafter, working out the most favorable final text possible. As drafting is a continuation of negotiation and not merely a recordation of consensus, he who wields the pen is in an advantageous position to develop a favorable text. The effective negotiator is always ready to undertake the "burden" of drafting: "It's a dirty job, but I'll do it!"

Once the chip play and drafting are over and the negotiation is completed, the postnegotiation behavior of the sides must be monitored to assure smooth implementation and the development of favorable practice. In short, the negotiation continues with emphasis on the continuing pursuit of interest in either preserving the agreed result or attempting to modify it by favorable practice.

All of these concerns identified with "thinking negotiation" will be elaborated further in the pages that follow. The intent here is only to suggest the all-encompassing nature of the effective negotiator's preoccupation with advantage as part of the "think-negotiation" mindset. Understanding the full breadth of the concerns involved in "thinking negotiation," in effect the mirror of the demands of effective negotiation, highlights the importance of the mindset element in the negotiation process.[8]

"Thinking negotiation" keeps the focus on interest and advantage, the twin towers of direction in conducting the dialogue. It suggests the desirability of a negotiating game plan to control the interfaces of negotiation, external (side-to-side) as well as internal (intraside). The game plan's strategic approach (rather than tactical or ad hoc) facilitates full exploitation of situational opportunities throughout the negotiation.

Drawing upon the foregoing, the special focus of this Guide can be formulated as an equation: $CN + TN + EX = EN$. The end product, the effective negotiator (EN), possesses a conceptualized approach to negotiation (CN), the "think-negotiation" mindset (TN), and negotiating experience (EX).[9] The Guide conceptualizes the negotiation process, exhorts the effective negotiator's mindset, and provides vicarious experience through examples and extensive coverage of presentational considerations and techniques and basic tactics and ploys. The conceptualization also points up the relevance of prior experience, which, although not gained in negotiating situations, can be useful in conducting negotiations.[10]

NOTES

1. For the most part, Lenin's adversarial outlook continues to shape the thinking of Soviet negotiators. This reflects more the result of exposure to the conflict or contradiction orientation of the Hegelian dialectic than any conscious emulation of Lenin's negotiating or decisional style.

2. "Effective negotiator" is used throughout the Guide to refer to the paragon of negotiating virtue and skill, the Guide's role model. Had the deal concerning gender usage not been struck, the consequences of not using a single, gender-neutral formulation would have been considerable. For example, it would have been necessary to choose among a variety of possibilities: "effective negotiator"

and "effective negotiatrix," "effective negotiaperson," or "effective negotiating person," all of which strike the ear harshly, increase the cost of publication without substantive benefit, or represent misspent creativity. The suffix on "negotiatrix" has negative phonetic implications from the negotiation point of view. Thank you, dear reader, for going along with the deal as proposed.

3. I have been quoted as follows: "The real world is a giant negotiating table and, like it or not, you are a negotiator." "Negotiating on the Job," *Association Management,* June 1981, pp. 55–58, at p. 55. "Whether you're asking for a raise, buying a car or deciding where to go for dinner, you're always negotiating." Morton Hunt, "How To Come Out Ahead," *Parade Magazine, Washington Post,* September 4, 1988, pp. 12–14, at p. 12.

4. No distinction is made between friend and foe. Despite the surface cordiality and warmth of the relationship with friends or allies (long-standing as well as recent), they are best dealt with at the same arm's length as recognized competitors and adversaries. The atmosphere may be different, but the basic technique is not. Negotiators are neither paranoid nor cynical; they are merely sensitive to the folly of giving without getting for whatever reason, including friendship, real or contrived.

5. The concern for career advancement colors the effective negotiator's priorities. He frequently finds himself in dialogue with his principal to "keep him under control" and otherwise influence the instructions under which he must work. The effective negotiator seeks career advancement through success, which he equates to either (1) getting what his principal actually desires or is *influenced to desire,* or (2) demonstrating a tremendous effort to pursue the principal's interests in a situation perceived to be nearly hopeless. The perception-creation activities of the effective negotiator vis-à-vis his principal's expectations about the negotiation represent his involvement in *internal control maintenance.* A parallel *external control* activity relates to influencing the expectations of the other side. Together, they represent the negotiator's involvement in overall dialogue control maintenance.

6. The mechanics of the process apply also to intraside dialogues between and among principals and between negotiators and principals.

7. Stalin understood well the importance of perception creation and manipulation in his negotiations with the West during the post–World War II, Cold War period. When asked to explain his success in those negotiations, he is reported to have explained that "Our strength lies in the fact that they fear war more than we."

8. The effective negotiator's view of the world is shaped by this mindset because it has become second nature to him. The beginner would do well to consciously adopt this outlook. With it, he may be able to hold his own while perfecting the effective negotiating skills that only experience can bring.

9. The equation underscores (1) the importance of the nexus between experience and the conceptualized "think-negotiation" approach, and (2) the related distinction between experience and effectiveness: While experience is necessary for effectiveness, experience alone does not guarantee effectiveness.

10. Hereafter, the prior experience made relevant to negotiation through better understanding of process will be referred to as derivative experience.

2

The Negotiation Process

GENERAL

The negotiation process involves the pursuit of interest through dialogue management and control in situations that are clearly or implicitly competitive or adversarial. The pursuit of interest to favorable consensus requires persuading the other side to grant enough of what is sought. Generally, persuasion can be friendly or pressured. Friendly persuasion usually takes the form of generating rapport and exploiting or nurturing other relationships to get the other side to go along with a proposed consensus. A common example is "Do it for old times' sake" or "for friendship's sake."

Pressured persuasion, on the other hand, essentially involves the creation and manipulation of perceptions, uncertainty, expectations, and apprehension about the negotiating situation that inhibit or induce the action desired by the pressuring side. The cost-benefit analysis of the side being persuaded must be made to indicate that its best interests or needs are served (i.e., it has something to gain or less to lose) by accepting the proposed consensus. In pressuring consensus, the effective negotiator seeks to exploit the *objective truth* or reality of the situation but is prepared to be creative and develop *subjective truth* (i.e., perceptions of reality) to influence or affect the decisional equation of the other side. This is the essence of the negotiation mind game. When both sides are involved in pressuring tactics the mind game becomes more confrontational, at times escalating to open psychological warfare. The confrontation between President Bush and President Saddam Hussein in the Persian Gulf crisis of 1990 is a prime example of the mind game in this form.[1]

THE NEGOTIATION MIND GAME

The effective negotiating skills required for successful pursuit of interest can be enhanced by an approach that recognizes that the negotiation process is a mind game in both conceptualization and application. This approach is the complete handle on process because it provides guidance concerning *how to think about negotiation dialogues* and *how to control and manage them.*

The mind-game approach is the edge enjoyed by the effective negotiator. The essence of the approach is reflected in the "think-negotiation" mindset. The importance of mindset is that it orients the negotiator to be alert to the presence of competing interests, the essential condition of a negotiating situation. Thereafter, the mindset provides guidance for managing and controlling the related dialogue through friendly and pressured persuasion. Understanding the importance of mindset is the core objective of this Guide.

The mind-game approach is reciprocal in that it focuses on the subjective nature of the process and the decision making involved in both sides' conduct of the dialogue. The side armed with the mind-game focus can augment the traditional tools of negotiation with others that are geared to this subjective reality. The mind-game approach is effective because subjective perceptions about the negotiating situation are just as important as its objective reality. The approach facilitates persuasion by penetrating the decisional process of the other side as it balances cost benefits and trade-offs in planning and conducting the dialogue. The effort is to induce desired (and inhibit undesired) action by stressing the favorable elements of the decisions that must be made. Action does not result from arm twisting but from a favorably colored perception of the decisional choices.

The mind-game approach operates throughout the dialogue; it facilitates dialogue management and control through to consensus. For example, the question of which side has the burden of negotiation, a serious disability in conducting the dialogue, can be resolved favorably by causing the other side to believe that it has the burden. The same can be done with perceptions concerning the tone of the dialogue and the relationship between the sides to mask its basic adversarial nature. The approach can also be utilized to exploit personal and positional credibility, to achieve success with tactics and ploys, to create apprehension and uncertainty, to control expectations, to facilitate role playing, and to enhance the effectiveness of presentational techniques.

The development of favorable consensus is effected through the real or apparent adjustment or accommodation of differences. The effective negotiator projects his readiness to adjust differences either by making real, bargaining-effective concessions or by creating the impression that he is making concessions. The former usually reflects the successful realization of a key element in concession making (i.e., not to give without getting); the latter is a "smoke and mirror" exercise in illusory concession making using a variety of techniques that will be described shortly. Of course, where the objective reality of the situation is favorable, there is no need to risk going the perception-creation route. It is a comfort, however, to know that there is a back-up system should the negotiating situation not be favorable.

Some traditionalists may seek to defend less creative, mechanical approaches to the negotiation process by charging that the mind-game approach involves slipping into the realm of the "con." This stretches things a bit, as conning is usually defined to involve the commission of a crime by first winning the confidence of the victim. What I am suggesting here is the use of positive perceptions concerning interest to *sell* consensus. I am speaking about creative advocacy, not the sharp-and-unethical-practice implications of conning. In the memorable words of Patrick Henry, "If this be . . . [conning], make the most of it."[2]

AN OPERATIONAL DEFINITION

Before expanding the general definition of negotiation to emphasize the operational aspects of effective negotiation, let me add a few words concerning ambiguous or nonformal negotiating situations. Under the principle of universality, every dialogue involving competitive interests presents negotiating considerations and possibilities. In many bilateral and multilateral situations, one or more of the sides does not realize that interests are engaged and, therefore, are at risk. The side that is aware of this can take action to pursue its interests through negotiation.

The "think-negotiation" mindset of the effective negotiator sharpens his perception of dialogue and interest clash and, accordingly, his sensitivity to the need to treat the ambiguous situation as negotiation. In fact, the universality principle pushes him to view all situations and developments through the prism of interest-oriented dialogue and the applicability of negotiating concepts and techniques. The wariness of the effective negotiator recalls the behavior attributed to the wily Talleyrand, who, upon learning that the Russian ambassador had committed suicide, is reported to have mused, "I wonder what he is up to?"

As already noted, defining negotiation in terms of the pursuit of interest only partially states the nature of the process. The following complete definition includes all the operational elements: "Negotiation is the process of orchestrating the exploitation and manipulation of situational opportunities with the persuasiveness of presentational skills and personal characteristics to attain desired objectives in a dialogue. The process essentially involves dialogue management and control through the orchestration, exploitation, and manipulation of perceptions, uncertainty, expectations, and apprehension concerning the situation in the direction of a desired consensus." This definition meaningfully isolates the key elements, as well as the general techniques involved, in effective negotiation. Understanding the negotiation process and its mind-game elements constitutes a giant first step toward becoming an effective negotiator.

The key elements are dialogue and interest recognition, analysis of situational opportunities, presentational skills, personal characteristics, desired objectives, and the perception-related troika of uncertainty, expectations, and apprehension. The operational techniques are orchestration, exploitation, and manipulation. While not all of the key elements may be present or operational techniques usable in a particular negotiating situation (e.g., there may not be a situational opportunity that can be exploited by either side), checking for their possible applicability, both offensively and defensively, is an essential element in the "think negotiation" analysis and approach.

Dialogue and interest recognition are key to full realization of the interest-serving potential of negotiation concepts and techniques. Sensitivity to dialogue permits focus on the extent of interest engagement and, based thereon, the management or control measures to be undertaken in pursuit of that interest. In some situations the level of interest involvement may indicate only a passive, monitoring effort. In others deemed to be of greater interest importance, management through monitoring may have to give way to direct, active negotiation. For example, in a multilateral dialogue of low interest concern, one may only have to monitor the course of the dialogue. Even where the interest level is higher, there may be no need to play a more direct negotiating role if the dialogue is moving favorably or is being guided by another participant who shares a common interest. If this is possible, one can be advantaged[3] by maintaining a low profile while enjoying the benefits of favorable dialogue. Where important interests are engaged and there are no alternatives to active involvement, the choice is clear: The dialogue must be directly managed and controlled. In any case, the "think-negotiation" mindset provides early warning signals concerning dialogue importance and the extent of need to become more actively involved.

Situational opportunities are conditions or circumstances concerning the merits of, or participants in, the situation that can provide special advantage, or *leverage*. I say "can" because leverage is not self-implementing or self-executing; one must consciously make it a part of the negotiating effort through a two-step approach. Operationally speaking, leverage requires (1) recognition of the potential for exploitable advantage in a situation, and (2) the decision and implementing effort (the negotiating game plan) to exploit the advantage. In focusing on leverage, "thinking negotiation" identifies the advantage that is potentially available and the best way to realize the advantage potential.

Leverage can be best understood in terms of exploitable *substantive* or *procedural* advantage. Exploitable situational opportunities are not limited to substance (i.e., the merits of the case or the factual situation). Of course, the side with the stronger case is in a better bargaining situation because of the substantive advantage it enjoys. Furthermore, other aspects of the factual situation may provide substantive advantage. For example, the financial straits of a party (or his negotiator, if a fee is involved) may present the possibility of settlement at a lower figure than the merits warrant. Leverage can also be based upon the procedural aspects of the negotiating situation, including developments in the conduct of the negotiation. For example, a disparity in the skill level of the negotiating representation of the sides may provide procedural advantage or leverage. Similarly, a procedural or tactical slip by one side may present the other with an exploitable opportunity for a more favorable result. Limited focus on the merits would not suggest the possibility of more advantageous results based upon procedural advantage. The broader focus comes from the effective negotiator's continuing search for exploitable advantage through "thinking negotiation."

Generally, it may be said that special advantage or leverage potential exists when the real or perceived cost (monetary, political, or other) of disagreeing is or can be made to appear higher than the cost of agreeing. The party feeling the disproportionate cost trade-off tends to be more easily pressured into favorable consensus. Cost perception, like beauty, is in the eyes of the beholder. This can be demonstrated in the collective bargaining situation; here, labor's power to strike is arrayed against management's power to close down operations, relocate activities, or lock out the workers. The result will turn on whether it appears less costly for management to grant labor's demands than to accept the loss (of business or other) that would result from the threatened strike or the resort to countermeasures to thwart it.

As with all aspects of "thinking negotiation," the search for exploitable advantage involves consideration of offense as well as defense. Advantage or leverage can be enhanced by orchestrated actions to increase the real or perceived cost of not agreeing. Similarly, the other side's advantage or leverage can be blunted or countered by defensive action that reduces the cost impact. In the collective bargaining situation, for example, orchestration of the timing of negotiations can be critical to cost considerations. Success in scheduling talks (1) before a stockholders' meeting, or (2) just before the "season" for seasonal businesses might increase the perceived cost to management of not agreeing; however, scheduling before a union election or the onset of a recession might shift the cost concern to the labor side. As has been noted, the cost dimension of enhancing or defensive action is measured in monetary and other value terms such as relationship, image, and precedent. The effective negotiator is sensitive to the possibilities for manipulating the other side's perception of cost in a leverageable situation.

Presentational skills and techniques are the effective negotiator's tools for success; he knows that only a proposal or position that is a "giveaway" sells itself. Consequently, he has to present his proposal or position most persuasively, utilizing position-enhancing, presentational techniques. Without being sensitive to the importance of presentational considerations, a negotiator deprives himself of all the mileage that might be obtained from a given proposal or position. Good presentation involves not only a persuasive manner (i.e., salesmanship) but also attractive packaging, a careful concern for timing, and effective use of tactics and ploys. All of these must be integrated into the presentation portion of the negotiating game plan.[4] For example, when increasing a dollar offer in a negotiation, the negotiator must (1) convey persuasively that the offer is fair and reasonable and all that can be expected under the circumstances, and (2) present, or package, it attractively. If one is increasing an original offer of $100 to $300, the following judgment must be made: Would the new offer be better packaged if described as a 300 percent, or three-fold increase, or as an increase of $200? Although the percentage formulation might seem attractive to the reader, a known preference of the other side for $200 or its symbolic importance could mean that describing the offer in terms of its dollar value would be most attractive in this circumstance. Any timing need of the other side would be critical to the timing of the higher offer, whatever its form, as the combination of good packaging and timing would substantially enhance its acceptability. Specific presentational techniques will be covered in detail in subsequent sections.

Personal characteristics[5] that generate good rapport and convey reasonableness, open-mindedness, candor, honesty, sympathy, understanding, and forthcomingness (hereinafter referred to as "pizazz"—a contrived term that is struggling for academic legitimacy) are useful in negotiation because they can facilitate persuasion by improving the overall negotiating relationship. Pizazz may also make it possible to influence the other side's negotiator to be less hostile or suspicious, or even to be "won over." If the negotiator can be made less hostile or suspicious he may attach greater credibility to positions advanced, scrutinize them less carefully, and (more important) make positive recommendations to his principal that may facilitate approval of favorable consensus. Of course, if the negotiator for the other side can be won over and made a de facto ally, the effort to persuade his principal is immeasurably simplified. Notwithstanding the Dale Carnegie precept for making friends and influencing people, in most cases pizazz alone will not produce the desired consensus; persuasion in negotiation is more frequently pressured than friendly. If pizazz does carry the day and produces favorable consensus, it should be enjoyed as any other windfall but should not be viewed as a sure-fire, operating principle.

What can be said is that pizazz usually improves the tone of the dialogue and may lower the level of hostility or alertness of the other side. The ideal situation is achieved when the other side is made to believe that the interface is friendly and that there is a shared need for cooperative effort to resolve a common problem.[6] Stimulating the other side in this manner to a more open and forthcoming posture may produce exploitable benefits both in ascertaining negotiating positions and in developing concession exchanges. The resultant advantage suggests that a friendly, pizazz-laden approach should be the preferred tone in negotiation dialogue. Nothing is sacrificed by this approach; one can shift to a more openly adversarial style if necessary.

Where it appears that the other side is hostile and cannot be influenced positively by a friendly style, one has the option of "playing victim" or reacting in kind. The choice is based on the circumstances: principally, where the burden of negotiation lies and what tactical benefits can be derived from the option plays. One can buy decisional time by continuing to play the role of victim to see if the offending side will attenuate its level of hostility in response to negative signals (pained looks and other expressions of displeasure). Continued role playing can also provide a reading on audience sensitivity that the opting side may wish to exploit. The risk, of course, is that continued victim play can convey to the offending side (and important audiences) that the burden of the negotiation lies with the victim as the natural tendency is to react in kind. Thus, the effective negotiator will shy away from too much victim play unless it can be made clear to the other side that important audience considerations are involved rather than the negotiating need or plight of the playing side.

Where reaction in kind (i.e., hostility) is chosen because of the burden of negotiation or audience or other concerns, it must be shown in a variety of ways that the tone or approach of the offending side is proving to be counterproductive. This can be done most effectively if the reaction is combined with a slowdown in substantive or procedural progress in the dialogue. For example, the reacting side may choose not to respond to proposals or may delay responses. In addition, it may raise the decibel level through controlled angry outbursts to underscore further deterioration of the negotiating situation.

To summarize, although success in negotiation is not dependent on having pizazz, the negotiator who is sensitive to it, who defends against it, or who consciously weaves it into his negotiating style has an easier task. The insensitive negotiator who lacks pizazz or who does not exploit it has to work harder. The effective negotiator always seeks to harness his positive personal characteristics to the negotiating effort in keeping with his hybrid approach (forthcoming on the outside, hardball on the inside) to exploit potential relationship advantage.

Understanding of *desired objectives* helps bring success in negotiation. It involves careful analysis, preparation, and planning related to interest identification and pursuit. Preparation for negotiation should be based upon a detailed analysis of the situation: special needs of the sides; their probable objectives and exploitable vulnerabilities; the issues and issue sensitivity of the sides; and the consensus possibilities. The negotiator must have his negotiating objectives clearly in mind so that the dialogue can be structured and implemented accordingly. A negotiating game plan must be developed. Its principal element is the development and formulation of desired objectives; that is, what the side wants to get from the negotiation based upon a realistic assessment of the consensus possibilities. To do this effectively, realistic minimum and maximum objectives must be formulated to serve as the landmarks of acceptable consensus and negotiating flexibility. These landmarks define the area from which bargaining chips may be drawn; they reflect their relative worth. Without establishing minimum and maximum objectives, the negotiator is not in a position to (1) assess bargaining-chip cost and make advantageous concession trades based on that assessment; (2) attempt to control the dialogue by limiting its issue parameters; or (3) recognize and effectively exploit the weaknesses or mistakes of the other side.

In speaking of the attainment of desired objectives, we must not understate the importance of maintaining the negotiated result. It is not enough for the effective negotiator to attain the desired consensus; he must also be sensitive to the need to protect it against any erosion or encroachment by practice during the implementation phase. Erosion connotes sloppy implementation, which results in deterioration of the quality of the negotiated result; encroachment, the active effort of a side to improve the result by attempting to develop divergent practice (through exploitation of sloppy implementation, for example). As we will see, conceptualization of the negotiation process must treat implementation as a continuation of the dialogue because of the exposure to erosion and encroachment.

Uncertainty, expectations, and apprehension play a significant role in the negotiation process. Puzo's Godfather enjoyed the luxury of being able to make offers that couldn't be refused; the effective negotiator does not. He must work in the realm of consensus building and must persuade the other side that its best interests are served by accepting the proposed offer. The essence of negotiation, therefore, is persuasion, more frequently pressured than friendly. However, the pressuring requires a defter hand than that of Don Corleone and his family.[7]

In this most challenging aspect of negotiation (i.e., effecting persuasion in the face of competing interests), the negotiator is involved in a planned effort to change the other side's perception of the situation (i.e., its cost benefit analysis and, ultimately, its consensus objectives). At the outset, that side should be encouraged to believe that the negotiation is not zero-sum in the sense that both sides can win because their "realistic" goals and objectives are realizable. (This encouragement serves to nuture and exploit any win-win possibilities in the situation as well as reduce the start-up costs of getting the other side into the dialogue). Thereafter, an attempt is made to shape the other side's perception of what would be a "realistic" (i.e., reasonably attainable and mutually successful) conclusion of the negotiation. If the negotiator is successful, he may achieve most of his objectives and still have the other side leave the table happy and feeling "success."[8] Moreover, the effective negotiator may even benefit from the appearance of being a practitioner of the win-win approach. Actually, win-win is not really a separate, innovative approach to negotiation. It merely reflects what constitutes effective negotiation in situations where the sides' needs (relationship, burden of negotiation, and other) and the limited potential for hard bargaining dictate more balanced accommodation of differences in developing consensus. The reciprocal needs of the sides call for a problem-solving approach that can be made more exploitable by packaging as enlightened win-win.

Let's look at the following example of pressured persuasion through perception creation and manipulation. In a negotiation involving the sale of an item, uncertainty over (or apprehension concerning) its continued availability can be utilized to get a better price from the buyer. In effect, he is manipulated into quick acceptance of a selling price (higher than he might otherwise get through further negotiation) because he is made to believe that he must do so to acquire the desired item. (The countereffort on the part of the buyer involves conveying to the seller a low level of interest in making the purchase based on ready availability of the item elsewhere, perhaps at a better price and in better condition. Again, the purpose is to "persuade" the seller that it is in his interest to make the sale now and at a reduced price.)

Pressured persuasion that utilizes uncertainty, expectations, and apprehension actually involves perception creation concerning the cost benefit of the proposed action. In this example, the buyer is made to perceive the need for, or desirability of, a quick purchase; this inhibits him from "waiting out" the seller or further haggling with him. The technique is commonly encountered in the marketplace and can be practiced on used car lots, at flea markets, in real estate offices, and in antique shops.

Orchestration, exploitation, and manipulation are the general operational techniques for dialogue management and control. To be used effectively, they must be coherently combined in a negotiating game plan that elaborates a strategy for managing and controlling the dialogue. Through this approach, the negotiating effort is assured direction and purpose geared to interest. It is usually unproductive to enter a negotiation armed only with a vague concept of objectives and how the dialogue is to be conducted.

Negotiating skills and knowledge of tactics and ploys require a strategic framework to be maximally effective; otherwise, the would-be negotiator is simply going through the motions and leaving his negotiating destiny to chance. The key is appreciation of the critical distinction between strategy and tactics in understanding the negotiation process.

Orchestration relates to the *strategy* of pressuring persuasion; manipulation and exploitation provide the *tactical* means for effecting it. Accordingly, one essential element of the negotiating game plan is the subplan for orchestration of the entire dialogue. Planned orchestration is necessary to facilitate and enhance the exploitation and manipulation of available substantive or procedural leverage in a given situation by providing strategic, objective-oriented direction to the pressuring effort. The following examples demonstrate effective orchestration.

Consider the negotiation of a personal injury settlement where it is known that the financial situation of the claimant is such that he needs a prompt settlement. The insurance company attempting to work out the settlement might orchestrate the overall effort by (1) keeping the expectations of the claimant on the low side by rejecting high demands, disputing liability, questioning claimed injuries, and delaying settlement offers (manipulation), and (2) finally making an offer that, although below the market for the case, may be welcomed by the financially burdened claimant (exploitation).

Similarly, orchestration in an international negotiation might involve exploitation of a special personal relationship at a senior-government level: The negotiator might suggest the desirability of a meeting or other contact between senior officials at a critical point in the negotiation. The purpose here is to increase pressure for favorable action at the negotiating or working level (manipulation). Suggesting a meeting or contact is used at the working level to create (1) apprehension concerning loss of control over the negotiated result—generally, an unwanted career development, or (2) uncertainty about how outstanding issues would be resolved at the higher level—the usual staff concern when summitry is involved. The resultant apprehension or uncertainty is then manipulated and exploited by either pushing for the meeting or relenting, depending on the extent of forthcoming action at the working level.

Orchestration, manipulation, and exploitation need not involve a complex maneuver; it might amount to nothing more than timing or coordinating actions, such as enhancing the acceptability of an offer for the purchase of an item by having a check ready for the offered amount. Whatever the complexity, each negotiation requires coherent, interest-oriented orchestration and supporting exploitation and manipulation. The effective negotiator is sensitive to this need and prepares his game plan with the complexity and detail called for by the situation.

Obviously, the experience level of the other side will have a significant bearing on the success of the orchestration, exploitation, and manipulation effort. For example, involvement of an experienced negotiator on the other side will tend to dilute the successful exploitation of perception, uncertainty, expectations, and apprehension. This is because he is familiar with the pressuring process and, being sensitive to the play involving it, can resist or counter the effort effectively. His ability to resist or counter, however, should not rule out the effort. Orchestration of the exploitation and manipulation of perceptions, uncertainty, expectations, and apprehension is the operational heart of the consensus-pressuring process: No other tools are available for conduct of the dialogue.[9] The fact that the other side has the ability does not mean that it has the requisite degree of sensitivity, alertness, attention to detail, motivation, preparation, or desire to take effective defensive or counter action. Experience level of the other side is to be treated as any other situational element that the negotiator must consider as he structures the pressuring effort and assesses the potential for its success.

In conclusion, our definition of negotiation distinguishes between dialogue (which is the formal aspect of the process) and orchestration, exploitation, and manipulation (which are the operational aspects). Emphasis on the latter points up the definition's broadly operational orientation, which distinguishes it from narrower definitions that tend to be synonymous with the formal dialogue or aspects of the process involving concession trading. Actually, the validity or usefulness of many statements concerning negotiation turn on the breadth of the basic definition.

For example, a frequently encountered admonition to "negotiate only with those who have authority" makes sense only if negotiation is defined in the narrow sense of concession trading. In this case the admonition should then read: "Don't *try to trade concessions* with those who have no authority to do so." As reformulated, a valid point is made. Trying to trade concessions under the circumstances will, at the very least, waste bargaining chips, telegraph positions, and otherwise increase the probing take of the other side concerning negotiating objectives. Under this Guide's broader definition of negotiation, which incorporates the principle of globality (i.e., every contact or communication has negotiating potential), that first admonition would be too limiting. The broader definition connotes using any channel or means of communication, including persons without specific negotiating authority, to influence the decisional level of the other side. Under the global approach, negotiation includes any dialogue, communication, or action that can get the pressuring "message" to key actors on the other side. Failure to attempt to get that message through by all available means limits the scope of the negotiating effort.

The broader, global definition also conveys the "always-be-negotiating" posture that gives an edge to the practicing side. Orchestration, exploitation, and manipulation are continuing features of the interface, making it unnecessary to distinguish between formal sessions at the negotiating table and discussions, including "small talk," during recesses and social meetings. The best results are achieved if negotiations are conducted on a sustained basis, with each contact or possibility for contact being treated as a negotiating opportunity. In this global view of negotiation, there is a continuity of action that reflects the operational focus on orchestration, exploitation, and manipulation. Next steps fall into place as part of the negotiating game plan. The question "What do I do next?" is preempted by the operational focus of the game plan, which tends to exhort: "Orchestrate, exploit, and manipulate!"

PURPOSES OF NEGOTIATION

The main purposes of effective negotiation are consensus-oriented: to conclude a transaction; settle a controversy; or reach agreement on an individual, organizational, or international position, policy, scheme, or regime. The types of consensus tend to reflect the nature of the pursuit of interest in the private, intraorganizational, and international negotiating environments. Examples of concluding a transaction or settling a controversy abound by environment, as deal cutting is the usual culmination of the negotiation process. The third purpose (i.e., position, policy, scheme, or regime formulation) is reflected in negotiated arrangements such as premarital agreements between individuals, and technical cooperation or research and development agreements between firms (private); organizational staffing exercises that produce agreement on a position, policy, system, or procedure (intraorganizational); and bilateral or multilateral agreements or consensus between and among nation-states concerning international positions, policies, or regimes (international).[10] It also includes in all environments the less formal consensus reflected in behavior or action conforming to that desired by one of the sides.

Reaching agreement on a position, policy, or regime has both an external and internal dimension to which the effective negotiator must be especially sensitive. Negotiations directed toward the development of a position, policy, scheme, or regime constitute the external, side-to-side dimension. Behind this lies an important internal, intraside dialogue or dynamic that must be taken into account if one is to fully understand the negotiation process.

For example, in private negotiations the negotiator participates by advice and counsel in developing his side's negotiating goals and objectives. His career concern (to be successful, or to appear to be so) will tend to be reflected in his advice and counsel; he will seek to have his principal accept a consensus position that will advance both his career interests and the principal's dialogue. The problem for the principal is that he may not share the same standard of success or zest to "go for it" that the negotiator demonstrates. The negotiator will tend to be influenced by his career self-interest to push for a softer position that will promote quick consensus rather than one that risks dialogue breakdown in the effort to achieve a more favorable result. Although it may not be apparent to the principal, the diversity of interest puts him and his negotiator in a position of negotiating against each other. Realistically, the principal cannot ignore his negotiator's recommendations without endangering the relationship he wishes to maintain in the interest of dedicated and effective representation.

The solution for the prudent principal is to recognize the diversity of interest and to screen and modify his negotiator's recommendations and actions to provide for his own negotiating needs. If the dialogue does not produce a comfortable balance of competing interests, the principal should seek a different negotiator. (He might also feel the need to do so if his negotiator has not pursued the intraside dialogue, reflecting thereby a lack of effectiveness in appreciating and handling the interest situation as it affects the parties!) It is important for the principal to be aware of the competing interests in the principal-negotiator relationship in pursuing the external dimension of the dialogue.

The intraside dialogue is an important aspect of negotiations in other environments as well. In intraorganizational negotiations, the internal dimension is driven by two forms of interest: careerism and its related institutional manifestation, parochialism. Pursuit of these interests has impact on the staffing dialogues within organizations. The tendency is to assign priority to the personal and parochial interest at the expense of a more objective approach to the organization's interest. Here, unlike the private negotiating environment in which the prudent principal can be the champion of his own interests, no one can be relied upon to do the same for the organization; it is hostage to the behavior of its officials and their special interest preferences. Pursuit of personal and parochial interest encumbers the effectiveness of organizational action and detracts from the focus on mission accomplishment.

In the international negotiating environment, development of the position that is presented in the external, nation-state dialogue results from the interaction (i.e., negotiation) between and among various government organizations involved in the foreign policy formulation process (i.e., the internal dimension). All bilateral and multilateral international negotiations are supported by policy-formulation dialogues within the participating states.

To further complicate the situation, the intraside interest clash tends to occur during both the intraorganizational, policy-formulation, in-country dialogue and the government-negotiator relationship in the subsequent nation-state dialogue. Interest clash at either level may stimulate an effort by the side sensitive to the clash to exploit the situation in a divide-and-conquer maneuver to split the side. Awareness of the key actors and divisive issues on the other side permits the negotiator to shape the dividing side's own positions to play to those actors and, thereby, attempt to penetrate and influence the internal dialogue.

This Guide's consensus-oriented approach excludes as pseudonegotiation those dialogues conducted only for the sake of dialogue (i.e., where the interest of one or all of the sides goes no farther than being in dialogue concerning a particular situation). In such cases the dialogue is an end in itself, being used to convey to "others" the impression that action is being taken to resolve a situation or issue. For example, Country X, for political (domestic or international) reasons, may feel the need to be in dialogue on an issue with respect to which it cannot afford the political cost of inaction or a settlement. Therefore, it may wish to appear to be negotiating toward a resolution of the issue. Country Y, the other side, may be either a party to the sham or may acquiesce in it. The others here could include the other side when it is not aware that the dialogue is sham and, of course, any audiences interested in the dialogue.

The classic example of the pseudodialogue in private negotiations occurs when settlement discussions are conducted with a view to delaying the commencement of a lawsuit. In this type of pseudonegotiation, only one of the sides is aware of the sham. Pseudodialogues may also be used for reaching a particular audience or for disseminating or gathering information (i.e., to exploit the "show and tell" possibilities inherent in probing.) These dialogues must be recognized for what they are so that appropriate defensive action is taken to prevent the aware side from exploiting sham to the prejudice of the defending side.

For the effective negotiator, the distinction between negotiation and pseudonegotiation is not operationally significant because the universality and globality aspects of his "think-negotiation" mindset impel him to look upon all contacts as potential negotiations to which negotiating considerations should be applied. Of course, it is useful for him to make a tentative judgment concerning a dialogue, lest he make a disproportionate effort or, more important, waste chips in an "all-show, no-go" nonsubstantive situation. This does not end the matter, however, as he must be alert to the possibility that pseudonegotiation is being used to set the stage for actual negotiation in the future.[11]

Furthermore, under the globality aspect of "thinking negotiation," the pseudodialogue can be exploited to serve or pursue communication or signal-sending interests.[12] For example, parallel pseudodialogues can serve as convenient vehicles of communication. In the 1990 stand-off between Lithuania and President Gorbachev on the question of independence and secession from the Soviet Union, Gorbachev used parallel direct threats to the other Baltic republics to intimidate Lithuania and to create apprehension in other republics with large secessionist movements (e.g., the Georgian and Moldavian republics). As will be discussed subsequently, pitches directed at audiences who are not party to a dialogue, for negotiating impact rather than consensus development are actually parallel covered dialogues. The bottom line is that "thinking-negotiation" requires all negotiating dialogues, actual as well as pseudo, to be subjected to the scrutiny of interest-serving management and control.

MEDIATION AS NEGOTIATION

Mediation is a form of negotiation in which the parties-in-interest seek the involvement and assistance of a third party to advance the dialogue toward consensus. Mediation is not third-party judgment, as the role of the mediator is to facilitate the dialogue, leaving to the sides the final decision concerning its outcome. The mediator's role may be passive or active.[13] The passive mediator essentially ensures that the procedural flow and momentum of the negotiation dialogue are maintained. He keeps the sides in dialogue by ensuring that negotiating schedules and deadlines are observed. In effect, he acts as a process-oriented monitor of the dialogue.

The active mediator goes beyond the monitoring role and becomes substantively involved in the dialogue through suggestions, proposals, and other advice to the sides. He is actively engaged in structuring the consensus and seeking to persuade the sides to change positions and make concessions toward that end. In effect, he negotiates with each side to gain acceptance of his advice. A good example of active mediation is the effort of former secretary of state Alexander Haig in connection with the Falkland Islands crisis of 1982.

To assure that control is not lost over the negotiated result, the sides may agree to limit the mediator to a passive role. The dynamics of mediation may prevent them from achieving this result, notwithstanding their agreement. This constitutes one of the principal exposures of going the mediation route. The exposure stems in part from the difficulty of attracting a competent, prestigious individual or organization to undertake (with or without compensation) a purely passive mediation role. In such cases the sides may be induced to acquiesce in a more active role to attract the desired mediator. Even where the mediator does accept a passive role, the operational dynamics of mediation tend to make him more active the longer he is involved in the mediation effort.

The mediator, whatever his agreed or assumed initial role, is pushed toward an active role because of the felt need of the sides to "play" to him and involve him in their effort to reach consensus. This is usually done by advancing proposals through him and seeking his support for them. As there are significant pressures to go along with the mediator's suggestions, he becomes substantively involved in the proposals that both sides "clear" through him as they vie for his support. The sides realize that the mediator's support can be most persuasive; neither would wish to risk alienating

him or create the impression of being uncooperative. The process becomes self-reinforcing as the sides become increasingly dependent upon
the substantive support and input of the mediator. Time constraints on
the mediator's continued involvement in the dialogue also push him toward
an active role in seeking an early conclusion. Thus, the dynamics of mediation tend to produce an active negotiating role for the mediator.

Apart from the fact that the sides may not be fully able to control the
active or passive nature of the mediator's participation, there are other
exposure concerns in accepting mediation. The participation of the mediator opens the dialogue to an audience who is privy to all the proceedings
and, in effect, provides a witness to them. As a result, the sides will be
burdened by the constraint of having to maintain a good (and perhaps
exploitable) relationship with him. This will tend to (1) dilute substantive
positions (both in their initial formulation and in sticking to them once
tabled) to demonstrate a forthcoming posture, and (2) inhibit questionable
or sharp tactics and practices. Thus, the very participation of the mediator
pushes the sides toward a more balanced consensus and away from dialogue collapse or a one-sided result. Moreover, failure of the dialogue
becomes potentially more onerous for the side wishing to resort to the
usual charges regarding the other side's fault in instances of postnegotiation collapse. Participation of the mediator will also inhibit postnegotiation
plays to develop favorable practice on the basis of one side's claimed understanding (or misunderstanding) of the consensus arrangement. In both
cases, action will be inhibited by the "living record" of the mediator's participation.

Exposure concerns are not limited to the parties-in-interest. The mediator has certain exposures to consider before accepting the role, whether
active or passive. There is an understandable reluctance to be involved in
a difficult situation; the possibility that the dialogue may collapse must be
weighed by the mediator-to-be. Such a failure could carry adverse career
consequences by reflecting adversely on his or his organization's policy or
effectiveness. He must also consider the potential relationship cost of any
settlement he might help engineer that disappoints one or both sides and
for which he may later be blamed. Thus, all the actors, parties as well as
the mediator, are involved in an interface that involves negotiation considerations and concerns.

Notwithstanding real exposure for all the actors, mediation is frequently
chosen in the negotiation process. As may be expected, the frequency of
resort to mediation gives evidence that an interest-oriented balance can be
struck in favor of its utilization. For example, mediation can be useful to
bridge a personality or emotional clash between the sides or their negotiators. It can also be helpful when there is a disparity of power between
the sides; that is, it can be used by the weak side to protect against power
plays by the stronger side. The stronger side may be willing to accept the

mediator's participation because it will have a basis (and a witness) for claiming that there was no duress in reaching consensus. The stronger side may also look to the mediator to protect it from any irresponsible acts by the weaker side to increase its negotiating leverage (e.g., refusal to negotiate by resorting to delaying tactics or exaggerated victim play). Furthermore, mediator participation may facilitate agreement because concessions can be made in a more face-saving, politically acceptable manner (e.g., made at the suggestion of the mediator rather than pressured by the other side). The mediator himself may accept participation because his interests are engaged in the subject matter of the negotiation and he may desire to be in a position to influence its resolution in a manner consistent with those interests.[14] He may also be motivated toward participation by the desire to accommodate a relationship with one or both of the parties-in-interest. Furthermore, if he is a professional mediator, he may accept involvement because he believes it would be career-enhancing or otherwise highly remunerative.

When requested by his principal for a recommendation concerning the use of mediation in a particular negotiation, the effective negotiator carefully considers the trade-offs as they impact his career and his side's interests. His principal concern is the constraint of the mediator's involvement that may negate the advantage the negotiator himself might otherwise enjoy by virtue of his greater experience and skill. On the other hand, the mediator could serve as a useful "fall guy" in a difficult negotiating situation, thereby easing the career pain of an unhappy ending. In response to his principal's request, the effective negotiator should prepare a balance sheet of the potential benefits and drawbacks of mediation with a recommendation concerning whether it is in the side's interest to undertake it. The decision to undertake or reject mediation should be made by the principal (with the "assistance" of the negotiator); this will provide some insulation for the negotiator should the mediation turn out badly. In addition, the principal should be briefed about the dynamics of mediation as it impacts the negotiator's role so that the former can better appreciate the representational effort required on his behalf.

NOTES

1. Tony Horwitz, "Iraq Is Sending Mixed Signals on Kuwait Withdrawal," *Wall Street Journal,* November 2, 1990, p. A10.

2. *Pocket Book of Quotations,* ed. Henry Davidoff (New York, London, Toronto, Sydney, Tokyo, Singapore: Pocket Books, 1952), 404.

3. For example, noninvolvement in a dialogue that is going well amounts to the happy state of getting without giving (i.e., the side enjoying the benefit does not have to expend bargaining chips for the favorable developments in the dialogue).

4. In the interest of stressing presentational techniques directed toward en-

hancing the cosmetic appeal of proposals and positions, the discussion here purposely omits the important, complementary orchestration and credibility aspects of the presentational effort. These are covered elsewhere (e.g., Presentation Phase and Tactics and Ploys).

5. Special gifts of nature such as the honest face, sincere eyes, the disarming smile, the innocent look, ready humor, and an engaging personality are exploited by the effective negotiator who structures his negotiating style and approach around them. Apart from its value for generating rapport, humor is an effective way of retrieving a trial balloon using the "only-kidding" approach. "Doing it in the name of play provides an easy retreat," permitting one to decommit. (Caryl S. Avery, "The Art of Laughter," *Eastern Review,* December 1988, pp. 34, 52–60, at p. 34).

6. In his address to the United Nations on December 7, 1988, General Party Secretary Mikhail S. Gorbachev sought to improve the tone of the Soviet Union's relationship with other nation-states by stressing the interdependence of states sharing "universal human interests" as the basis of international relationships rather than the ideologically mandated international class struggle. (*Washington Post,* December 8, 1988, p. A32.) The Soviet press translation of the speech used the terms "common interests of the whole of human kind" and "humankind's common values" ("Speech by Mikhail S. Gorbachev at the UN General Assembly," *Moscow News,* No. 51, 1988, Supplement, pp. 1–4, at p. 1).

7. Trivia pursuitists might be pleased to learn that in the old gangster movies before there was a Godfather series the pistol was variously referred to as a "rod," "heater," or "persuader," all having a pressuring connotation. (The term "gat" was a form of slang derived from the gatling gun, which had a revolver-like operation.)

8. The effective negotiator is not a mood engineer without reason. He is sensitive to the importance of a good continuing relationship for postnegotiation implementation. Therefore, he tries through perception creation and manipulation to make the other side feel happy with the "good deal" that was struck. It is not unusual for the effective negotiator to accomplish this by commending the other side for its strong representation and even, where appropriate, its contribution to a win-win resolution of the differences between the sides. Characterization of the dialogue as win-win is both flattering to the other side and still another way of saying that it made a good deal.

9. In the case of a specific ploy or tactic, on the other hand, reduced chance of success may militate against its use when the desirability of that use is balanced against the concern about adverse impact on the negotiating relationship or other counterproductive effect.

10. The intended normative impact of negotiation on the ordering of international relations is reflected in the formulation "international legislation." As a practical matter, negotiation is the only means of "ordering" international relations among the sovereign-state actors whose consent is a condition to being bound. Even where there is no formal consensus, the concepts of political and negotiating cost tend to act as sanctions to inhibit or deter certain disruptive state action, thereby exerting a passive ordering influence. In this sense, the negotiation process is part of the glue that holds the international system together.

11. The dialogue with North Vietnam concerning U.S. involvement in that country started as a pseudonegotiation with a focus on situs questions, table shapes, participating parties, and other nonsubstantive issues as each side used the dia-

logue for its own political agenda. The dialogue began to address the substantive issues as the sides started to move toward consensus development.

12. "A purpose of negotiation is obviously to reach agreement. Where difficult issues are involved, however, that agreement may not be possible in the short run. Equally important, therefore, the negotiating process must be used to communicate concerns . . . so as to lessen the likelihood of ambiguity." (Max M. Kampelman, "Negotiating World Order: A View from Madrid," *Christian Science Monitor,* November 14, 1983, p. 22.)

13. Some detractors of former president Jimmy Carter might suggest another role, that of the "angel," for his generous foreign assistance commitment to Anwar Sadat and Menachem Begin. This contributed to the success of his mediation of the Camp David talks in 1978.

14. This may explain the generosity of an angel mediator and, perhaps, why he is acceptable to both sides.

3

The Negotiating Environments

THE ENVIRONMENTS

Effective negotiation divides the negotiation universe into three operational environments: private, intraorganizational, and international. This division facilitates a single, process-oriented approach to negotiation that has across-the-board applicability and relevance. For full realization of the potential of that approach, an operational adjustment in the application of general concepts and techniques of effective negotiation must be made to take account of the essential features of the environments and the differences between them.

In *private negotiations,* which usually involve dialogues concerning transactions or dispute resolution, at least one of the parties is an individual or a corporate or other private organizational entity.[1] In this environment, the dialogue may range from the formality of a structured dialogue (e.g., collective bargaining) to the simple bargaining of the flea market or bazaar.

The *intraorganizational environment* reflects the operational reality that the staffing and coordination of organizational business actually involve negotiations because competitive interests, both organizational and personal, are actively engaged and pursued. Thus, any corporate, organizational, or governmental bureaucracy is engaged in "management or government by bargain"; the competitive, and therefore adversarial, nature of the process is the result of the double impact of careerism[2] and parochialism[3] upon organizational operations. Generally, corporate or government officials vie with each other for career and status advancement. They tend to promote the parochial interests of the particular organization they represent because their positions, as a practical matter, depend upon the quality of the results achieved.

Dialogues in this environment are usually multilateral because, as staffing exercises, they involve broad participation to ensure that all substantive organizational interests are represented. The essential feature is development of an organizational position or policy. Dialogues can involve the staffing and coordination exercises within organizations as well as those between organizations operating at the same level (i.e., both intra- and interorganizational dialogues are included under the intraorganizational classification). In form, they can range from formal meetings and conferences to informal telephone discussion and coordination of organizational positions.

In some situations, both intra-and interagency dialogues are involved in a two-stage process: internal dialogues developing positions for an external dialogue. The best example is the U.S. foreign policy formulation process, the second stage of which meshs into a coherent *national* policy the *agency* positions developed in the first stage, internal dialogues of the participating agencies. Assume a situation in which the United States is negotiating a base rights presence in Country X. The U.S. foreign policy formulation process will involve dialogues within and with those agencies that have an interest or role in this policy area. Certainly, the Departments of State and Defense, the Central Intelligence Agency, and the National Security Council would be included in the staffing exercise. In each of these agencies there will be an intraorganizational dialogue[4] to develop an agency position for presentation at the interagency dialogue that develops the national position or policy.

International negotiations involve the consensus-oriented dialogues between nation-states in the conduct of their foreign relations. These dialogues can range from daily contacts of diplomatic representatives with their foreign-office counterparts, on one end of the spectrum, to formal bilateral discussions or proceedings in multinational forums, on the other. The dialogues in this environment, reflecting diplomatic custom and protocol and the impact of cross-cultural contacts, tend to involve greater formality and more ceremony and ritual than those conducted in either the private or intraorganizational environments.

There is a special nexus between the intraorganizational and the private and international environments. In every pursuit of a private interest against any structured organization, there is involved on the part of that organization an internal staffing exercise or dialogue to develop an organizational position or response for the dialogue (negotiation) with the private party. The staffed response, which becomes the negotiating position of the organization, is the product of intraorganizational dialogue. Similarly, in international negotiations there is an intraorganizational process to develop agency positions and meld them into a national position (i.e., foreign policy)[5] that is presented in the international dialogue.[6] In both cases, the intraorganizational dialogue actually supports the principal, external dialogue. It is not unusual, therefore, for claimants (in the private negotiating environment) or for governments (in the international negotiating environment) to attempt to structure and orchestrate negotiating positions to influence the policy formulation process (intraorganizational dialogues) of the other side.

For example, the parochial interest of one element participating in the supporting, internal dialogue may be reachable and, therefore, exploitable through a carefully shaped position intended to divide and conquer or win over some of the participants in that dialogue. The same approach may be used to exploit a special career interest of one of the key participants in the dialogue. These possibilities suggest the importance of learning as much as possible concerning the roles and interests of the individuals and elements involved in negotiating the organization's policy position.

In the private negotiating environment, the effort to influence internal policy dialogues is covered in the discussion of "Mr. Outside's" role as the private petitioner seeking to influence favorable organizational action through reliance on pressure points related to individual and organizational concerns about careerism, parochialism, imagery, and precedent. In the international negotiating environment, the same pressure points are relevant to a nation-state's effort to influence the internal policy dialogues of other states and international actors.

Mediation, as a form of multiactor negotiation, is most frequently encountered in the private and international negotiating environments. The usual multilateral nature of dialogues in the intraorganizational environment does not negate the possible use of mediation, which has been successfully used in multilateral as well as bilateral negotiations. For example, in 1988 a U.S. mediation effort was successful in arranging an interim cease-fire in Angola; Cuba, South Africa, and Angola were the participating states. Nevertheless, mediation is seldom utilized in intraorganizational negotiations because the structured nature of the interface obviates the need for a procedural monitor or pusher toward consensus. The built-in suspense system and its monitors keep the staffing dialogue moving. However, one can conceive, of a mediation situation in which a trouble-shooter is appointed to help resolve an issue between organizational entities.

The breakdown by environment is generic. It should not be confused with any special regimes (i.e., rules or practices) that may pertain to the conduct of a negotiation or that may affect the dialogue in any of the environments. For example, a bargaining statute[7] or market practice governing certain negotiations in the private environment should not be viewed as creating a subenvironment. Such a statue or practice should be considered a situational element to be taken into account in developing the strategy and tactics of the negotiating game plan. The statute or practice should be analyzed to see whether it can be used as a sword or a shield in structuring the dialogue. If it cannot be exploited as a cutting edge, at the very least an effort should be made to blunt any potential negative impact. Similarly, in the intraorganizational environment, internal staffing procedures (e.g., suspense systems and clearance requirements) all affect the conduct of the dialogue and must be taken into account in developing the negotiating game plan. The same applies in the international negotiating environment, where custom and "international legislation" in the form of multilaterally approved rules for dispute and other settlement processes affect the conduct of negotiations. Again, any constraints external to the negotiation process should be treated like other factual elements in the situation (i.e., subject to orchestration, exploitation, and manipulation in the pursuit of interest).

DISTINGUISHING THE ENVIRONMENTS

Application of negotiation concepts and techniques to the three environments is affected by the special nature of each environment. The negotiator must be sensitive to the specific environmental features that require adjusting the techniques used to manage and control dialogues. As his experience grows, he better understands the environments and the significant operational distinctions that impact the effectiveness of dialogues conducted within them.

The following discussion deals with the manner in which basic negotiating considerations are affected by the operationally relevant features of each environment. In elaborating more fully these basic considerations and the nature of the environments, the discussion has across-the-board utility for all would-be negotiators, whether they operate in a single environment or across the environmental spectrum. For example, they benefit from the increased understanding of dialogue management and control in the context of the varying demands of each environment. Furthermore, given the operational nexus between the private and intraorganizational and between the intraorganizational and international environments, most everyone involved in negotiation is, at one time or another, a two-environment player. Even the unidimensional negotiator (e.g., one whose dialogues exclusively involve the transactions and disputes of private individuals) must understand the special operational considerations applicable to the private negotiating environment.

Privacy of Negotiation

The size of the negotiation audience and its scrutiny affect the management and control of dialogues. The larger the audience, the more inhibited is action that may reflect adversely on the negotiating position and personal reputation of the negotiator and his principal. This inhibition affects the strategy and tactics of conducting the dialogue.

In a very real sense, audience scrutiny constitutes a rudimentary form of process constraint because the behavior of the sides is driven by concern about the negotiating or relationship cost of substantive and procedural moves that might offend that scrutiny.[8] Consequently, and because negotiators generally seek to minimize operating constraints, negotiation in all environments tends to be as private as conditions permit, with the degree of privacy varying with the specific situation. Generally speaking, privacy is most attainable in bilateral settings; it is less so as the number of participants increase, as in mediation and multilateral settings. The operative principle is that audience exposure tends to increase with the number of participants in the dialogue if only because the additional interest involvement tends to attract other audiences.

Audience exposure concerns are reflected in the judgments brought to bear in deciding whether to adopt a particular course of action, procedurally (e.g., whether to gamble or employ a sharp practice) or substantively (e.g., whether to propose a certain concession or result). Central to the decision on the former question are concerns for the reputation of the negotiator and his principal and the impact on the negotiating relationship—all items of negotiating cost. As to substance, the concerns are augmented by the potential negative precedential impact of a proposal or result—a more tangible cost exposure that must always be carefully weighed. A side having a similar involvement with others who are not parties to the negotiation may be deterred from proposing or reaching a settlement that may have future costs in those other involvements.

For example, in private negotiations, an insurance carrier may not wish to concede liability or settle a claim in an unclear area of the law because of potential settlement exposure in similar cases. Likewise, in intraorganizational and international negotiations, establishment of a substantive precedent has consequences that go far beyond the particular issue or situation under negotiation. In an intraorganizational negotiation, the precedent, where relevant, tends to establish the organizational approach to subsequent actions. Organizational bureaucrats enjoy the sanctuary of the "sanctity" of precedent! The regime established for international relationships soon becomes the standard for (or at least the regime demanded by) nation-states similarly situated. In the final analysis, concern for exposure to adverse audience impact or reaction is largely a function of the perception of its potential relationship or other negotiating cost.

The "think-negotiation" vulnerability analysis performed during the preparation phase requires consideration of the defensive and offensive implications of audience scrutiny and the related tactics and ploys available to the respective sides in the negotiating situation. The defensive approach to audience exposure is to insist on privacy in the mutual interest of the sides using the following rationale. "Concession trading can be inhibited if it has to be concerned with audience reaction to each trade; both sides benefit from the more balanced view of how the bargaining went as reflected in the final agreement." However, when exploiting that exposure is a part of the negotiating game plan (as in a "victim" play), the exposure is courted offensively to inhibit the other side.[9]

Audience exposure is usually smallest in the private negotiating environment because of the nature of the dialogues (i.e., individual transactions or claims) and limited external interest. This may not be the case in private negotiations involving large corporations or the government; here, publicity is generated because of the newsworthiness of the negotiation or because it can be used as a pressure tactic by a claimant. Audience exposure is somewhat greater in intraorganizational negotiations, depending on the extent of the involvement of the bureaucracy (such dialogues tend to be multilateral) and the publicity accorded to the particular issue; it is greatest in the international environment because of the widespread interest and, at times, multilateral involvement in the conduct and results of negotiations.

Although the privacy attainable in negotiation is relative and varies with the negotiating environment, the negotiator should be aware that he always has to play to an audience. Exposure to an audience is a constant element for him as distinguished from his principal because, even in the most private of negotiations (i.e., where the principal's position is secure from all audiences other than the other side), the negotiator's principal is an audience judging the effectiveness of his representation.[10] (In this sense, the principal is also a party, receiving proposals from the negotiator who actually negotiates with him in an effort to keep him satisfied with his representation and otherwise "under control".) Thus, the effective negotiator thinks in terms of a broad spectrum of audience scrutiny as he conducts the negotiation: scrutiny by his side, the other side, and other involved audiences. For him, every negotiation is multiparty[11] insofar as his personal exposure is concerned. As a consequence, he tends to look in all directions to view the internal and external exposure of his negotiating behavior and posture. In short, he "thinks exposure" as he contemplates the scrutiny of the various audiences to which he must play.

Imposed Result or Other Alternatives to Negotiation

When parties resort to negotiation, they should recognize as part of their exposure the possibility that a result may be imposed or the dialogue otherwise disrupted by alternatives to negotiation. This possibility—either through deadlock or impasse, litigation or other recourse to authority, or self-help (including the use of force)—influences the conduct of the dialogue. If one side has a greater stake in, or need for, a negotiated result, the possibility that a result may be imposed or the dialogue otherwise disrupted should be regarded as a serious vulnerability. The side with the greater stake may be said to carry the burden of negotiation, which will dictate caution and conservative action in conducting the dialogue lest it trigger costly disrupting action by the other side.

Operationally speaking, the burden of negotiation is a subjective matter (i.e., a side can be made to believe that it has a need greater than it actually does). It is not unusual, therefore, for a side to attempt to improve its negotiating position by masking its own need and causing the other side to feel that it has the burden. Many ploys (e.g., studied disinterest and apparent readiness to take certain action inconsistent with a negotiated result) are utilized for this purpose. Of course, requests for "a settlement," "resolution of the matter," or "discussion," in the face of a threat by the other side to break off the dialogue or resort to available remedies, are avoided lest the real need of the side for a negotiated result be conveyed. If the actual need of a side does not permit playing this game, it must work with the burden.

Having to accommodate the burden involves lowering one's perception of what is attainable in the negotiation; the burden does not permit the luxury of holding out for the best possible deal. In some cases, the impact of the burden is so great that the negotiation takes on the character of a salvage operation, with the burdened side trying to salvage "something" from the situation.

The effective negotiator considers the possibility of a disrupted dialogue a key vulnerability because the side most committed to a negotiated result will be inhibited from (1) chancing action that threatens to disrupt the dialogue through deadlock or impasse, or (2) otherwise pushing the other side out of the dialogue to the available recourse. He knows well that the relative ease of recourse to an alternative to negotiation, in terms of its institutional and practical availability in the negotiating sense, affects the commitment to a negotiated result. If no remedy is practically available, the burdened side has a greater need for the dialogue. For him it may become the "only game in town" with the increased exposure of having to nurture the continuation of the dialogue.

For example, one who wishes to avoid litigation in the private negotiating environment does not lightly adopt, and stick to, a hard-line position or the tactic of a proposal tied to the threat of terminating the dialogue or filing a law suit. Similarly, in intraorganizational negotiations, the side wishing to shape the result by personal participation in its negotiation must refrain from proposals and tactics that may cause other participants to "kick the problem upstairs" for executive decision. In the international environment, there is the same concern that the hard line or tactics such as brinkmanship may cause the other side to terminate the negotiating dialogue or resort to undesired policy action, including self-help.

Thus, vulnerability to disrupted dialogue is an important element to consider in preparing for negotiation. It is helpful to understand the alternatives to negotiation in each of the environments. The effective negotiator is at his best in (1) environments where the sides have relatively few alternatives to negotiation, or (2) situations in any environment in which the other side believes, or can be made to believe, that it has the burden of negotiation or that the alternatives to negotiation are not practically available.

Exposure to the vulnerability of disrupted dialogue varies from environment to environment because it reflects the completeness of the system of recourse and other alternatives to negotiation in each environment.[12] Given the three purposes of negotiation—to conclude a transaction, settle a controversy, or formulate a position—the greatest exposure to disrupted dialogue lies in the intraorganizational environment even though the dialogue itself is mandated by the internal process of the organization. Actually, it is because of this mandate that disruption through deadlock or impasse is not realistically possible. Any deadlock or impasse quickly leads to an imposed result through executive intervention and decision. Furthermore, in this most structured setting, recourse to executive decision is always available (1) offensively, to dictate the deal, settlement, or position that will terminate the dialogue, or (2) defensively, to redress any abuse or violation of organizational practice or process. Also, the courts and other competent authorities are available to review substantive actions of the organization.

In the private negotiating environment, the courts and other authorities are usually available for adjudication of controversies and protection against, or redress for, impasse or unlawful self-help. Except for special cases (e.g., actions for the specific performance of real property agreements or declaratory relief), available remedies in the private negotiating environment do not usually extend to concluding a transaction or formulating a position.

The international negotiating environment, being the least structured and most consent-oriented in terms of remedies, offers the least recourse to third-party adjudicatory or other dialogue-disrupting authority. The reduced exposure to such authority means less vulnerability to action by the other side to impose a result. But the blessing is mixed; defensively, the general absence of recourse also means the absence of effective redress for victims of impasse and self-help. Although nation-states generally strive to conduct their foreign relations by negotiation, history does record impasse and the resort to force, third-state intervention, and other forms of self-help as alternatives to a negotiated solution. The protective, inhibiting element here is not organizational or institutional authority, but concern for political (negotiating) cost, which, being the critical policy determinant, usually[13] discourages states from greater resort to self-help.

The Continuing Relationship and Linkage

In all negotiations, there is a concern for the continuing negotiating relationship. First, the negotiator always seeks to impress his principal with the quality of his representation as a means of securing subsequent business or improving career prospects. Second, a nonadversary-appearing interside relationship is generally considered to be more conducive to favorable consensus than one in which the sides face each other with open hostility, suspicion, and distrust. The former concern repeats the point that a negotiator, driven by career interests, actively negotiates with his principal; the latter, that a general negotiating technique is to try to exploit friendly persuasion by using a relationship basis to encourage a cooperative spirit in conducting the dialogue. A frequently encountered approach, worn by its overuse, relies on the "buddy (old buddy)," "friend," "kinfolk" or "family," or "nice (good) people" formulations to build a relationship basis for persuasion: "Friends, we've been doing business for years. Don't treat me like a stranger, give me the family or kinfolk price!"

Apart from the general tactical interest in the quality of the negotiating relationship, parties already enjoying a beneficial[14] continuing relationship have a more specific reason for ensuring that subsequent dialogues do not adversely affect the relationship. The extent of the effort to defer to the relationship in the handling subsequent dialogues will reflect the perceived stake in its continuation. This perception should be based on interest and a monitoring dynamic. All ongoing relationships should be subjected to a continuing review of the benefit they provide. For example, if an additional cost develops in the relationship or results from a subsequent dialogue involving its parties, the situation should be reassessed to determine whether the relationship is worth continuing.

Deference to the continuing relationship is a form of procedural linkage; the effective negotiator understands that it has the potential for substantive exposure. Where there is a continuing benefit from the relationship, its maintenance may be deemed important enough to impact the conduct of a subsequent negotiation involving discrete issues. That case should be distinguished from one in which other aspects of the relationship are so interrelated with the issues to be negotiated (or those that the other side can be expected to put on the table as a bargaining move) that they involve, and potentially risk, the substantive basis of the ongoing relationship. The effective negotiator recognizes the former as procedural linkage because it reflects considerations related solely to the value or desirability of maintaining the relationship; the latter as substantive linkage because the complexity of the substance of the relationship does not admit of easily treating issues separately.

Procedural linkage is simpler to deal with than substantive linkage because an effort to defer to the maintenance of the relationship usually involves only atmospherics—a positive, forthcoming approach to generate a good tone for the subsequent dialogue. If the dialogue cannot be concluded, other aspects of the relationship do not necessarily become involved because there is no substantive nexus. Despite the failed dialogue, the ongoing relationship may be sustainable on its own merits because the issues are discrete and separate. Of course, any mishandling of the subsequent dialogue that generates personal animosity between the sides could undermine the ongoing relationship.

In substantive linkage, the concern is that any issues to be negotiated may have a disruptive, spillover effect on other issues involved in the relationship. In some cases, the spillover concern may be great enough to inhibit any dialogue at all; the concerned side may have to "swallow" some problems to avoid putting the overall relationship at risk. If the problems cannot be swallowed, the entire relationship must be reviewed to assess the cost benefit of continuing it. Another difficulty with substantive linkage is that subsequent dialogue may cause other substantive issues between the sides to become involved, with the possibility that desirable aspects of the relationship can be upset. The negotiator has to make a judgment whether it is in his side's interest to take the offensive and invoke substantive linkage by expanding the dialogue or to take defensive steps to prevent the other side from doing so. Essentially, this judgment involves a cost-benefit analysis of actively linking the specific issue to be negotiated to other substantive aspects of the relationship. The immediate plus of gaining additional bargaining chips by invoking linkage has to be balanced against (1) the exposure and vulnerabilities on other issues that are put at risk by becoming involved in the dialogue, (2) procedural considerations relating to dragging out the negotiation because of its expanded scope, and (3) the possibility that the entire relationship may be weakened because it may be perceived as too fragile or exposure-laden to survive specific disagreements or disputes.

Rarely do both sides feel the same degree of need to preserve the continuing relationship; usually one side feels, or can be made to feel, a greater need. Generally, it is desirable to encourage the other side to develop this feeling of need: It will influence its conduct of subsequent negotiations because relationship maintenance, in effect, becomes one of its goals or objectives that affects substantive positions and negotiating strategy and tactics. The side that is successful in making relationship maintenance an objective of the other will be more secure in managing the ongoing relationship and will be well positioned to reap a bargaining benefit should its continuation become an issue.

As in most aspects of negotiation, decisional alternatives have to be viewed from the standpoint of offense and defense. Whether procedural or substantive linkage is invoked depends on the perceived value of the relationship to the invoking side and its view of the manipulation potential by the other. The effective negotiator, sensitive to linkage play, can manipulate the situation to his advantage because he knows that decisions can be based on perceptions as well as facts. Therefore, he can either exaggerate or downplay the importance of the continuing relationship, depending on the signal he wishes to convey to influence the other side's action on the issue.

The distinction between procedural and substantive linkage has important implications for the so-called win-win approach to negotiation. Those who exhort win-win draw their best examples from situations in which a continuing relationship provides the stimulus and basis for a more creative and constructive attitude toward the accommodation of interests and consensus development. Essentially, their rationale is that the shared desire to maintain the relationship provides an interest dimension that makes it cost effective to work toward mutually beneficial results. Thus, win-win has a cost feature in the sense that the shared relationship interest transcends the usual inclination to get as much as possible from the dialogue. It follows that the universe of win-win is further[15] reduced by the reality that not all beneficial continuing relationships are worth (in the negotiating sense) enough to support the cost element that may be involved in any win-win approach to subsequent dialogues.

The importance of the continuing relationship (i.e., procedural or substantive linkage) varies with each negotiating environment. In the private negotiating environment, many dialogues are one-shot encounters in which there is no continuing relationship beyond that of the dialogue itself. Private individuals usually resolve their differences unburdened by extraneous concerns. This tends to be less the case where (1) one side wishes to favor or exploit a business or other relationship, or (2) one side is large enough to have a broad range of relationships that may be adversely affected by a sullying of its reputation or image, or by the precedential impact of the negotiated result. In both cases, some deference to the relationship becomes a feature of the negotiation.

For example, insurance carriers are inhibited from sharp or unfair dealings with first-party (insured) as well as third-party claimants, and automobile manufacturers carefully handle warranty disputes with their customers. In some private negotiations, the existence of a beneficial continuing relationship is clear; to the extent of its importance, the parties are influenced by it in their dealings with each other. Labor negotiations fall in this category, as do dealings between attorney-specialists and the governmental and private entities with which they regularly conduct business.

Relationships in the more structured intraorganizational and international negotiating environments are usually continuing in the procedural and substantive senses. Consequently, it is important to defer to maintaining the relationships and to consider linkage-exposure possibilities. Organizational business tends to occur between the same offices, elements, and officials; hence there is need, in the mutual interest, to maintain good working relationships, both institutional and personal, and to reduce adverse substantive linkage exposure. All this provides fertile ground for use of the win-win tactic. The same is true of dealings between nation-states that maintain diplomatic relations and a web of economic, political, and other relationships based upon, and reflecting, their interdependence. One tends to encounter more substantive linkage in the international negotiating environment. Here, as contrasted with the intraorganizational environment, there is less agenda discipline in addressing issues between the sides. If they wish, nation-states can put the entire relationship on the table.

Exposure to procedural and substantive linkage is quite different in international negotiations where the hostile or adversarial character of the sides' relationship is reflected by the absence of recognition or diplomatic representation and a paucity of interstate ties. A classic example is the manner in which U.S. military base issues with Panama and Cuba have been handled. Both states have demanded renegotiation of treaties, concluded at the turn of the twentieth century, that make provision for a long-term U.S. military presence in country. The need to preserve the relationship and other ties with Panama brought the United States to the negotiating table. As a result of the dialogue, the 1903 treaty was replaced by the new Panama Canal Treaty, which was concluded in 1977. The absence of the similar need in the case of Cuba (because of the openly hostile relationship and minimal linkage ties) permits the United States to insist on its full treaty rights in maintaining the status quo with respect to the naval installation at Guantanamo.

In conclusion, concern for the continuing relationship influences negotiating objectives, strategy, and tactics. The effective negotiator weighs the extent of this concern as he analyzes the negotiating situation. Should it appear that his side alone has this concern or that its concern is greater than the other's, he will treat it as a vulnerability and a potential constraint on conduct of the dialogue. Similarly, should the greater concern be on the other side or made to appear to be, he will view it as a strength to be exploited during the dialogue. Furthermore, the effective negotiator understands that, notwithstanding the differences in negotiating environments, there are relatively few negotiations in which concern for the continuing relationship is not a factor to be considered.

Viability

Concern for the continuing relationship is related to the larger question of viability. The effective negotiator is aware that it is possible to ask for and get too much with counterproductive results. The exposure is twofold: The other side may be driven out of the dialogue, or the negotiated result may come apart earlier than expected. As to the latter, a frequently stated suggestion is that negotiated solutions are likely to last longer when each party feels that it has a stake in maintaining the agreed result. This attempt to develop commitment to the negotiated result is often used as an argument for the win-win approach, which exhorts satisfying the other side's needs to ensure agreement viability. I believe, however, that a more operationally meaningful approach to viability involves focus on satisfaction of critical, specific needs rather than the more abstract win-win exhortation. Win-win implies a sharing or fair division of the bargaining chips to ensure postagreement harmony. Applying win-win in that general, more abstract sense can be very costly and can lead to position slippage. (See discussion of win-win in the preceding section and in the chapter on tactics and ploys.)

The question of viability is tantalizing, as it requires restraint and judgment in the face of the tendency to (1) try to get the most out of the situation by adhering to the most favorable position (e.g., "sticking" too long with the highest or lowest figure), or (2) "run with a good deal," the "one-in-the-hand" approach. The requisite restraint and judgment are a product of experience and "thinking negotiation." Together, they provide a feel for what the traffic should be made to bear, which is the key issue on the question of viability.

As in many other areas, viability can best be approached by distinguishing between process and substance. From the procedural point of view, viability involves considerations related to maintenance of the continuing relationship. Even where there is to be no continuing relationship after the negotiation, there is need to maintain a good negotiating relationship to facilitate the persuasion process. The concern about substantive viability relates to the acceptability and feasibility of proposal and consensus substance. The nexus is that it is a rare situation in which pushing too hard or winning too big does not entail present (i.e., during the negotiation) or follow-on interface or relationship cost. Accordingly, each proposed tactic or other negotiating action and consensus proposal must be subjected to a scrutiny that takes into account the continuing relationship as well as the substantive feasibility and viability of the proposed solution. In effect, the concern about viability requires balancing advantage and goal realization against the risks and cost of counterproductive action or results. As we will see the "think-negotiation" checklist includes a focus on both the continuing relationship and viability.

To improve substantive viability, proposals must be practical, oriented toward the needs of the other side, and packaged as attractively as possible to enhance their acceptability. The requirement for practicality should be self-evident; an impractical proposal has little credibility and can be rejected on the basis of lack of workability without getting to the underlying issues. Rejection on such a basis deprives the proposing side of the benefit of the other side's serious consideration of, or response to, the proposal and of the possibility of probing the issues related to it. In addition to practicality, a proposal should reflect an effort to meet the needs of the other side and have the highest possible cosmetic appeal. Proposals that ignore the needs of the other side or are not attractively formulated place the proposing side in the position of either risking termination of the dialogue or, where the burden of negotiation is on the other side, pushing that side into a consensus that may not survive postnegotiation pressures.

Thus, the concern for viability has a relationship and substantive orientation reflecting the potential for negative dialogue and postnegotiation consensus implications. Of the two, the latter is more serious. Once the negotiation is over there is no available, underlying, or ongoing dialogue (as with the former) to correct or cover the nonviable development. A nonviable arrangement usually produces a time bomb and runs the risk of having a "blow-up" or, at the very least, a renegotiation.[16]

The exposure implications of the foregoing cause the effective negotiator to weigh carefully the attempt to make "the big steal" or drive the "hard bargain." He must make a viability judgment by balancing the possibility of an immediate gain against a potentially difficult negotiating and postnegotiation situation. If he can live with the potentially adverse impact on the negotiating relationship, he can be comforted somewhat by knowing that (1) by running with a good deal or driving a hard bargain he shifts the burden of action to the side that might wish to renounce it, and (2) that side will have to overcome the inhibition and reluctance to undertake renunciatory action, that is, the normal discomforture of departing from the "done-deal" approach. To assess the level of inhibition and reluctance, he must consider the actual, political, or other cost that the other side would incur by taking that action. He must also map out the countermeasures to be taken to increase the perception of that cost and thereby further inhibit renunciation.

These cost concerns and countermeasures are affected by the particular environment. Generally speaking, there is a greater chance in the private negotiating environment that parties will sit on their rights or be inhibited by countermeasures from renunciation because of ignorance, naivete, commitment to the conventional view that "a deal is a deal," and the need, cost, and effort to get professional assistance and pursue a remedy (considerations relating to the practical availability of process). In many cases, just having to face the other side again can be an inhibiting factor that kills dialogue renewal. That is less the case in the intraorganizational and international environments; here, the parties and negotiators are more knowledgeable and professional, and an ongoing dialogue or contact can be used to attempt to reopen the negotiation.

Being aware that there are ways in which he can reduce relationship cost and the threat of renunciation, the effective negotiator may conclude that it would be advantageous to take a chance on a result that may not be completely viable. If he does, he protects his negotiating posterior by fully briefing his principal to make him a party to the risk venture; he then begins his damage control operation (i.e., increasing the other side's perception of the cost burden of renunciation) from the moment he gets the go-ahead to take the chance and gamble.

Instructions

The negotiator is an agent with limited authority who is bound to represent his principal in accordance with the instructions he receives from the principal. In practice this strict agency-principal relationship tends to be undermined by the negotiator's efforts to use the dialogue with his principal to advance career objectives. Generally, the negotiator seeks to impress his principal with the quality of the representation he is providing. He attempts to achieve this by keeping his principal under control and by influencing his thinking about negotiating goals, objectives, and what constitutes a successful negotiating effort.

Ability to control one's principal tends to vary with the environments because of the manner in which instructions are formulated and conveyed. Generally, the negotiator wants his principal to be satisfied with the substance of the negotiated result and with the manner in which his interests were represented. As the substance of the result is more important than the quality of his representation, the negotiator tends to devote most of his control effort to getting his principal to agree to achievable goals and objectives. He knows that a mighty effort on behalf of a cause perceived to have been lost has only limited appeal to a disappointed principal.

In the private negotiating environment, the negotiator actively counsels his principal who wishes to benefit from his professional experience. The situation lends itself to easy exploitation by the negotiator whose position approximates that of the proverbial fox in the chicken house. Through the cover of counseling, the negotiator can influence his principal's view of what is attainable through negotiation, thereby exercising considerable control over the side's negotiating position. The negotiator also benefits from the informality of the formulation of his negotiating instructions. They are seldom reduced to writing; in many cases, they amount to little more than a general mandate to obtain a result within fairly broad monetary or other parameters. This generality defers to the needs of the fox. It facilitates his manipulative skill in the counseling phase and reflects the usual lack of the principal's awareness of the fox's game. The privacy of the counseling dialogue (i.e., absence of the potential constraint of an audience) is also a contributing factor to fox success.

In the intraorganizational and international negotiating environments, the manipulative possibilities are considerably less. The negotiator is not necessarily a part of the position-formulation dialogue; where he does participate, his voice is only one in what usually is a group decisional exercise. This dilution of the negotiator's influence is a function of the numbers involved in position formulation and the inhibiting effect of the audience they constitute on attempts to influence organizational positions to take account of career or other personal interests. Furthermore, the position or instructions are usually put in writing. This reduces the possibility of the negotiator exploiting ambiguity or silence in his personal interest.

In all environments the dialogue between negotiator and principal concerning instructions continues throughout the negotiation. As part of his commitment to his principal's instructions, the negotiator is required to report back with dialogue developments, including proposals that he provisionally accepts *ad referendum* (i.e., for his principal's consideration and the issuance of appropriate instructions). The effective negotiator uses the *ad referendum* submission to provide advice and recommendations to his principal, ostensibly to assist him in formulating new instructions. Actually, this aspect of the negotiation process affords him the opportunity to further influence position formulation. In the private negotiating environment, continuation of the negotiator's role as counselor can be exploited to reinforce the advice already provided. In the intraorganizational and international negotiating environments, the negotiator may be able to establish himself as a key advisor by giving high-quality advice at this important stage in the dialogue. He may also be able to shape the report of dialogue developments to demonstrate that earlier advice, given but not acted upon, was on target, thereby qualifying his views for special consideration as the dialogue proceeds.

In summary, the goal of the effective negotiator is to have maximum control over the dialogue so that he can achieve positive results in the pursuit of his side's interests, including those related to his own career advancement. The private negotiating environment offers the negotiator an excellent position to dominate his principal. The number of actors in the intraorganizational environment makes it the most difficult one in which the negotiator can exercise control. The international environment tends to be equally difficult, but it may offer additional possibilities to influence foreign policy decisions because of the many channels of communication (i.e., potential dialogues) it encompasses. At times, a well-connected chief of mission or negotiator who is a good operator can bypass regular channels and communicate directly with individuals on his side's key decisional levels, thereby positioning himself to control the dialogue from the field.

The Use of Power and Law

Power. Power in negotiation involves more than exploitable disparity between the sides.[17] The key is the orchestration, exploitation, and manipulation of that disparity. As the effective negotiator well knows, power (like every other source of leverage) is not self-executing. It must first be identified and then consciously exploited. The two-step nature of leverage reminds us that "power can be weakness and weakness can be power." For example, the heavy-handed use of power may be self-defeating in the face of credible victim role playing to an audience to which the more powerful side is sensitive. In this situation, the power role is reversed and weakness becomes the dominant, controlling element.[18] The effective negotiator, therefore, looks at power as a potentially two-edged weapon as he seeks to either exploit it or neutralize it, depending on his side's interest. The "think-negotiation" focus on advantage assists him in handling a power imbalance.

The effective negotiator considers power the most usable tool in his inventory of bargaining counters. Whatever the strength of his personal commitment to ethics and morality, his professional judgment is that they are not as effective as power for influencing or pressuring persuasion. Experience has taught that the pursuit of interest by one side is rarely inhibited by reference to the ethical or moral deficiency of a proposed course of action. Although the reference to ethics or morality is an appropriate argument in a dialogue, especially when an audience is involved, it usually must be supplemented by a power- or leverage-oriented back-up (i.e., one that reflects a negotiating-cost dimension) to inhibit resort to undesired action. As power is the single best instrument for pressuring or influencing persuasion, it is difficult to conceive of a negotiating effort that does not involve an attempt to exploit it. Effective negotiation requires a clear understanding of the use of power in the negotiation process.

Power can be defined as a potential bargaining strength or advantage that may facilitate the achievement of negotiating objectives. Without orchestration, exploitation, or manipulation, however, a power advantage loses its bargaining potential. Power per se is not enough; it must be actively harnessed to the pursuit of interest. Although power implies leverage in that the side with the power edge usually can translate it into effective leverage, it is possible that (1) its existence or exploitability may not be recognized or utilized by the side possessing it, or (2) reliance on it can be inhibited or blunted by the defending side.

Bargaining or negotiating power is usually associated with a disparity in size, wealth, or strength. Actually, it can take a variety of forms besides the physical. It can involve occupying a key position; having the law or equity on one's side; having influence through family, rapport, or other connections; demonstrating readiness to act irresponsibly or irrationally; and playing the victim. Effective use of negotiating power starts with creating a credible perception that one enjoys a significant, exploitable power advantage. Once this is accomplished, power can be used to pressure the other side toward the desired consensus. As with leverage in general, power is what one makes of it either on offense or defense (i.e., it's another case of "use it or lose it!").

Effective exploitation of power requires recognition of its advantage potential and an effort directed at establishing the substantive and procedural aspects of power credibility: the existence of exploitable power (substantive credibility) and the capability and readiness to use it (procedural credibility).[19] Power that is not credible in this dual sense will not be exploitable or manipulable to achieve the desired effect.

Power credibility requires that the exploiting side be prepared to actually resort to the threatened power play and that exposure be carefully thought through. Of course, where the other side is impressed by threatened use of credible power, there usually is no need to actually make the power play because the desired perception and apprehension have already been generated. If there is doubt, however, the threat may have to be confirmed by action. For example, in the private negotiating environment the threat to sue, in the absence of a positive reaction by the other side, is usually followed by prompt filing of suit. Failure to do so will undermine the credibility of the power play and, perhaps, the entire negotiating position. For this reason, in many situations the effective negotiator will prefer veiled to express threats in order to have more negotiating flexibility (so that he does not have to take the action to demonstrate credibility).

The effort to counter or defend against the offensive use of power involves inhibition through creation of the perception that power is not exploitable or that its exploitation would be too costly. The former relates to the perception that the defending side cannot be intimidated or otherwise influenced by it because, for negotiating purposes, it does not exist. The latter, that exploitation would be too costly in actual terms and in terms of its relationship and audience impacts. Thus, offense involves establishing the credibility of power; defense involves masking its potential impact or exaggerating the negotiating cost of reliance upon it. During the Persian Gulf crisis of 1990, President Bush's strong rhetoric concerning the use of force to get Iraq to withdraw from Kuwait was countered by Saddam Hussein's stated readiness to (1) defend vigorously the incorporation of Kuwait as the nineteenth province of Iraq, (2) protect Iraqi installations from military attack with foreign hostages and prisoners of war, (3) blow up the oil fields and otherwise use the oil weapon, and (4) launch attacks against Israel and Saudi Arabia.

The negotiating environment is an important factor affecting the exploitability of power. The key is the extent of the presence in each environment of (1) audience exposure, (2) concern for the continuing relationship, and (3) practically available process to counter the use of power. All three factors tend to discourage the use of power. The private negotiating environment has the greatest vulnerability to a power play, as (1) audiences that could be inhibiting tend to be small or nonexistent, and (2) more frequently than not, there is no continuing relationship to be preserved. Furthermore, the practical cost of resort to process to serve as the equalizer to power (e.g., retention of counsel or commencement of litigation) often inhibits the attempt to blunt the use of power. Remedies that cannot be resorted to easily or in a cost-effective manner are not practically available in the negotiating sense.

Too frequently, the weaker side capitulates to its perception of the power situation, ignoring the potential for creative defensive action. This need not be the result. Even where there is no actual audience or continuing relationship and process is not practically available, the effective negotiator can still operate defensively. For example, he can attempt to develop a sympathy-evoking victim play that can be combined with the prospect of undesired publicity (through such vehicles as media hot lines, consumer affairs offices, and better business bureaus) to create the perception that audience or remedy exposure might neutralize or reverse the power disparity. The defense is to create a real or perceived negotiating cost for the reliance upon power by the stronger side. In effect, the weaker side uses its knowledge of the dynamics of power, including perception creation, to turn it on its head and run with it.

In the intraorganizational environment, on the other hand, the ever-present audience of organizational actors and the structured continuing relationships (the essence of the dialogue process) tend to inhibit open use of power in the conduct of day-to-day business, notwithstanding the theoretical availability of executive decision to terminate every dialogue. The overuse of executive decision is inhibited because it can disrupt the normal conduct of organizational business; it can undermine the integrity of the system that contemplates the routine resolution of most issues at the working (negotiating) level with prescribed institutional participation or representation.

Despite the inhibition, there is still some exposure to the power play. One cannot rule out the open use of power in a special situation deemed worth the negotiating cost (i.e., the opprobrium of short-circuiting organizational process). Furthermore, more muted and subtle uses of power occur in "behind-the-scenes" activity such as (1) backchannel and other efforts to generate internal and external decisional pressures on the organizational process, and (2) reliance upon name dropping and other ways of conveying the perception of a special relationship with, or access to, senior officials or an awareness of their views in order to pressure capitulation at the working level. Thus, despite the outward indication of reduced exposure to power because of the tendency to maintain the integrity of organizational process, the effective negotiator must be alert to covered power possibilities in the intraorganizational environment.

In the international negotiating environment, audience exposure and concern for the continuing relationship tend to reduce resort to power. The critical difference, however, is the absence of any practically available process that can control state behavior (in the form of an institutionalized system of third-party judgment or decision). Thus, the international system, incorporating the principle of governance through consent, knows no limit or constraint on the use of power and rule by the powerful.[20] Notwithstanding the foregoing, nation-states do not usually attempt to dictate solutions or resort to self-help in dialogues with other states. Instead, they tend to be restrained by the desire to avoid incurring political cost, bilateral as well as multilateral, with states that comprise the scrutinizing audience as well as with states that are directly impacted by their action. (There is also concern about incurring domestic political cost in connection with the naked use of power in conducting foreign relations.[21]) The result is that state concern for the avoidance of political cost supplements the restraining impact of audience exposure and concern for the continuing relationship, with cost avoidance emerging as the principal motivator of international behavior. In effect, cost avoidance replaces the practical availability of process as a deterrent to the use of power in the international negotiating environment.

Accordingly, state and other international actors only exceptionally substitute a power play, including self-help through military force or other sanction, for negotiation. Generally, they prefer dialogue and political settlement (i.e., negotiation) because it provides a means for large and small states alike to exploit the situational control arising from power through active and creative participation in the negotiation process. Diplomacy, defined as the conduct of international relations, is actually negotiation, in the form of nation-state dialogues for the conduct of day-to-day relationship business or for the resolution of specific issues or controversies in the pursuit of foreign policy interests. As states and other international actors seek negotiated results by using power to pressure acceptance of desired positions or actions, it is not surprising that power is inextricably involved in foreign relations. However, effective state use of power depends on its credibility; power that is not substantively or procedurally credible cannot be used to produce the desired pressuring effect. Failure to maintain both aspects of credibility often leads to the need to wield power—a costly result in political and economic terms that states usually seek to avoid.[22]

As a practical matter, power includes the entire spectrum of actions—political, economic, and military—that a state can take to pressure or influence a situation. It relates to the carrot[23] as well as the stick and can be utilized in either form to achieve desired results. The carrot aspect involves utilizing power to (1) grant what the other state seeks, or (2) otherwise reward it as a quid pro quo for the inaction or action desired. The range of possibilities is endless, but as a practical matter nation-states tend to be very reluctant to utilize power in this manner because of their concern for the precedential-impact cost of generous settlements or rewards. They do not usually "buy" solutions; rather, the emphasis is on controlling expectations and effecting settlement by exploiting uncertainty and apprehension through political, economic, and military pressures.[24]

Although power is traditionally associated with size and economic and military capability, recent history demonstrates that possession of scarce resources, having a key geographical location, or playing a politically important role in a situation enables states of all sizes to wield power. Furthermore, states can significantly increase their power impact by combining in blocs to pressure or influence a situation.[25] Therefore, power is not only the prerogative of large states, although their options are greater and more varied than those available to small states attempting to exploit power. Some typical examples of small-state power plays include acting irresponsibly (e.g., Iran in the American hostage situation); embarrassing a larger power by demonstrating to the world audience that negotiation is a cover for diktat (e.g., Panama's raising of negotiating issues in the Security Council during the Panama Canal negotiations); courting adversary states (e.g., Philippine overtures to the Socialist Bloc during base negotiations with the United States); and bloc or concerted action with respect to resources or in international forums (e.g., Organization of Petroleum Exporting Countries oil embargo and Group of 77 solidarity in the Law of the Sea negotiations).

Small and large states can also gain power by putting the entire relationship on the negotiating table through procedural and substantive linkage to the specific issues under negotiation. In a sense, linkage provides a built-in source of power; it draws upon the relationship itself, or substantive aspects of the relationship, to pressure or influence the result with respect to a specific issue. On the procedural side, the importance of the continuing relationship is always a factor. A good relationship and the felt need to maintain it will be a constraint that will impact the conduct of the negotiation.

As to substantive linkage, there seldom is encountered an international situation in which one can assume that an issue can be negotiated discretely or in isolation. The tendency is for one or both sides to enhance their leverage situation by linking issues in a balance-sheet approach, using the carrot and stick as appropriate. Moreover, even where there is no formal diplomatic relationship, issues can be linked. For example, when the Carter Administration attempted to develop a dialogue with Fidel Castro to control the 1980 Mariel exodus of Cuban refugees, it ran into the suggestion that the dialogue include the Guantanamo base issue. Removal of the U.S. naval base at Guantanamo was proposed as the price for dialogue on an agreement for a more orderly exodus.

It should be apparent that effective negotiation requires that power be orchestrated, exploited, and manipulated (not necessarily employed) in pursuing desired consensus. The negotiator who is not versed in the play of power of who shuns that play is ill positioned to gain what is sought through negotiation. As a very practical fact of negotiating life in all environments, leveraging one's position to gain desired results starts and ends with considerations of power.

Law. Having the law on one's side has special importance in the negotiation process because it constitutes a form of power that is orchestratable, exploitable, and manipulable in conducting the dialogue. The effective negotiator is prepared to argue "the facts, equity, or the law," depending on his side's interests in the light of what the situation is on the merits. Reference to the merits brings to mind the classic question, "What happens when two effective negotiators face off against each other?" The "think-negotiation" response is that the negotiated result will approximate the situation on the merits. The quality of negotiated results tends to reflect the skill level of the participants rather than the state of the law or other standards for third-party judgment.

The use of law as a lever of power is linked to the availability of effective process or other negotiating-cost consequence of its invocation. In the private negotiating environment, availability of the courts and other decisional bodies enhances the leverage potential of having the law on one's side. As a consequence, most demands in this environment tend to be accompanied, directly or indirectly, with a threat to "see you in court" or resort to other dispositive process. Even here, there is a useful distinction for effective negotiation. The fact that the case is actionable and a competent tribunal exists does not necessarily mean that effective process is practically available in the negotiating sense.

The concept of practical availability relates to the readiness, disposition, or ability of the invoking side to take advantage of the process by which the stronger position on the merits can be exploited. It involves the will to make use of the process in light of such considerations as probability of success, strength of the opposition, ease of access, cost, convenience, and attendant notoriety, all of which might otherwise inhibit resort to it. For the effective negotiator the question is not existence of process but whether the process is perceived by the other side to be practically available. The issue of practical availability becomes the refuge of the side with the weaker legal position. It defends against the invocation of process by shaping the invoking side's perception of practical availability by stressing the difficulties and burdens of resort to process. This exercise in perception manipulation is most frequently encountered in burden-of-negotiation discussions, which often turn on perceptions concerning the practical availability of effective process as a viable alternative to a negotiated result.

In the intraorganizational environment, resort to process is facilitated because staffing procedures contemplate additional process that can be exploited (e.g., referring to a higher level for a decision or having other elements participate in the dialogue, such as organizational counsel for an opinion). In the negotiating sense, this environment affords greater practical availability of internal process for the side with the strongest position of the law. However, some considerations of restraint must be weighed by the potential invoker of process to avoid action that may prove to be counterproductive over the longer term. Among these are loss of policy or operational control at the action level (an important career concern), disruption of continuing staff relationships, and interruption of the staffing rhythm by the precedent of a different procedure for disposition of difficult issues. The principal exposure here is the career impact of invoking extraordinary process (that which departs from normal staff-resolution procedures) and, perhaps, being considered a whistle-blower. Insofar as invocation of process external to the organization is concerned (e.g., involvement of the courts or the General Accounting Office), there is the additional exposure of the career consequences of going outside the system.

Use of law in the international negotiating environment has some special wrinkles because of the (1) lack of process in the sense of the absence of a system of compulsory adjudication or settlement, and (2) manner in which the effective negotiator approaches and uses international law in conducting the dialogue. In no way can an international actor be subjected to third-party judgment on the merits, as the consensual basis for involvement in the international system precludes compulsory process.[26] As to the use of international law, the effective negotiator measures the importance of law principally in terms of considerations of political cost and credibility. Normative impact is secondary because of the consensus-oriented environment in which he is operating. This is understandable in light of the limited efficacy of legality to pressure or influence persuasion. Law is only marginally effective in this regard; there are relatively few situations in which states are so sensitive about their reputation for lawful behavior that the opprobrium of involvement in an "illegal" act either inhibits or induces action perceived to be contrary to the national interest. Thus, the advice that a contemplated course of policy action would be regarded as a violation of international legal principles does not, of itself, lead the effective negotiator to reject that option. It merely invites the follow-on question concerning the nature and extent of the political or negotiating-cost impact of pursuing it.

It may be said that when states have the luxury of choice, they usually opt for the action that accords with the practice of states or accepted principles of international law. This behavior pattern reflects the reality of interdependence and the general desire to (1) reap the political benefit of the reputation for legality and (2) enjoy the enhanced acceptability of a proposal when it can be presented as compatible with international law. In other situations involving special national interests and more limited choices, however, states tend to weigh legality along with the other elements in the decisional equation as part of their cost-benefit analysis. While illegality is not dispositive in itself, it can have a scale-tilting, collateral effect; unlawful behavior may adversely impact other involvements and important continuing relationships. The judgment here is based on political cost, not legality or other normative considerations.

The effective negotiator views legality as an important facilitative tool in conducting the dialogue. In reacting to proposals or positions, he will raise the legal issue if it can be exploited or manipulated favorably. For example, on defense, a claim of illegality may be used as an argument to discredit a proposed position, introduce a new issue, or expand the dialogue to probe the other side's position more deeply. On offense, the negotiator attempts to enhance the acceptability of his own proposals and positions by clothing them with the trappings of legality—at times with great creativity (e.g., during the Vietnam War the United States used the maritime-law doctrine of hot pursuit to justify territorial incursions into Cambodia). Where legality cannot be used to support his position, he will attempt to remove the issue from the dialogue by ignoring it or discounting its importance because of the transcendent political importance of the national interest involved in his position or proposal. In doing so, he is actually seeking to explain the special need to depart from traditional international law or any creative application of it in an effort to reduce the political cost of the departure.[27]

The effective negotiator's perception of law is decidedly oriented toward process and negotiation cost and understandably so. His vision parameters are set by pragmatic considerations of operational need and the requirements for success rather than by theoretical considerations related to legality, system building, or other values. This is to be expected, as in the personal dimension of his "think-negotiation" mindset his focus is on career advancement through success in negotiation.

There is, however, one area of legality to which the negotiator is extremely sensitive: the development of practice during the implementation phase of an agreement. A frequently overlooked implied objective of negotiation is maintenance or preservation of the negotiated result. As a consequence, the "think-negotiation" approach, being sensitive to the legal effect of the practice developed under an agreement, treats implementation as a continuation of the negotiation process. By carefully monitoring the postnegotiation practice as it develops to ensure its compatibility with the negotiated result, the side whose interest it is to defend that result is in a position to challenge and defeat attempts to dilute it. Similarly, the side seeking a change through the development of favorable practice has to be careful: The attempt actually involves flirtation with a possible charge of breach of the agreement, which could sour the entire postnegotiation, implementation relationship.

The effective negotiator attempts to lay the groundwork for such a post-negotiation effort by the manner in which certain issues are handled during the negotiation. For example, stressing the difficulty of including a certain requirement in the agreement can later be used to explain the nonconforming action used to test the practice under the agreement. The test can be presented as confirmation or proof that the agreed requirement is overly burdensome or unnecessary. A positive result could be a reopening of the issue in the "common interest" to ensure a smooth postnegotiation relationship. (It is not in the interest of the defending side to open a dialogue concerning the requirement. Opening the dialogue tends to raise expectations and thereby jeopardizes the negotiated result. The best defense is a firm "no" and "a deal's a deal"—in other words, dialogue avoidance.) If carefully handled as suggested, the maximum exposure involved in an unsuccessful attempt to create favorable practice is the need to implement the arrangement as originally negotiated.

Interest (Parochialism)

Although it has been highlighted in connection with the intraorganizational environment, parochialism is basically a manifestation of the larger element, interest, that pervades all the environments. Interest and the pursuit of interest drive negotiations and give them an adversarial, competitive character. While the pursuit of interest does not exclude accommodation of all or some of the other interests involved in a given negotiation (generally, negotiations are not zero-sum), it is more conducive to goal/objective realization to think about negotiation as an adversarial process. Any approach to negotiation that stresses as a principal concern the cooperative, rather than competitive, harmonization of interests (e.g., Roger Fisher's focus on the duty of the negotiator to work out a "wise agreement" [28]) and the requirement that everyone leave the table a winner detracts from the goal-oriented focus with negative bargaining implications.

In the first instance, the negotiator as an advocate and proponent should not have that role blurred by the need to make Solomonic or other judgments unrelated to the pursuit of a side's interest. Second, such an approach underestimates the possibilities for creating and exploiting the perception that the negotiation has turned out well for the other side. Furthermore, operating from the premise that all sides must win or be satisfied tends to lower defenses against a strong goal/objective thrust by the opposing side.

The basic approach to effective negotiation should reflect a win-oriented thrust in support of interest, leavened by all of the "think-negotiation" concerns about viability and relationship costs reflected in this Guide's continuing checklist (to be discussed in detail later). The key word is "leavened"; without the balance provided by the caveats concerning viability and negotiating-relationship maintenance, a strictly "win-lose," "go-for-the-jugular" approach is usually counterproductive. The very consensus and accommodation orientation of the negotiation process precludes reliance upon unbridled greed in defining and pursuing interest. The Gordon Gekko (Wall Street) dictum about greed [29] is not the answer to effective negotiation.

A balanced approach to interest is the principal focus of "thinking negotiation." It drives the dialogues in all the negotiating environments. In the private environment, pursuit of the principal's interest drives the push for consensus. In intraorganizational dialogues, pursuit of the special interest of the organizational entity being represented produces the phenomenon of parochialism. In the international environment, dialogues are the means states use to pursue their national interests. Cutting across all of these principal-oriented, interest-driven dialogues is the interest of the negotiator in advancing or protecting his career. Pursuit of this interest is one aspect of the intraside dialogue that encompasses other diversity of interest within the side (e.g., where there are multiple principals). Recognizing, sorting out, and accommodating all the interests in a negotiation constitute the main preoccupation of the effective negotiator, whose basic orientation is the crafting of favorable consensus in pursuit of his side's interest.

Careerism

Careerism is a feature of all negotiating environments. Negotiators desire to advance their professional careers by receiving high marks and tangible rewards from their principals. The intensity of this desire varies with the environments because of the differences inherent in them. An appreciation of this variation is essential in assessing whether the career concerns of the other side's negotiator can be exploited in conducting the dialogue. Moreover, the prudent principal who wishes to (1) reduce his exposure to the career pressures of his negotiator and (2) defend against any vulnerability on this score has to be aware of the impact of environment on that exposure.

In the private negotiating environment, the negotiator's concern is to develop a good reputation for effectiveness in order to acquire future business (if he is a private practitioner) or achieve career advancement (if he is operating as part of an organization, corporate, governmental, or other). In the former case, except when he is involved in a high-visibility negotiation, a negotiator in a one-shot relationship (i.e., retained for a specific negotiation without the prospect of a follow-on, continuing relationship with the principal) may consider his exposure quite low: All that may result from an unsuccessful effort is loss of the principal's future business (which is not expected anyway, because of the one-shot nature of the relationship) and, perhaps, his criticism of the negotiator's representation. Given the limited nature of his exposure and consequent apprehension, the negotiator's minimal career concerns may be exploitable by the other side in the sense that the negotiator's commitment to the effort may not be as strong as if he were carrying greater career risk. This may be manifested by a readiness to dispose of the matter quickly or make a pro forma effort without the tenacity of an all-out effort to get the most out of the dialogue.

The possibility of this exploitation is most discouraging to the negotiator's principal, who is in a relatively weak position to harness the former's career interest to produce a strong negotiating effort on his behalf. Short of action to increase the negotiator's career interest through a bonus or other incentive, the prudent principal should carefully monitor the negotiator's performance and encourage him to make a strong representational effort. The principal can also prop up the negotiator's resolve by controlling his authority to conduct and, of course, conclude the dialogue. The key to the principal's protection is alertness and understanding of the dynamics of his interface with the negotiator. Whenever the effective negotiator is pressed by an alert, prudent principal, he usually raises the apparent level and enthusiasm of his representation and stresses, whenever credibly possible, the difficulty of his negotiating assignment and the side's position.

The situation is considerably different where the negotiator is an employee of his principal (e.g., claim adjuster for an insurance company). The continuing employment relationship (i.e., conduct of the negotiation as part of his work for the principal) will have an important impact on the negotiator's career advancement and therefore will be a source of considerable concern to him. In this private negotiating situation the principal can realize maximum exploitable mileage from the career concerns of the negotiator. Again, vigilance is in order for the principal: It is also possible for the negotiator to be inhibited or bluffed by the other side because of an understandable desire to follow a conservative course and not gamble with his principal's interests and, more important, his own career. The principal must be sensitive to this possibility as he monitors his negotiator's work and tries to stimulate a strong representational effort by stressing the rewards for success and the consequences of lesser results. When a negotiator is risk averse insofar as strong representation is concerned, the consequences include dismissal or transferral to other duties. The same situation prevails in the intraorganizational and international environments, where the negotiator always operates in a structured relationship with his principal.

The foregoing is only a sampling of the considerations involved in the exploitation of careerism in the negotiating environments. "Thinking negotiation" should always take into account the vulnerability presented by the self-interest orientation of the negotiator.

Coping with the Intraorganizational Environment

The intraorganizational environment, involving dialogues with and within large structured organizations, private or governmental, appears to the uninitiated to be an awesome arena in which to operate. The thought of taking on a "corporate giant" or "fighting City Hall" from the outside or being involved in bureaucratic infighting within an organization implies the hopelessness of a battle against insurmountable odds. The general reaction is that such encounters are unpleasant, dangerous and, more important, unwinnable. However, the effective negotiator has a different view. Although he prefers the simpler assignments usually encountered in the other environments, he is comfortable working in both the external and internal dimensions of the intraorganizational environment because he knows that such situations can be handled effectively through the application of negotiation concepts and techniques.

By substituting negotiation for petition or other submissive approaches, he can pursue his interests outside and within an organization with significant success. The key to coping with dialogues in this environment is to realize that (1) organizational actions result from internal multiparty or multilateral dialogues, and (2) these dialogues can be influenced because the participants are motivated by, and are sensitive to, four basic concerns: career interests, parochial organizational interests, organizational imagery, and the precedential cost of organizational activity. These concerns provide *pressure points* for use from the outside or within the organization in pursuit of favorable organizational action or inaction. These pressure points are orchestrated, exploited, and manipulated as part of the dialogue management and control effort to produce the desired action or inaction.

It is useful to view operations in the intraorganizational environment as involving attempts to influence organizational action (i.e., the internal staffing exercise or dialogue) from both outside and within the organization. In effect, a "Mr. Outside" and "Mr. Inside" approach and mentality are suggested. Whenever there is a Mr. Outside effort to influence the organization, there is a corresponding organizational reaction in the form of an internal staffing exercise or dialogue to develop a response. The effort to develop that response is led by the official who is responsible for the particular subject matter; he is usually known as the action officer. In accordance with organizational structure and process, he is responsible for preparing and staffing an action paper. If he is sensitive to the negotiation reality of the internal decisional process, he would be a Mr. Inside working with or against any other equally sensitive Mr. Inside who is involved in, but not responsible for, leading the staffing action. Any competition between officials in the internal dialogue tends to polarize the process.

Thus, pursuit of a private claim against a large corporation or government entity actually involves two dialogues: (1) the attempt to influence favorable organizational action from the outside, and (2) the organization's internal decision-making process, which produces the response. There are two negotiations: one in the private negotiating environment, the other in the intraorganizational.

The Private Negotiation Dialogue: Coping from the Outside. Mr. Outside analyzes the operations of the organization to become familiar with its process and identify the key actors. Thereafter, he develops action options that are available to the organization under the circumstances, and seeks to uncover personal career implications for the key actors and image and precedential concerns of the organization, with respect to the options. This approach will reflect the leverage possibilities for exploiting process and the pressure points in dealing with the key actors. Mr. Outside then combines these possibilities with what is favorable on the merits to develop his negotiating game plan. Throughout preparation of the game plan he must work closely with his principal, making sure that the principal is aware of the difficulty of the dialogue and has realistic expectations concerning the attainable results. Principals usually tend to be most cooperative, given the David-and-Goliath nature of the operation.

In this difficult private negotiating situation (where the parties are so unequal), all available pressures and influences, both real and created, must be brought to bear to stimulate the desired organizational response. As in all negotiations, this involves the creation of apprehension and uncertainty, the control of expectations, the creation of favorable perceptions of the situation, and the inhibition of undesired action. Above all, a special effort must be made to convey strong and confident resolve in pursuing the matter despite the inequality of the situation. Where there is little that can be used to pressure for the desired response, the negotiator may need to conduct a "salvage" operation to try to get something out of the negotiation for his principal. In fact, if the other side is led to believe that the negotiation will be long and difficult, it may offer a relatively low-cost settlement to avoid it. The impetus for settlement is the desire to terminate involvement in a potentially burdensome dialogue. Release from such involvement has a value that is usually referred to as the nuisance or inconvenience value of a negotiating situation.

For example, Mr. Outside might determine that the nature of the process contemplates productive dialogues by organizational operators and provides adequate opportunity for the presentation of a case. If this is so, he may be able to bring about a favorable, quick disposition of his principal's matter by demonstrating a readiness to utilize all the time and procedures permitted by the process to present a case that, on the merits, cannot produce anything more than a marginal result for the organization. This technique involves demonstrating to the operator that his career interests cannot be advanced by devoting all the time that appears to be necessary for the "unproductive" dialogue. The happy result could be an early disposition on terms acceptable to Mr. Outside. This technique may be successfully exploited in responding to Internal Revenue Service tax audits in which operator performance is judged on the basis of productivity of the results.

Having said the foregoing, let me caution that one should not hastily conclude that the negotiation has to be a salvage operation just because of the perceived disparity in relative strength of the sides. First one must carefully probe the organization's perception of the situation, lest one's own pessimistic perception become a self-fulfilling prophecy. Confirmation by probing enables one to reap the benefit of any windfall in the form of an exploitable, unexpectedly favorable perception of the situation (e.g., apprehension, uncertainty, or controlled expectation) on the part of the other side. Probing will also shed light on the organization's commitment and readiness to pursue the dialogue and may uncover "talking points" for the salvage operation if, in fact, one must settle for that.

The Intraorganizational Dialogue: Coping from the Inside. When working as Mr. Inside to develop consensus on a response or other organizational policy, the negotiator has the following career pressures: to control the action (to demonstrate competence at the working level and derive job satisfaction), and to produce the desired result or, at least, demonstrate to the organizational audience a "best effort" to do so. An important part of controlling the action is to shape the organizational leadership's perception of what is or should be desired as well as the great difficulties involved in achieving the desired objective. In helping to shape this perception, Mr. Inside will try to exploit the special interests and image and precedential concerns of the organization and its leaders. His objective is to lighten his negotiating task within the organization (and ultimately with Mr. Outside) by bringing about a favorable, career-friendly conclusion of the intra-side dialogue concerning the side's objectives and the difficulty in attaining them.

Once Mr. Inside receives his negotiating instructions from the overall organization he represents, the basic technique he uses to develop the organizational position is a *search for allies* among the other elements involved in the organization-wide staffing exercise. As development of organizational consensus tends to be a domino process wherein interested and involved elements lean toward the easy course of concurring with (rather than preparing) a proposed decisional document, Mr. Inside should prepare the staffing proposal. If he is the action officer, this will be expected of him and he will not have to betray the advantage it entails by making a special effort to seek the assignment.

The proposal should have broad appeal to all participants in the dialogue in order to win adherents (allies) and start the snowballing of the desired consensus. The essence of searching for allies is to "poll the house" (i.e., discreetly ascertain the positions or approaches of the elements involved, as well as special interests and needs, including those of key individuals) and then shape the desired position with features (reflecting the results of the poll) that maximize its group appeal. In addition, past organizational behavior should be scrutinized to see who are the leaders and followers among the group and, in terms of the specific issue, which participants are most substantively involved. There is little need to expend shaping chips on the followers or those who are only marginally affected. The former can be reached by the shaping directed at the leaders; the latter require only token shaping, as there is little reason for them to stand in the way of a snowballing general consensus. Lacking an interest involvement, the marginally affected can be expected to join the herd in its movement toward consensus.

The next step is to have all participants respond to the document drafted by Mr. Inside, that is, to get them to negotiate from his draft. If this can be accomplished, Mr. Inside has an enhanced possibility of attracting support for his shaped position and, ultimately, having his way. The technique's effectiveness is immeasurably enhanced if Mr. Inside is the action officer; in that capacity, he will have little difficulty in getting other dialogue participants to work from his draft (which, of course, has been shaped and loaded in his favor). From the negotiation point of view, he is in the driver's seat.

Less easy but still manageable is the task where Mr. Inside is not the action officer. The technique is the same. As organizational bureaucrats sometimes prefer to "let George do it," volunteering to be the George who drafts the working paper may provide access to the driver's seat. If this is not possible, the shaped position must vie for group acceptability as a counterproposal. If the action officer is not playing the part of Mr. Inside (i.e., not seeking to exploit the negotiating advantage of having his shaped draft as the working paper), he may entertain a counterproposal. The counterproposer may have to make his paper especially attractive so that it will be preferred over the one being pushed by the action officer. This need for greater attractiveness may carry increased substantive cost. If a strongly competitive situation develops, the search for allies may become a more costly, "divide-and-conquer" effort to separate the action officer from his supporters.

In both the Mr. Outside and Mr. Inside operations, special attention should be paid to management and control techniques that facilitate acceptance of the desired result. The effective negotiator is well aware of the potential exploitability of careerism, and he reacts appropriately. In organizational activities, innovation is generally less easily embraced than a familiar precedent or approach. Organizations tend to be creatures of habit because career concerns, stemming from peer pressures and a competitive environment, shade dialogue participants' choices on the side of safety and low risk. In a highly structured organizational setting, errors tend to be recorded or "remembered with consequences"; this generally inhibits bold action. The tendency away from risk assumption by the target group should be one of the principal considerations in position shaping. A high-risk position will be more difficult to sell to potential allies within and outside the organization.

Thus, when trying to influence or pressure organizational action from the outside or the inside, the effective negotiator must be sensitive to the possibilities of exploiting the traditional conservatism of the career bureaucrat.[30] Furthermore, he may be able to exploit the bureaucrat's desire to avoid having a superior become personally involved in the dialogue. The bureaucrat would not want the personal exposure that results from the direct "audience" surveillance, and he would not want the superior's involvement to be viewed by colleagues as an indication that he is unable to "hold up his end." Moreover, the bureaucrat may be expected to resist the loss of personal job satisfaction in not completely controlling the action. If involvement of superiors is a career concern, the effective negotiator can exploit it by stating that he intends to stimulate progress in the dialogue by "going upstairs" or scheduling a meeting with, or even calling, the superior directly; this threat provides leverage for the desired movement at the working level. In addition, if he knows that dialogue participants do not want to be responsible for discrediting or embarrassing their superiors or the organization, he can create exploitable, inhibiting apprehension by involving the media or arranging other audience exposure.

Exploitation of Process

In effective negotiation, there must be sensitivity to the need to exploit process, whether it be process internal to negotiation or some formal or informal external process related to an available recourse or remedy. In terms of internal process, the effective negotiator knows that he can best orchestrate, manipulate, and exploit perceptions, apprehension, uncertainty, and expectations when he is in contact or in dialogue (i.e., negotiating) with the other side. Thus, exploitation of the negotiation process involves maximizing the number of contacts or dialogue opportunities. Each contact under the globality principle is a part of the negotiation; it provides probing, perception-creating, and pressure-persuading opportunities. Common examples are (1) slowly exiting an office or store after making a low offer (thereby giving the other side additional time to accept the offer as it contemplates the vanishing deal), and (2) arranging "a chance" meeting or being in contact on another matter (thereby giving an opportunity to demonstrate or ascertain interest or lack of interest in renewal of a stalled dialogue).

Exploitation of negotiation process is frequently overlooked because of the traditional focus on exploitation in the form of techniques, ploys, and tactics of formal, across-the-table dialogue. The emphasis here is on multiplying the informal contacts, preferably face-to-face,[31] to achieve full exploitation of the "always negotiating" posture of the globality principle. Informal contact may catch the other side off balance and provide excellent probing opportunities.

Ad referendum is another feature of the negotiation process that lends itself to useful exploitation. The general need to refer proposals for approval by the side's principal can be exploited to gain time in responding to proposals, to distance oneself from a difficult principal ("good guy–bad guy"), to attempt to become a surrogate mediator by expressing opinions on what would and would not be acceptable to the principal, and to claim to have limited authority with respect to troublesome issues. The foregoing can be used to force the other side to (1) persevere only with respect to its most important demands, dropping the lesser ones because of the time and effort involved in their pursuit; (2) make exhaustive presentations in support of positions (thereby providing more material for probing); and (3) direct antagonism away from the negotiator to his principal in the interest of cultivating a friendlier tone at the negotiating table. All these possibilities would facilitate the conduct of the dialogue by reducing chip expenditure, increasing probing take, and improving the negotiating relationship.

Apart from exploiting the process internal to negotiation, the effective negotiator is alert to formal and informal external processes that can and should be exploited. In the private negotiating environment, the availability of a judicial, administrative, or "hotline" forum or other process for redress can be utilized as a lever in conducting the dialogue. "If you do not settle, we sue"; "Go to the Better Business Bureau"; "Involve the Bar Association"; or "Call Channel X." In such cases, exploitable leverage comes not only from the possibility of an adverse finding or disposition but also from the cost and inconvenience factors (including undesired notoriety) that may result.

In the intraorganizational negotiating environment, formal process is key because staffing and other organizational dialogues tend to be conducted in accordance with established procedures. Recognized mastery of these procedures often gives exploitable advantage; the less knowledgeable may "go along" rather than get involved in a losing procedural dogfight or one that reveals their lack of operational skills. Mastery of process also indicates that one knows how to generate (formally and informally) the types of internal and external pressures that can be exploited to impact organizational action. In addition, knowledge of the organization and its process enables the negotiator to identify the key actors who should be involved (or avoided!) at critical points in the dialogue. For example, a deftly placed memorandum at the proper organizational level—an apparently nonthreatening, dialogue maneuver—can be dispositive because of the attention it attracts and the pressures it generates. A similar result can be obtained by placing in, or "inadvertently" failing to remove from, the file a helpful internal document, a "plant." In short, procedures must be viewed from the "think-negotiation," interest/advantage perspective to identify how they can be used directly and indirectly to support the negotiating effort.

The conduct of international relations involves (1) the formal process of international organizations and entities and (2) the protocol, ceremony, and ritual of the diplomatic practice of states. Insofar as external formal process is concerned (e.g., international organizations, international tribunals, or arbitration), states cannot be forced to submit to process against their will. This is different from the private and intraorganizational environments where binding process can be invoked against a side and that side must respond. What is the same, however, is the availability of, and the need to use, internal process creatively[32] to generate internal and external pressures for the desired consensus. It is fairly easy to orchestrate, exploit, and manipulate diplomatic contacts, protocol, and formalities, including social functions, to pursue negotiating objectives under the globality principle.

For example, threatening to involve the secretary of state and his foreign counterpart in resolving an issue on which stalemate has been reached at the negotiating level can create pressures for movement at that level. Similarly, the possibility of exploiting meetings of senior-level officials scheduled for other purposes can be brought into the dialogue by suggesting that the status of the negotiation be added as an agenda item. Moreover, lack of progress in the negotiation can be made an agenda item for an appropriately timed meeting of a relevant international organization. Social contacts can also be exploited. An unhappy turn in an ongoing negotiation can be reflected in cool, less friendly social contacts or their complete elimination.

In the international environment, where there is a preoccupation with nuance and signal sending and reading, the effective negotiator can have a field day in conveying the pressuring signals deemed productive for managing and controlling the dialogue. The basic approach here is to convert conventional contact points and activities into manipulable dialogue process that can be orchestrated in support of the negotiating effort.

Importance of Precedent

Precedent is a concern in every negotiating environment because it impacts both process and substance as a source of negotiating exposure and cost. On the process side, it can establish a practice concerning how certain transactions or disputes are handled. On the substantive side, a precedent can be dispositive on the merits during either the negotiation or any subsequent resort to remedies concerning the negotiated result. Practice and precedent tend to have the greatest impact in environments in which a scrutinizing audience demands observance of, or adherence to, the particular practice or precedent. This implies a certain level of knowledge and alertness that is more frequently encountered in the professionalism of the actors in the intraorganizational and international environments. Actually, this is a bit misleading because many of the special organizations that provide advisory and consulting service to consumers and other nonspecialist actors serve as a surrogate scrutinizing audience. Moreover, there is sufficient specialization, sensitivity, or self-interest in the private marketplace to make precedent a concern because one who expects to prosper there cannot ignore business practices or customs.

In the private negotiating environment, precedent in the form of a market or business practice can dictate the substantive terms to be included in negotiated arrangements. Precedents concerning party responsibilities in standard transactions tend to fix the textual boilerplate for the onus and scope of those responsibilities in the relevant arrangements. The effect of the practice (precedent) is to take the issue out of the negotiation and impose a tremendous chip-cost burden on the side that seeks to depart from the practice in an effort to tailor an arrangement. Similarly, parties must take account of legal precedents that, in the remedy-oriented private environment in which they operate, can be controlling or persuasive in the negotiation of the arrangement and in any subsequent litigation or other process to resolve controversies arising from it.

Precedent can also control the process for dispute resolution. For example, the recognition through precedent that certain claims fall under insurance policy or warranty coverage establishes the process for resolving such claims. As a consequence, insurers and warrantors are most sensitive to dialogues that have the potential to become precedents for expanding the claimant population. They recognize that many claimants would be deterred from pursuing their claims if they had to establish the existence of a right or remedy to do so as a precedent condition. There is also the matter of cost, expenditure of time, and other inhibiting factors in undertaking judicial rather than administrative or other less formal process in pursuing a claim.

The general absence of sensitivity to the exposure potential of precedent on the part of individual actors without professional knowledge, assistance, or representation reduces the importance of precedent in many private negotiations. This does not apply to negotiations involving the larger actors; they have learned that their very size makes them objects, if not targets, of public interest groups. They have to consider the notoriety generated by the press and its activism. Also, administrative agencies and groups such as consumer relations and better business organizations are a source of precedential apprehension for them, because they act as the scrutinizing audience in intervening on behalf of, or providing assistance in connection with, what would otherwise be poorly pursued claims.

In the intraorganizational environment, precedent plays an important part in the staffing dialogues. Precedent, which serves as the safe haven for risk-shy bureaucrats, can easily be manipulated by those both inside and outside the organization who desire to develop favorable consensus. In many instances, precedent takes on the character of (or is represented to be) organizational policy, which then is used to dispose of the issue on the basis of fiat rather than consensus. The inside operator must research organization files to ascertain the existence of relevant precedents that can be used by him or against him in the intraorganizational dialogue. In effect, he acts as the scrutinizing audience to ensure that, at the very least, favorable precedents surface and are considered in connection with the dialogue.

As organizations face outward, they are very sensitive to the exposure potential of precedent in expanding organizational obligations and responsibilities. They are most careful to avoid establishing a precedent even at the expense of honoring claims in a low-key manner or off the record. The low key is preferred because notoriety and publicity attract claimants. This sensitivity can be exploited by claimants who are willing to accept favorable organizational actions in a covered fashion that does not establish a general practice or precedent. In fact, their willingness to do so can serve as an effective bargaining chip. For example, I myself was able to get two transmissions replaced by one of the Big Three automobile manufacturers as a matter of ad hoc customer friendship in return for not informing the National Highway Transportation Safety Administration or other consumer affairs organizations that a product defect was involved. The manufacturer's sensitivity to the potential exposure of a recall action made it amenable to being customer friendly. The heart of the corporate concern is to avoid audience involvement that might result in the development of a costly precedent.

In the international environment, precedent becomes a part of the practice of states; as such, it becomes a sort of international standard of state behavior for specific arrangements. This standard is demanded by states in similar situations lest the treatment accorded them be viewed as unequal or nonstandard. As a consequence, states usually have to accord this standard in their other international relationships. This is especially burdensome to states that have similar involvements with many international actors because they have to take account of the potential exposure of new arrangements that could become costly precedents for other relationships.

Consider a bilateral setting involving a base rights negotiation for a U.S.

military presence. There would be understandable reluctance on the part of the United States to enter into an arrangement containing a special concession to the host state. The real cost of the concession must be viewed in terms of the potential future need to accord that same treatment to all other similarly situated host states. The cost reality of the situation provides a rational basis for credibly refusing to grant the concession. The refusal of the government of New Zealand to permit the visit of military ships or aircraft carrying nuclear weapons was a limitation that the United States felt was too costly to accept, even though the actual cost to the United States was the undermining of the Australian–New Zealand–United States security relationship. If the host state cannot be refused because of the basing state's need for its strategic location, the impact of the precedent may be attenuated by linking it to some concession on the part of the host state that might dampen the enthusiasm of other states to insist on equal treatment. For this approach to be effective, the host state must be put on notice and accept that the full terms of the arrangement will be made known to other states as a protection against their adverse use of precedent against the basing state.

The nature of the international negotiation environment encourages efforts to exploit favorable precedent. States jealously scrutinize state practice to see how they can convert other states' practice into a de facto, third-party beneficiary situation. The fact that very few international agreements are classified and most are made public facilitates the scrutiny of the would-be beneficiary states. This complicates foreign policy formulation for large states because in their viability analysis of proposed policy they must consider the potential precedental exposure to third states.

NOTES

1. The dealings between layered organizations (e.g., subordinate and superior governmental entities or subsidiary and parent corporate organizations) take on the character of private negotiations. However, dealings within an organization, or between equal organizations involved in a structured decisional process at the same level, are intraorganizational in nature.

2. Careerism is both a positive and negative factor as negotiators seek, in their career self-interest, to excel in serving their principals. In the final analysis, negotiators can only do two things for their principals: either achieve the desired consensus or demonstrate the strongest possible effort to do so (i.e., that the principal "got a good run for his money"). Because the former brings the greatest career rewards, there are pressures on a negotiator to (1) shape the principal's perception of the desired consensus (i.e., he negotiates with his principal for a more attainable or "negotiable" position), and (2) pull out all stops to achieve that consensus (i.e., he tends to accept expediency as the categorical imperative). These pressures produce the positive tendency of bringing the sides closer to consensus and the negative of introducing sharp and, at times, unethical practices into the negotiating

dialogue. Career pressures operate at their best and worst in the relatively laissez-faire private negotiating environment; they are somewhat muffled by the structured, institutional framework of interfaces in the intraorganizational and international environments.

3. Similarly, parochialism has both a positive and negative impact. On the positive side, it contributes to the full airing of issues in the sense that individuals and organizational entities contending for the adoption of preferred positions make presentations favoring adoption that can enhance the balance and rationality of the solution. On the other hand, parochialism can negatively affect the solution by injecting a divisive, subjective pull away from a unified effort to attain objective rationality.

4. These dialogues can be rather complex. For example, in the Department of Defense there would be internal dialogues within the army, navy, and air force for the preparation of service positions. These are then considered at the departmental level to develop the agency position—in effect, two stages before getting to the national-level dialogue.

5. The term "foreign policy" can be and is used in a variety of ways. One can speak of the "foreign policy of the United States" to refer to a specific policy or to a trend in U.S. relations with other states. Emphasis on dialogue awareness, management, and control in the "think-negotiation" mindset leads to a preference for treating each foreign relations decision as a foreign policy and using the formulation "foreign policies" when a collective reference is intended.

6. Foreign policy is made whenever a nation-state makes a decision, adopts a position, or takes action with respect to an aspect of its relationship with another state, group of states, or other international actors. From the operational point of view, these decisions, policies and actions are driven by the policymaker's analysis of their perceived cost in terms of national interest and politics. To be effective and viable they must satisfy the following criteria: (1) be consistent with the national interest in addressing the aspect of the specific relationship; (2) be consistent with the national interest in terms of their impact on the national image and on similar involvements with other international actors for which they could be the precedent basis for demands for equal treatment; and (3) be supported by a domestic consensus of all constituencies that, de jure and de facto, are involved in the *foreign policy formulation* process.

These criteria constitute rational process in foreign policy formulation. By definition, they exclude the decisionmaker who is above process; that is, who is in a position to make these decisions, adopt these positions, and take action without any institutional or policy constraints. As history has produced relatively few such decisionmakers (e.g., Hitler, Stalin, and the Ayatollah) and technological advances are making states more interdependent, rationality in foreign policy formulation is becoming the norm.

Foreign policy implementation requires effective negotiation, which includes entry into the dialogue with maximum bargaining power and other advantage. Frequently, in societies where the domestic consensus phase involves open discussion and negotiation between and among many participating contituencies, including a free press, the best position from the standpoint of effective negotiation is diluted by the deal making and public disclosure that are incident to domestic consensus development. This, of course, prejudices the follow-on international negotiation.

This operational fact of life makes it more difficult for open societies to negotiate with counterpart states that are more authoritarian, with a correspondingly reduced exposure from consensus development. For example, in the United States–Soviet Union context, it is more difficult for the United States to formulate a policy that gives it negotiating advantage because the domestic dialogue (1) is so broad and contentious, and (2) tends to be driven by domestic political interests rather than the national interest. On the other hand, in the Soviet Union there is greater unity and discipline in developing consensus on foreign policy. The reason is that fewer constituencies are involved in consensus development. This is the case now and it was more so when the Communist Party of the Soviet Union was unchallenged in its leadership role. The point is that in all systems with meaningful decision-making process, however limited the participation, there is need for some degree of domestic consensus in support of foreign policy. The Soviet experience in Afghanistan is a case in point. The critical difference is the nature and breadth of the policy process and its impact on the negotiation that implements the policy decision.

Domestic consensus can be more effectively developed if it is handled as a government-people dialogue using negotiating concepts and techniques that provide a more focused, persuasion-oriented effort than a public relations approach. The domestic consensus requirement in foreign policy formulation imparts another cost dimension that tends to inhibit reckless foreign policy decisions and adds greater stability to the international system.

7. Such bargaining statutes might require that the parties stay in dialogue (e.g., neither side can break off or walk out), exchange certain information, negotiate certain issues, and observe certain procedures and time limits, all of which can be limiting or exploitable in conducting the dialogue.

8. The impact tends to be greatest in the intraorganizational and international negotiating environments because there is the widest audience involvement and scrutiny. To the extent that nation-state behavior is affected by concern for audience reaction (relatively few agreements are not made public after negotiation), it may be said that the consequent negotiating (political) cost has a stabilizing, quasi-normative effect on the international system.

9. It is not an overstatement to view audience plays as parallel dialogues that complement the side-to-side interface and for which provision should be made in the negotiating game plan.

10. As this audience pressure is considerably increased when the principal actually sits in on the dialogue (because he has the vantage point of a witness), the tendency of a negotiator is, for this and other reasons that will be discussed later, to oppose summitry (i.e., direct principal involvement.) He prefers to have his principal depend on his reports of developments in the dialogue when assessing the quality of his representation. The aversion to witnesses also inclines the negotiator to prefer to go it alone rather than be involved in dialogues where the sides are represented by negotiating panels or teams. In many cases he cannot avoid this involvement because of the need to have technical-specialist involvement in complex dialogues.

11. The technical terms "bilateral" and "multilateral" relate to the number of formal parties to a dialogue (i.e., those directly involved in working out the consensus in the external, side-to-side dialogue). "Multiparty" is used in the broader

sense of the parties actually involved in, or affected by, a negotiation, including its external and internal dimensions (e.g., the dialogue between negotiator and his principal and between several principals on the same side). The effective negotiator following the global principle of negotiation would recognize another category, multiactors. These are nonparties whose participation is essentially passive; they serve as conduits of information intended to create perceptions, uncertainty, and apprehension or control expectations on the part of a party to the negotiation. Multiactors are only collaterally involved in the dialogue; they are the messengers under the globality principle.

12. For example, the possibility of deadlock or impasse leading to a disruption of the dialogue is present in every environment because it is inherent in the consensus development process. What does differ by environment is the institutional and practical availability of recourse, which affects the readiness to push the dialogue to the break-off point.

13. The invasion and occupation of Kuwait by Iraq on August 2, 1990 ended in the use of force in the aftermath of a failed dialogue. The Iraqi leader, Saddam Hussein, displayed an insensitivity to the actual and political cost of defying the action by the United Nations that effectively isolated Iraq and called for member-state military action to force it to quit Kuwait. A coalition of states led by the United States attacked Iraq following the failure of diplomatic efforts to convince Hussein to withdraw from Kuwait.

14. An ongoing relationship, one that in the normal course of events can be expected to continue, is beneficial if it (1) involves implementation of a desired arrangement (the benefit here is to enjoy the arrangement and be in a position to monitor the smoothness of the implementation, including the practice under it), or (2) can be the source of other dealings or business.

15. As noted elsewhere in this Guide, the win-win approach is based on a relationship interest that is not present in all dialogues, including those where the relationship between the parties is adversarial and those where at least one of the parties defers to the Gekko creed and seeks to exploit the cover of a surface-relationship connection. In view of the limited applicability of win-win, I have concluded that it is more appropriate to treat it as a tactic or ploy rather than as a general approach to negotiation.

16. A hard-pressed side may actually accept nonviable consensus as a ploy to gain leverage from playing the victim in the renegotiation. For example, in the private environment, "stealing" the settlement of a personal injury claim may result in the release being renounced or judicial action to have it set aside; in intraorganizational dealings, an involved element alienated by the consensus may seek executive action to set aside the negotiated staff result and impose one; and in the international environment, domestic or international political pressures may result in renunciation of the negotiated arrangement. In all these examples, the side that pushed hard and "won" will tend to be on the defensive in coping with the unhappy turn of events produced by the win.

17. The power differential can be substantive (e.g., on the merits) or procedural (e.g., better negotiating skills)).

18. Mahatma Gandhi demonstrated that weakness can be power by departing from the traditional symmetry of power reflected in the "meeting-force-with-force" formulation. Instead, he confronted British power with nonforce in the form of

passive disobedience and resistence. British sensitivity to societal (audience) approval or disapproval provided the necessary level of restraint and decency that made Gandhi's weakness an effective counterforce to power. Gandhi's lesson for effective negotiation is that access to an audience to which the other side is sensitive is an essential condition for meaningful victim play. (See John Kenneth Galbraith, "What Ghandi Means Today," *Parade Magazine, Richmond Times-Dispatch,* December 25, 1983, pp. 12–13.)

19. Unilateral rejection of the exploitation of a power advantage may produce the warm inner feeling of having taken the high road, but there is no real "advantage take" unless the rejection is related to a negotiating play (e.g., is used as a bargaining chip). The key to advantage is the manner in which power (its use as well as its rejection) is orchestrated, exploited, and manipulated. For example, restraint in the use of power may produce desired results in terms of audience approval. On the other hand, express rejection of a power option within the expectation parameters of a situation may signal either a lack of capability or will or a lack of understanding of the negotiation process—in either case, a source of comfort and encouragement to the other side and others who might be contemplating challenge or confrontation.

20. See "Thinking To Do," *Wall Street Journal,* February 25, 1991, p. A8, which notes that "Force is a legitimate tool of [foreign] policy; it works."

21. See, for example, the domestic criticism of the "contemptible" nature of the Persian Gulf air war: "After a month of obliterating Iraq, and now downtown Baghdad, the U.S. air war has been revealed as a coward's war." (Colman McCarthy, "The Cowards' Air War," *The Washington Post,* February 17, 1991, p. F2.)

22. "Few things are more dangerous to a nation than an international reputation for blustering and backing down. . . . The irresolute reputation of American foreign policy may have encouraged Panamanian dictator Manuel Noriega in his last round of outrages that finally provoked U.S. military intervention." (Thomas Sowell, "The Panama Predicament," *San Juan Star,* December 29, 1989, p. 20.) "Ambiguity may be a clever negotiating ploy, but clarity of American intent is the way to stop war from happening." ("The Other Summit," *Wall Street Journal,* May 31, 1990, p. A14.)

23. An aspect of the carrot is the attraction of power. A state with a relatively weak power situation copes with the resultant disability by an association of varying degrees of closeness to a more powerful state or bloc of states. In some cases, the association is dictated by geopolitical realities (i.e., the power implications of geographic location); in others, there is freedom to choose a side and even play it against another. A state with the reputation for credible power attracts to its "umbrella of power" allies and other states disposed to be influenced to support it in its pursuit of foreign policy objectives. The disposition tends to be an implied term of the relationship. Thus, a state recognized for its credible power has an easier task in pressuring or influencing other states' conduct. The increased difficulty of the United States in this regard reflects the perception that developed during the Carter Administration that U.S. power capability and the will to employ it had declined. The following administration of President Reagan sought to reestablish U.S. credibility by resorting to the military option from time to time (e.g., the liberation of Grenada and the air strike against Libya).

24. Common examples of the stick are reduced or suspended diplomatic rela-

tions or activities, condemnation or withdrawal of support in international organizations, and reduced cooperative activities and contacts (political); trade and technology-transfer embargoes, primary and secondary boycotts, freezing of assets, and withholding or withdrawal of assistance (economic); and show of force, withdrawal of military assistance or providing it to a potential adversary of the state being pressured, deployment of forces in the area for interdiction, staging or other hostile operations, and punitive actions (military).

25. The effective negotiator distinguishes between issue-sensitive and nonissue-sensitive bloc action. A bloc of the latter type (e.g., the Socialist Bloc during the Cold War) tends to maintain its solidarity without regard to the issue under consideration. Habitually, these states vote as a bloc without regard to the specific issue. Therefore using bargaining chips to attempt to win over a socialist state tended to be an exercise in giving without getting; however, it is possible to coax away from a bloc a state that has joined to benefit from bloc solidarity on a specific issue. In such a case, bargaining chips may be productively used to shape a position to meet the needs of that state on another issue and, perhaps, bring about its defection from its bloc association when reacting to the second issue.

26. There is no established system for enforcement of organized sanctions. When sanctions are levied they are imposed individually by the states and only if they elect to do so. This is sometimes described as a system of personal or individual sanctions. The UN resolutions against Iraq in the Persian Gulf crisis of 1990 were obligatory upon the member states but they could not be forced to comply with them.

27. The effective negotiator would, in effect, be echoing Machiavelli's advice to the Prince concerning the "reasons-of-state" rationale; that is, that political action be freed from moral considerations and primacy be given to the political imperative. See Niccolo Machiavelli, *The Prince,* classic ed. (Toronto, New York, London, Sydney: Bantam Books, 1981), 6–7.

28. "A wise agreement can be defined as one that meets the legitimate interests of each side to the extent possible, resolves conflicting interests fairly, is durable, and *takes community interests into account*" (emphasis added). (Roger Fisher and William Ury, "Negotiating an Agreement without Giving in," *California Lawyer,* November 1981, pp. 34–36, at p. 34.)

29. "Greed . . . is good. Greed is right. Greed clarifies, cuts through and captures the essence of the evolutionary spirit." ("Freed from Greed?" *Time,* January 1, 1990, pp. 76–78, at p. 76). While greed is a factor in negotiation, it must be bridled by the considerations involved in "thinking negotiation." The result is a rationalization and balancing of the pursuit of interest to avoid the pitfalls and counterproductivity of overkill, which usually ignores the importance of viability and continuing relationships.

30. Essentially, the typical bureaucrat seeks to maintain a low profile, avoid organizational or personal embarrassment, and follow precedent or the leader.

31. In this connection, there arises the question of conducting negotiations by telephone. There is no substitute for face-to face contact, as (1) "voice reading" for reaction is more difficult than "face reading," and more important, (2) it is easier to say "no" over the phone than in person. These are the principal exposures in going the telephone route, which may otherwise be indicated because of considerations of economy of time and effort. History does not record any com-

pelling reasons for Miles Standish's reliance on John Alden in his courtship of Priscilla Mullins; it *does* underscore the efficacy of direct dialogue (i.e., speaking for oneself) in important matters, including those of the heart.

32. The process need not be that of the exploiting side. When representing the United States in developing a cooperative program with Country X, I was involved in a situation in which a federal agency overcommitted the government by agreeing in principle to accept promptly an invitation to send a delegation to commence cooperative activity. The corrective-action scenario called for some tap-dancing to cool the rush to consensus in order to allow time to link this initiative with other bilateral developments. I was tasked to slow down the dialogue without appearing to renege on the U.S. commitment. I resolved the matter by responding in a timely fashion as promised, but not through the more direct, usual U.S. Embassy channel. Being aware of the bureaucratic maze in Country X and the special interest of its Washington embassy in getting credit for this development in the bilateral relationship, I sent the U.S. reply through Country X's embassy. By exploiting the available process I was able to slow down the dialogue as tasked and, at the same time, solidify my relationship with the embassy by deferring to its desire to be directly involved in the action.

4

Preparing and Conducting
the Dialogue

GENERAL

Conceptualization of the negotiation process involves understanding its
dynamics and formulating an interest-oriented approach to dialogue management and control. Under the approach suggested here, a strategic overview in both planning and conducting the dialogue is essential to the effective pursuit of interest and the achievement of desired consensus. The
overview ensures a continuing focus on goal realization.

Too many approaches to negotiation neglect understanding of process
and mindset in favor of the search for mechanical methods or basic principles for conducting the dialogue. Whether they emphasize distillation of
personal experience, analysis of historical precedents, or iteration of accepted basic principles, such approaches usually culminate in a statement
of the rules of negotiation. The most these rules can provide is some insight into the tactical aspects of negotiation; they cannot provide strategic
considerations to facilitate the interest-oriented orchestration, exploitation, and manipulation that are essential for a directed negotiating effort.

The conceptualization suggested in this Guide has no claim to exclusiv-
ity; it is merely one possible approach that takes account of the mind-game
character of negotiation and the strategic, tactical, and other operational
elements of interest-oriented dialogue. Other conceptualizations that are
similarly oriented toward an understanding of process, mindset, and strategy can be effective; readers should select the one that is most meaningful
to them. In my approach, the negotiating dialogue is divided into (1) four
component phases: preparation, presentation, reaching agreement, and implementation; and (2) a continuing checklist (involving consideration of
goal realization, consensus viability, arrangement adequacy, and negotiat-

ing-relationship cost) to test the efficacy and feasibility of action in each phase. The combination of a step-by-step, "thinking-through-the-process" approach with a continuing checklist guarantees effective management and control of the new dialogue.

The four-phased conceptualization also serves as an instructional tool to focus on the key mileposts of the negotiation process. Actually, it represents a by-the-numbers approach to what is a continuous, action process; its operational dynamics cut across and blur phase lines. The approach is operationally effective because it focuses on developing a mindset and method to promote interest-serving consensus. The emphasis is on interest and its effective pursuit to consensus in both the formulation of the negotiating game plan and the execution of the dialogue called for by it. With practice, the would-be negotiator will find that the demarcation of the negotiation process into phases supported operationally by a checklist will enable him to structure and conduct an effective, coherent dialogue.

PREPARATION PHASE

General

The first phase of negotiation, the preparation, involves analysis of the situation, development of a strategy for the management and control of the dialogue, and formulation of a negotiating game plan. In many respects, this is the most important phase. Here, goals and objectives, issues, vulnerabilities and leverage, and presentational considerations are melded into a game plan that coherently combines the operational aspects of the effort to manage and control the dialogue.

Central to preparation is researching and investigating everything about the merits of the matter to be negotiated and the individuals involved, principals as well as negotiators. As a practical matter, the research and investigation initiated during the preparation phase continue throughout the negotiation as new developments unfold and are supplemented and cross-checked by probing during the dialogue. Probing provides an updated informational base for developing and adjusting side positions and reacting and responding to those of the other side.

Unlike the litigating attorney, the negotiator does not have to contend with rules concerning admissibility of evidence or other exclusionary rules as he develops, for incorporation into the dialogue, the facts and circumstances and the argumentation and discussion relevant to its issues. In negotiation, practically everything relevant to friendly and pressured persuasion (i.e., related to the merits of the situation and the involvement and needs of the sides) can be utilized and should be considered for possible exploitation in developing consensus. This requires an active, "think-negotiation" search for aspects of the situation that can be translated into exploitable leverage and advantage. These are known as the situational opportunities because they can be orchestrated, exploited, or manipulated in pressuring desired consensus.

For example, vulnerability with respect to the merits may be overcome through exploitation of the greater need (based upon financial, career, or other personal considerations) of the other side's principal or negotiator for prompt settlement. In such a case, the strategy is to make the side with the greater time need forgo its advantage on the merits in return for settlement. The example points up that situational control need not be based on the merits but can be achieved by exploiting any factor relevant to the consensus-reaching process—in this case, the timing of the conclusion of the dialogue. The search for exploitable factors both for and against a side involves a vulnerability analysis, which is an essential feature of the preparation phase. Judgments concerning goals, objectives, and leverage possibilities require a realistic assessment of each side's needs and vulnerabilities.

In learning all he can about the merits and the individuals involved, the effective negotiator makes full use of standard research and investigatory techniques and services. Depending on the importance of the dialogue, the preparation may range from a chat with his principal (to ascertain facts, issues, and needs), a survey of applicable governing principles (to find out the strength of his case on the merits), and a few phone calls (to learn something about the other negotiator and his principal), on one end of the spectrum; to an in-depth investigation of the case using professional personnel to fully research the merits and compile a complete "book" on the players of the opposite side, on the other.

The type and extent of research and investigation vary with the negotiating environments. In the intraorganizational environment, preparation usually involves nonprofessional means (e.g., personal research, phone calls, and conversations); preparation for private and international negotiations tends to involve greater use of professional investigatory services (e.g., private investigators, professional researchers, and intelligence agencies). The importance of the matters and the stakes involved will indicate practical limitations on the extent and nature of the preparation required.

Once exploitable factors (situational opportunities) have been identified, they become central to development of the negotiating game plan, which is the next operational step. The plan, representing the bargaining blueprint for the dialogue, consists of sections relating to goals and objectives; leverage plays; presentational techniques; tactics and ploys; concession trading; and closing maneuvers. The leverage portion of the plan seeks to take advantage of exploitable factors and enhance their pressuring-persuasion potential through careful orchestration, exploitation, and manipulation. It also provides for defense against exploitation by the other side. It is difficult to conceive of effective negotiation without a subplan relating to the orchestration of leverage, both on the offense and defense, which is the backbone of the overall effort to manage and control the dialogue.

Development of the game plan enables the negotiator to become aware of his realistic goals and objectives and to plan the means and methods to realize them. Thus prepared, he is in position to work backwards and focus on the opening position, which is the formal end of the preparation phase. The theory of the opening position is that it should lay the bargaining groundwork for the substance and process of the dialogue that follows. As the opening position is the threshold for the dialogue, it should not foreclose any of the substantive positions or tactical moves that the negotiating game plan envisages. For example, if the plan contemplates fallbacks at a certain level or use of certain ploys or other tactical plays, the parameters of the opening position must be broad enough to accommodate them; otherwise, the position would not support the plan. As we will see, if following the theory of the opening position does not produce a formulation broad enough to encompass any part of the game plan, that portion of the plan should be reviewed to determine whether it can realistically be supported.

Method of Preparation

In preparing for negotiation, the effective negotiator must be concerned with negotiating goals/objectives and needs, the issues generated by them, and the related vulnerabilities of the sides. To derive a meaningful negotiating game plan, he must have a clear understanding of (1) what he wants to achieve; (2) what issues he has to address; (3) what his bargaining strengths are (what can be exploited and manipulated in his side's interest; in other words, leverage); and (4) what vulnerabilities he has to contend with. The method of preparation that follows here is designed to provide the requisite understanding for developing the game plan and a supporting opening position.

The Negotiating Game Plan. Development of the negotiating game plan includes establishment of realistic maximum and minimum goals and objectives, identification of leverage possibilities, development of subplans relating to the strategy and tactics to be used in managing and controlling the dialogue, and formulation of the opening position. The linchpin tends to be the vulnerability analysis, which provides insight into where the advantage lies (i.e., what is exploitable and leveragable). This, in turn, is the basis for the overall strategy, the supporting orchestration scenario, and presentational and tactical plays. The game plan, although formulated during the preparation phase, is continuously reviewed as the dialogue unfolds to make sure that it remains relevant in light of developments in the dialogue, especially the probing take.[1] Stated most simply, the negotiating game plan reflects the practical rationality of thinking ahead in the negotiation process. It is an exercise in the evaluation and planning of ways and means to manage and control the dialogue to achieve the desired consensus.

Goals and Objectives. Negotiating goals and objectives must be clearly defined during the preparation phase to give the desired direction to the dialogue. Unless the negotiator knows what the parameters of acceptable consensus are (i.e., the acceptable minimum and maximum negotiation results), he will not be in a position to know how much can be traded on the way to that consensus or to assess the cost and value of specific concession trades along the way. With such knowledge, the negotiator will seldom find himself in the unhappy position of having given away the ball game by one slip in his bargaining-chip play. In negotiation, there must be keen appreciation of the costs involved in each play of the hand.

To assist in working out the parameters of acceptable consensus, a goals/objectives plot is suggested:

Goals/Objectives Plot

```
< – – – – – – – – – –   Area of Possible Consensus   – – – – – – – – – – >
    ┌   ┌
    B   M                                    M
    O   N                                    X
    P   O                                    O
       |B  – – Area of Acceptable Consensus– – B|
        └ – –Negotiating Room/Fallback Area–  ┘
```

In this plot, the upper line is an infinite one representing all the consensus possibilities; the lower line reflects the parameters of acceptable consensus (i.e., the area between the minimum, MNOB, and maximum, MXOB, objectives). Anything less than the minimum objective would fall into the break-off point (BOP) area, the point beyond which it is no longer in one's interest to negotiate.[2] The area of acceptable consensus (i.e., between MNOB and MXOB) provides the negotiating room or flexibility in the dialogue; this is the area from which negotiating chips or fallbacks can be drawn. The area plot conveys to the negotiator some appreciation of the bargaining cost of his chip plays. If the negotiator makes this type of goals/objectives analysis, he will be fully aware of where his interests lie in continuing the dialogue and in trading concessions. The foregoing assumptions hold only if the plot realistically reflects the consensus possibilities.

In setting realistic[3] parameters of acceptable consensus, one must determine what is achievable in light of the goals and objectives (i.e., interests), needs and vulnerabilities of the respective sides. Account must be taken of any overriding special need or advantage that may motivate one side or the other to settle for less, or seek more, than what the traffic can reasonably be expected to bear. The parameters plot of the side having the special need (or belief that it has a special advantage) would reflect lower or higher expectations, as appropriate, in the setting of maximum and minimum goals and objectives.

Investigation and analysis of the negotiating situation during the preparation phase and probing in subsequent phases are directed toward uncovering that type of need, vulnerability, or advantage in one's own position or in that of the other side. Again, the important reality in negotiation is not only the actual situation; it also includes what the other side's perception of it may be. Thus, exploitation can also involve creating the perception that a side has a special need or advantage; the defense to such a play involves an alertness to, and a readiness to counter, the other side's effort to create a supporting perception. The best counter to any perception-creation effort is simply not to react, thereby avoiding encouragement of that effort. Actually, the counter also serves as a form of reverse perception creation because the lack of reaction or response is an indication that the perception-creation effort will not be successful.

Thus, the analysis of real and perceived vulnerabilities and advantages has a direct impact on assessing acceptable consensus. For example, if a claimant in private negotiation is in financial straits and needs a quick settlement, he cannot realistically hope for consensus based upon the top-dollar value of his claim. The maximum and minimum objectives in his consensus plot should reflect the reduced value of the claim resulting from his vulnerability due to financial need and the implied bias toward a quick settlement at a lower figure. Similarly, in international negotiations involving a small power and a large power, the leverage situation resulting from the basic mismatch (tempered by the large power's concern for its audience exposure in negotiating with the small power) and any other exploitable aspect of the relationship should be taken into account when the range of realistic consensus is worked out for the respective sides. In short, the goals/objectives assessment involves developing realistic maximum and minimum objectives based upon considerations of interest as impacted by actual or perceived vulnerabilities and advantages.

As the negotiation process is dynamic, the goals/objectives plot does not remain fixed. Depending upon developments in the negotiation, including whatever the probing take uncovers, there may be a need to adjust the plot. For example, if the other side plays its hand badly and a windfall is in the offing, there must be an appropriate reassessment of objectives. A side may find itself in the happy situation of being able to realize a result closer to its maximum objective (MXOB). At the very least, it should be able to hold out for more as its minimum objective (MNOB). Similarly, should the bad play be on his side, the negotiator will have to rethink his situation and adjust his objectives accordingly. He may even have to rethink the break-off point (BOP) if his plot of acceptable consensus has been badly compromised.

The goals/objectives plot also provides some insight into the degree of success achieved in the negotiation, because consensus closer to the maximum end of the spectrum theoretically indicates that one has gotten more than he was prepared to give. Furthermore, it is said that the test of bargaining skill is the negotiator's ability to return for his side a portion of its bargaining cushion. Again, the correctness of this view depends on the consensus plot being realistic. A plot with a maximum objective (MXOB) on the low side would give a disproportionate indication of success; similarly, an unrealistically ambitious MXOB would give an incorrect reading concerning lack of success. The foregoing suggests that the careerism of the negotiator, which pushes him toward seeking a low, rather than high, maximum objective, tends to distort the usual measure of negotiating success.

Issues and Vulnerabilities. Assessment of issues and vulnerabilities is inextricably involved in the goals/objectives plot. The negotiator first must identify the issues generated by his goals and objectives and those of the other side in order to prepare for the substantive content of the dialogue. He must also determine the vulnerabilities in the situation generated by the issues and make an analysis of both sides' vulnerabilities and advantages. The vulnerability analysis will provide insight into where the potential negotiating advantage or leverage lies, both in terms of each issue and overall. It is here that judgments are made concerning the perception-creation possibilities (including those with respect to which side has the burden of negotiation or special advantages, needs, or vulnerabilities) and what steps are necessary to exploit them or defend against their use by the other side. The analysis will also indicate to the negotiator which issues he should avoid or try to downplay or finesse. In short, it will reveal that which is orchestratable, exploitable, and manipulable in the situation, both for and against his side.

During the vulnerability analysis, an effort is made to identify the other side's special needs and interests (i.e., consensus requirements, including cosmetic concerns), their priority and order of importance, and any sensitivities related to them. These needs and interests are then matched with one's own to determine the points of clash and accommodation. From this matching process, an idea can be obtained concerning possible trade-offs and other bargaining factors. For example, ascertaining the existence of a special cosmetic need of the other side makes possible the orchestration of a substantive concession in trade for the desired cosmetic formulation or approach—which, in the hands of the clever drafter, may involve only a formal adjustment in a side's position without any substantive change or cost.

If possible, one should seek to uncover a key concession exchange.[4] This exchange, subject to verification during the probing and other parts of the dialogue, can serve as the focus of the entire negotiating effort and may even provide an effective way to close it (i.e., serve as the closer). If the other side does not have a similar focus, the negotiation will have a happy ending whether one is on the defense or the offense. Side strength here is a function of recognizing the criticality of the issue and conducting an interest-oriented pursuit or defense of it in the face of a lack of recognition of its criticality by the other side. The negotiator having that focus will be in a position to protect his side against inadvertently "giving away the farm" and to reap windfall and other benefits against his less analytical, nonfocusing adversary who may not attempt to exploit the issue or defend against its exploitation by the focused side. Should both sides have the focused approach, management and control of the dialogue will probably be in the hands of the side with greater strength on the merits.

The Opening Position. The preparation phase formally ends with the formulation of the opening position. That formulation naturally flows from the assessment of possible and acceptable consensus. The theory of the opening position is to start the dialogue at a point in the area of possible consensus that (1) maximizes negotiating room (i.e., bargaining chips or fallbacks) for the achievement of acceptable consensus, and at the same time (2) is attractive enough to draw the other side into the dialogue. Without this balanced approach, the other side may not find a negotiated result to be in its interest and therefore may have no incentive to become involved.[5] Obviously, an opening position that is well within the area of acceptable consensus does not satisfy the first objective; an opening position well beyond the maximum objective (MXOB) may be too extreme to be an acceptable starting point for the other side. Should the other side not be willing to enter into dialogue, the inviting side may have to incur higher start-up costs by sweetening the invitation. This usually occurs when attractive alternatives to negotiation are practically available in the negotiating sense or when the inviting side has the burden of negotiation. It may also be necessary, in the case of a reluctant participant, to make (as an additional start-up cost) some early concessions after the dialogue has started to demonstrate its potential productivity by the "movement" toward consensus.

As a practical matter, the opening position (OP) in a well-thought-out, realistic preparation should fall within the goals/objectives plot area beyond the maximum objective (MXOB). Schematically, the ideal opening position plot should look as depicted in the figure showing the areas of acceptable and possible consensus. The minimum (MNOP) and maximun

Opening Position Plot

Area of Acceptable Consensus

```
                              ┌─────────────────────────────────┐
M                             M
N                    M        X        O        M
O                    N        O        P        X
B                    O        B                 O
                     P                          P


<─ ─ ─ ─ ─ ─ ─┘─ ─ ─ ─ ─ ─ ─ ─ ─ ─ ─ ─ ─ ─ ─ ─ ─┘─ ─ ─ ─ ─ ─ >
```

Area of Possible Consensus

(MXOP) opening positions bracket the maximum objective (MXOB). The range between the minimum (MNOP) and maximum (MXOP) opening positions reflects the balancing of (1) negotiating room and flexibility for the proposing side, and (2) attractiveness of the proposed starting point to the other side. If the result of this balancing produces a final opening position (OP) congruent with or short of the maximum objective (MXOB), it is probable that the analysis that produced the range of acceptable consensus was not realistic, having a bias to the high side. In such a case, there is a need to rethink the goals/objectives plot. If one follows the approach just suggested, formulation of the opening position (OP) can serve as a check on the realistic nature of the formulation of goals and objectives during the preparation phase. The effective negotiator welcomes this and every other opportunity to cross-check and double-check his negotiating play.

PRESENTATION PHASE

General

The presentation phase involves considerations related to the actual conduct of the dialogue in accordance with the negotiating game plan. Although the following material is keyed primarily to the formal dialogue for instructional purposes, one should recall that presentation is conducted throughout all phases of the negotiation process. It may precede the formal dialogue as sides jockey for position by commencing their management and control efforts before ever taking their places at the negotiating table. Actually, presentation starts with any effort to create, orchestrate, and manipulate perceptions, apprehension, uncertainty, and expectations, however and whenever conducted. For example, a press release prior to the first formal meeting of the negotiators is considered part of the presentation if that release is intended to influence or impact the decisional level of the other side. During the formal dialogue, presentation involves the direct and indirect communication of positions and supporting and pressuring argumentation. In reaching agreement and during implementation, presentation is involved in achieving side goals such as closing and establishing or preserving postnegotiation practice. Thus, presentation is a continuing feature of the negotiating process because it is the operational medium for developing and monitoring consensus.

The principal and more limited objective of the presentation phase is to advance the dialogue toward establishment of the haggle zone. This can be defined as the delineation of broad parameters of consensus that are generally acceptable to both sides and from which they move toward closing the final agreement. The operational elements of effective presentation are friendly and pressured persuasion based upon coordinated orchestration of objective and subjective reality; attractive packaging and other techniques to enhance position acceptability; continuing effort to establish and maintain personal and positional credibility; full awareness and use of tacit communication; deft probing of positions and personal interests; and acute sensitivity to, and exploitation of, exposure, vulnerabilities, and leverage. The tone of the dialogue is related operationally to the foregoing; it involves creation and maintenance of a friendly negotiating atmosphere and relationship. In muting the basically adversarial nature of the interface, this forestalls the hostility and suspicion that generally impede the persuasion process. The techniques employed for friendly persuasion are rapport-oriented ones generally associated with salesmanship, that are conducive to persuading the other side that its interests are better served by accepting the proposed consensus or a slight modification of it. Furthermore, the effective negotiator draws upon all of his persuasiveness, presentational skills, and pizazz to gain friendly acceptance of the desired consensus. Failing that, he is prepared to turn up the heat and make the transition from friendly to pressured persuasion. He attempts to maintain the initial friendly approach to facilitate and mask the pressuring effort.

The principal elements of presentation are covered in the sections that follow.

The Formal Dialogue and Orchestration

The formal dialogue is the "at-the-table" portion of the negotiation process. It involves the discussions, presentations, and responses of the sides related to the issues on an implied or express agenda. It tends to have a surface formality that belies its operationally significant internal and external dimensions. The focus here is on exploitation of those dimensions to gain a negotiating edge.

The effective negotiator's preoccupation with interest and advantage and his consequent desire to manage and control the overall dialogue require that he do the same with respect to the formal dialogue. Management and control can be achieved by the fullest use of orchestration directed at both dimensions of the formal dialogue: the direct interface at the table and the arranged contacts away from the table. The effective negotiator seeks advantage through the creation and exploitation of additional negotiating contacts to complement the formal dialogue. These contacts are especially important because they are "covered" in the sense that the other side may not be aware that they are part of the negotiation in accordance with the globality principle.

Thus, orchestration can provide an edge to the side sensitive to the need to operate in both dimensions of the formal dialogue. The expectation is that there is a good possibility that the effective negotiator may have the field to himself and catch the other side off balance. This is frequently evident by the relief expressed by inexperienced negotiators who enjoy the "relaxation" provided by breaks, social activities, and periods between the sessions. The effective negotiator seeks to exploit these windows of covered-dialogue opportunity by continuing to negotiate during them.

Orchestration is central to negotiation because it is the principal operational vehicle for implementing the negotiating game plan. It enhances the effort to effect friendly or pressured persuasion through the coordination of efforts to create perceptions, apprehension, and uncertainty and to control expectations. Furthermore, manipulation and exploitation of leveragable situational opportunities are covered by the orchestration portion of the game plan. It can only help to continue the drumbeat of artful orchestration during the covered portion of the formal dialogue. Access to a relaxed, potentially less-alert ear portends well for the effort.

For example, the common claim letter,[6] if used as a negotiating vehicle[7] to maximize apprehension about the seriousness of a claim or to set up a meeting with the other side's negotiator to discuss off the record and away from the table the "uncontrollability" of his client, can serve a useful, covered-dialogue purpose. Furthermore, in the intraorganizational negotiating environment, reports and rumors can be used to exaggerate the importance of specific issues to senior officials or their preoccupation with larger ones and their nonavailability to consider the one being staffed; both are a means of pressuring the desired consensus at the working level. In international negotiations, the well-timed leak, the "just-for-you" information, the trial balloon at lunch or during the cocktail hour, or a press report or rumor can be utilized to color perceptions and influence reactions relevant to the formal dialogue. In all these examples, the purpose is to obtain a substantive or procedural advantage in the formal dialogue through a coordinated, supporting covered effort.

One can also use the covered dialogue to enhance orchestration of a timing play involving a negotiating ploy or tactic to influence the response to, or complement, a development in the dialogue. Changes in the fortunes or needs of the sides, including their negotiators, or in their negotiating positions are the developments frequently involved in orchestration plays. For example, in a base rights negotiation on behalf of the United States, I arranged the timing of a closing package deal to coincide with the known availability of a senior diplomatic assignment in which the chief negotiator for the other side was interested for career and other personal reasons. During a luncheon meeting it was ascertained that his daughter was scheduled to attend a university in the country of the other assignment. The hope (which was well conceived but unrealized) was that the chief negotiator, who was in line for the assignment, might be influenced to report the closing proposal with more enthusiasm than might otherwise be the case in order to end his base rights negotiation assignment more quickly.

My failure to achieve the desired result in the example just given should not discourage the use of covered dialogues to complement formal dialogue. If all my negotiating activities were portrayed as resounding successes, this Guide might suffer from a credibility gap. I believe that the formal dialogue with the reader concerning the utility and merit of the Guide is enriched by this report of failure.

The Role of the Negotiator

The negotiator's role in conducting the formal dialogue is to (1) present his side's position in his most persuasive manner, (2) listen attentively[8] to the other side's response or reaction, (3) probe with inoffensive questions the other side's line of thinking (e.g., not, "I don't believe that . . . ," but rather, "I didn't realize that . . . please explain it in greater detail") (4) report to his principal the specific communications (tacit and express) and general reaction to the probing, and (5) make recommendations to his principal concerning how his side should react (e.g., stand fast, try new approaches, or propose a concession trade). The process is much the same in receiving proposals from the other side. They are carefully listened to, noted, probed, and reported with recommendations.

When reacting to proposals, the negotiator should try to control as soon as possible the expectations of the other side. Accordingly, the effective negotiator reacts to a proposal as quickly and as definitively as his instructions permit. If the proposal is clearly unacceptable, it should be promptly rejected.[9] If he is uninstructed on the particular issue, the negotiator should so inform the other side to avoid having its expectations raised by a delay in rejecting or countering a proposal. If the proposal has some promise or potential, this should be signalled to the other side in an appropriate manner to encourage further movement. For example, if the proposal is a step in the right direction, this should be signalled either expressly or tacitly. In most situations, the amount of "give" detected in the other side's position will suggest the nature of the response. If more is offered than was expected and the prospect is that more can be gotten, the signal should be that a good start has been made toward reaching consensus (e.g., "At least it's a start." or "Now we may be able to move forward."). Where it appears that the other side is playing its last chips, the encouragement to make additional concessions should be more positive (e.g., "If we make a little more progress, we may be able to wrap this up quickly." or "We are getting pretty close."). Of course, at any stage of negotiation, one must not fail to grab and "run with a good deal." Seizing the magic moment is a function of having the preparation and experience to recognize when it arrives and, when one is negotiating on behalf of a principal, the authority to do so. Having a principal under control enables the negotiator to react quickly and positively in such a situation.

In all his actions connected with the making and receiving of proposals, the negotiator is preoccupied with exposure, that is, the question of who is being advantaged or disadvantaged by acceptance or rejection of a given proposal. This specific aspect of "thinking negotiation" is a continuing feature of the negotiation process. It becomes more critical during the presentation phase when one sits eyeball to eyeball with the other side, because the failure to counter quickly a high-exposure situation enhances expectations that will have to be paid for later. The negotiating table should be looked upon as a "sea of flame" consuming all that comes in contact with it in the sense that inaction, positions stated, or signals conveyed cannot usually be rectified without negotiating cost.[10] This feature of negotiation causes effective negotiators to opt for the low-exposure formulation (i.e., with the least amount of commitment and prejudicial uncertainty) and to avoid open-ended formulations that either favor the other side or create uncertainty concerning the extent of the exposure undertaken.

For example, commitments in all negotiating environments that incorporate by reference undefined requirements or conditions are to be avoided. (These can include phrasing in all environments: in private negotiations, "in accordance with customary market practice"; in intraorganizational negotiations, "regular clearance procedures will be followed"; in international negotiations, "subject to the laws of Country X.") Acceptance of these commitments constitutes buying the proverbial "pig in a poke." The effective negotiator seeks to limit his exposure by defining it with closed formulations. Lack of sensitivity to exposure usually leads to giving without getting, a cardinal sin in the effort to make cost-effective use of bargaining chips.

Negotiators act for their principals in accordance with the instructions and other authority received from them. In theory, control lies entirely with the principal. The extent to which the negotiator is constrained by his instructions depends upon the negotiating environment and the amount of control the negotiator has over his principal. In private negotiations, the negotiator often has a freer hand because the client-principal, not usually an experienced audience who can assess the professionalism of his attorney-negotiator's representation, tends to rely on the latter's expertise and judgment. In some situations, the instructions may be no more explicit than "settle the case" or "get me out of this." In intraorganizational negotiations, the relationship is more structured and the principal more knowledgeable. Accordingly, the entity or agency representative (negotiator) usually has more detailed instructions. In international negotiations, the principal-negotiator relationship is the most structured and controlled; formal written instructions are the rule. Of course, in some situations (e.g., special presidential envoy or representative) the instructions may be as general as those for the private negotiating environment. For example, during the round of negotiations with Panama in 1965, Ambassador Robert B. Anderson, who served as U.S. special representative and head of the three-man team of negotiating principals (of which I was one), had simple, general instructions from President Johnson: "Work out an arrangement with Panama that will fly on the Hill."

In all environments, the negotiator must work at controlling his principal's expectations to ensure that the goals and objectives are realistically attainable. This serves the cause of negotiation because "shooting for the moon" is not conducive to a negotiated result or continued dialogue. Failure to have a client under control can also be costly at settlement time. The classic situation that comes to mind is the attorney who commences suit for a sum (which is biased to the high side to provide some negotiating room for settlement) without controlling the client's expectations concerning the amount in suit as it relates to the settlement value of the case. The attorney has neglected to prepare his principal to accept the settlement he may ultimately recommend.

There is still another aspect to controlling one's principal. Negotiating leverage can be obtained if the other side is made to perceive that the negotiator does control his principal. If he is successful, the effective negotiator will avoid the unhappy situation of having the other side reduce his role to that of a mere channel of communication. The negotiator who creates this appearance of power gains an additional negotiating play. He can, in effect, make the other side bargain for his "support" of a proposal and, in the process, cause it to be modified in his principal's interest. For example, in private negotiations he can bargain for an increase in an offer by stating that if it is raised, he will strongly support it with his positive recommendation.

In the other two environments, similar results can be obtained. In intraorganizational negotiations, the reputation of being close to corporate or governmental principals can be used to (1) inhibit kicking the problem upstairs for resolution, and (2) pressure for acceptance of the consensus he proposes at the working level. The international negotiator who is known by the other side to be close to senior officials in his government enjoys clout that can be exploited in his country's interest. Again, he can stimulate the other side to bargain with him for his support. In all environments, bargaining for support also provides the effective negotiator with another opportunity for probing the other side's position.

There is a downside to the concept of principal control. The problem here is that negotiators tend to do more than facilitate the negotiation process because there is a selfish, career reason for their desire to control their principals. The attorney, corporate or government official, and international negotiator all are eager for the praise (and, of course, the economic rewards) of being able to get the job done (i.e., to satisfy the principal's negotiating goals and objectives). To facilitate gaining this praise, the negotiator seeks to be in control so that it will be easier for him to conduct a winning dialogue. Control in this sense has a negative manifestation because it frequently means getting instructions for doable tasks and having a "deliverable" principal—requiring, in either case, the negotiator's hand in shaping his principal's expectations concerning what to expect from the negotiation. Such control is desired by the negotiator because it enhances the possibility of a successful, career-serving conclusion of the negotiation. The tension of the intraside dialogue involving principal and negotiator is a dimension of the formal dialogue that is frequently overlooked or ignored.

The first opportunity to assert principal control is during the preparation phase when the negotiating game plan (including goals and objectives, strategy and tactics) is formulated. If the negotiator is consulted about, or otherwise involved in, that formulation, he will be in an excellent position to influence the substance of the instructions he will have to operate under in conducting the dialogue. The second and most common opportunity for negotiating with one's principal occurs during the presentation phase. It takes the form of the negotiator's *ad referendum* reporting of the other side's reactions to proposals and other developments in the dialogue and, most important, the making of recommendations concerning next steps, tactics, and proposals. At this stage of the negotiation, the principal's perception of the dialogue is mainly shaped by his negotiator's reports. For the purpose of exercising control, the situation is leveraged heavily in favor of the negotiator.

In most cases, principals are not aware that they are involved in an intraside negotiation. They are not aware that they are being pressured under the cover of receiving advice and counsel and "working together" with their negotiators to develop an effective negotiating game plan.[11] Although the career interests of the negotiator are best served by loose instructions that provide him with flexibility and room to maneuver, he must be concerned about the possibility that he may be criticized by whatever audience he may be sensitive to for poorly representing his principal because of the extent of the control he did exercise in developing the latter's negotiating objectives. As he negotiates in all directions (i.e., with his principal, relevant audiences, and the other side), the effective negotiator is careful about his personal exposure. He is guided by the continuing checklist and the standard of prudence in making the difficult judgments concerning the substantive, procedural, and ethical issues involved.

The negative implications of the negotiator's careerism are balanced somewhat by his operational incentive to make full use of his instructions in accordance with the principle that authority should be used to bring about the desired consensus. In the ideal situation, a side's objectives can be realized without expending all the bargaining chips. Effective negotiators, perhaps betraying their "on-stage" orientation as it relates to role playing in negotiation, are sensitive to the frequent need for an encore as a closer (or for next steps in an ongoing negotiation), and they attempt to save some of their bargaining chips for this purpose. Moreover, it is a good feeling to leave the table with something left over for a contingency need.

However, a variety of circumstances relating to the merits of the situation and the skill level of the representation on the other side may require the use of all the authority that has been granted. This departure from the ideal must be endured because the objective of the negotiation process is the desired consensus, not a display of toughness in holding firm. Hanging tough is not an end in itself; it makes sense only as the tactical part of a well-conceived negotiating game plan. Moreover, there is little point in getting doable instructions if full use is not made of them to achieve the desired consensus. Inexperienced negotiators may feel the need to demonstrate toughness to their principal or other audience and, by doing so, pass up opportunities to use their authority to make advantageous concession trades in pursuit of the desired consensus. "Thinking negotiation" provides the judgement crucible for wise use of authority to maximize its bargaining potential. The effective negotiator is ready to use his authority fully and creatively to achieve his side's negotiating objectives.

The negotiator who violates or exceeds his instructions or other authority commits the cardinal sin of effective negotiation. This disservice to his principal (by breaking the rules of his agency) and to himself (by the career prejudice resulting from his action) must be avoided. However much he may chafe under tight principal control, the effective negotiator must be disciplined enough to fulfill the terms of his agency (i.e., abide by his instructions) even though it may entail negative career consequences. Of course, he can always resign from his representational role, but reputation and economic considerations may limit the feasibility of this alternative.

Enhancing Position Acceptability

Effective negotiation through friendly and pressured persuasion involves developing favorable consensus by use of the carrot and the stick: The carrot relates to friendly persuasion and the stick to pressured persuasion. The carrot reflects concerns for (1) maintaining the quality of the negotiating and postnegotiation relationships (i.e., tone of the dialogue and personal rapport), and (2) enhancing the appeal and acceptability of specific proposals, which is the focus of this section. The carrot represents the "honey" which in friendly persuasion is usually the means for getting more. Exploitation of situational opportunities and vulnerabilities provides the leverage stick for pressured persuasion. The effective negotiator's preference for the carrot, whenever possible, requires that he be versed in the techniques involved in enhancing position acceptability.

There are two routes to enhancing position or proposal acceptability and appeal: the cosmetic and the substantive. The former involves chip-free efforts to make proposals as formally attractive and appealing as possible by using general presentational techniques and drawing upon knowledge of specific cosmetic needs and preferences of the other side. The latter relates to situations in which a substantive chip may have to be played to enhance acceptability—a preference of last resort for the effective negotiator. In most variations of the attractive formulation approach, the main effort is to package or otherwise provide a cosmetically appealing feature or cover to sweeten a position or proposal. The objective is a cosmetic formulation that contributes to the selling of the position or proposal, not its purchase through the expenditure of bargaining chips.

If, for example, the other side has a known preference for certain formulations (e.g., deletion of the word "socialist" from the official name of a country), positions or proposals should be drafted to reflect that preference. Similarly, in responding to a position or proposal, the courting side should try to retain as much of the language of the original formulation as is consistent with its counter or response, thereby conveying the impression that most of what the other side proposed was acceptable. Furthermore, explanations of the rationale of a position or proposal should be as detailed as possible with a strong presentation concerning its fairness, reasonableness, and correctness. As most cosmetic plays involve deferring to an audience concern of the courted side, the sweetening can best be conceived and accomplished by putting one's self in the position of the side with the need to play to that audience.

Other cosmetic approaches to enhanced acceptability include sweetened formulations that avoid flat noes and suggest less costly alternatives that (1) imply the desire to be forthcoming but (2) contain conditions that assure that there will be no commitment involving substantive cost. For example, in responding to a simple request for a loan one may describe a difficult personal financial situation that prevents loaning any amount or permits loaning a clearly insufficient amount. Another variation is to preempt possible demands by taking the initiative to describe difficult financial or other situations that would presage a negative response, thereby inhibiting the formal demand as a useless exercise. Still another is to defer to the special situation or reputation of the other side with low-key flattery to evoke a desired reaction: "A person of your means wouldn't be interested in what little I could do to help."

The second approach to the carrot involves the use of substantive concessions, not just attractive formulations to sweeten a position or proposal. These are best approached operationally from the standpoint of the theory of concessions. This theory, which will be presented later in the Guide, essentially bars giving without getting or giving more than one gets. When a concession trade involves cosmetic and substantive chips, the side exploiting the cosmetic need is usually advantaged. The effective negotiator generally avoids that kind of sweetener because it negates the whole approach to concession trading, which in this type of situation seeks to trade cost-free cosmeticity for facilitated persuasion.

When the other side has the burden of a cosmetic need, however, the effective negotiator is not averse to seeking substantive gain for any cosmetic courtesy extended. While not wishing to "pay" for the enhanced attractiveness and acceptability of his side's positions, he is ready to exploit a similar need of the other side. The difference, of course, is that being able to get a substantive chip for a cosmetic play is still another way of achieving the bargaining ideal of getting more than one gives.

In one international negotiation that I handled, the concern of the negotiator for Country X was to avoid any long-term grant of operating rights to the United States. This was resolved by providing a very short express term (five years) with the stipulation that if the activity was not completed within that period, the United States would have an additional five-year period in which to do so. In this way, the United States was able to control the situation and get the ten-year term it desired without placing on Country X the cosmetic burden of justifying to concerned audiences a "long-term," express grant of rights. In still another case, Country Y wanted to avoid an express provision in an agreement concerning a sensitive arrangement desired by the United States. The issue was resolved in the interest of the United States because it was ready to cover that matter outside the agreement through a favorable exchange of letters or diplomatic notes. Again, the United States was able to trade cosmetic flexibility for substantive gain.

Even where the other side has no apparent cosmetic need but only a preference, probing may uncover the possibility of changing that preference to a perception of need. For example, the probing side may be able to convey credibly that it also has a cosmetic interest with respect to the same issue, thereby requiring that the issue be treated as contested in the negotiation. If the other side takes the bait, one has a variation of the bootstrapping or false-demand technique, which permits (in this case) exploiting cosmetic preferences as an issue to get a bargaining chip. The point is that an inexperienced negotiator may not recognize, and therefore be made to pay for, the other side's real or feigned interest in a cosmetic issue, all in the name of avoiding impasse and advancing the dialogue.

Credibility

During the presentation phase, the negotiator is involved in presenting and explaining the positions, reactions, and responses of his principal. To serve his principal well, the negotiator has to impress the other side with his personal credibility and professionalism and the reasonableness, logic, practicality, and viability (i.e., substantive credibility) of his side's positions. Personal and positional credibility are essential to advance the persuasion process.

The negotiator's objective here is to impress the other side that he is sincere, honest, reasonable, forthcoming, businesslike, and professional and that he represents a position that should be considered seriously and given a substantive response.[12] The impression conveyed of the negotiator and his side's position is important because it influences the reporting of developments in the dialogue to the other side's principal as part of the *ad referendum* process; it is a basic way of reaching and impacting that principal's perception of, and decisions concerning, developments in the negotiating situation.[13] For example, if a negotiator conveys the impression of being frivolous, tricky, or unprofessional, the positions he espouses will tend to be tagged with the same attributes. His positions will be viewed with suspicion and not treated as serious negotiating developments when they are reported by the other negotiator to his principal.

On the other hand, the negotiator who creates a positive impression will generate both respect and rapport, which are very important in effecting persuasion. It will help to foster a desirable professional relationship and, perhaps, a cooperative spirit. This may result in a reduced level of alertness, which can be exploited in the course of the dialogue. The effort at disarming the other side usually contributes to building personal rapport and generating a nonhostile tone for the dialogue, which is helpful in effecting persuasion. Windfalls of successful rapport building in the form of exploitable confidences about the substance of, or the persons involved in, the dialogue may also be in the offing. If they do materialize, they should be considered a happy bonus of the building effort. Of course, the effective negotiator, always concerned about exposure, will cross-match these confidences with other information to judge whether the other side is really confiding or merely setting him up. The skill level demonstrated by the other side provides some insight into the spontaneity and reliability of its confidences. Generally, a skilled negotiator's confidences should be treated as suspect.

Projection of a credible, businesslike, and professional image has another positive effect. It will inhibit sharp practices and ploys by the other side because of the induced belief that there is little possibility of success and the concern that their impact could be counterproductive. For an example in private negotiations, the claimant's attorney who demonstrates his businesslike professionalism (e.g., competence and readiness to sue) will less frequently encounter a "take-it-or-leave-it" offer by an insurer who is inclined to settle the case. On the other hand, the attorney who betrays a lack of experience or determination to see the case through to trial will have to try more cases than his more businesslike and professional colleague. Actually, any perceived weakness in the handling of the dialogue may induce challenge on the part of insurers who might not otherwise do so. This is because the demonstrated weakness reduces the apprehension that is usually associated with attorney involvement.

In intraorganizational negotiations, the corporate representative who demonstrates he knows his way around the organizational bureaucracy and its process will be more effective at the working level; the others involved in the dialogue will be inhibited from bureaucratic challenges designed to influence him by placing career and other pressures on him. Similarly, in international negotiations, the professionalism of the negotiator will generate respect and the apprehension that ploys and other maneuvers will turn out to be counterproductive. The result may be promotion of a nononsense dialogue on the merits. The side that feels constrained to stick to the merits because of the credible professionalism of the other side is at a disadvantage; it will be inhibited from using ploys and other maneuvers that might produce an exploitable edge. Limiting a side to arguing only the merits produces a procedural barrier that has positive substantive implications for the inhibiting side.

The persuasion process is also enhanced by demonstrating the credibility of one's position (i.e., that it is sound, reasonable, and fair). The purpose, of course, is to improve the proposal's acceptability to the other side and to satisfy any special audiences that may have to be considered. The starting point is to make sure that all proposal-related data and other information are correct. Reliable research and other data-acquisition means should be employed so that credibility is not compromised by a routine error of fact or gap in the relevant information. Being assured of no exposure on this score and aware that the negotiator for the other side will have an audience (starting with his principal) that will have to be persuaded, or at the very least neutralized, the proposing negotiator attempts to improve the proposal's appeal by a presentation that stresses its soundness, reasonableness, and fairness.

Usually, much of the early stages of the formal dialogue involves argumentation concerning position credibility. The proponent seeks to show that he desires no special advantage in the consensus he proposes and that it is fair and just under the circumstances. The other side counters by showing the opposite or that there are compelling reasons why the proposed consensus, however fair and just, cannot be accepted. For example, in private negotiations, market-price or jury-verdict research can be utilized to support or question the demand in a sales transaction or a settlement in lieu of litigation. In intraorganizational negotiations, an effort may be to show that the proposal is or is not consistent with current corporate or governmental policy or the logical extension of it. In international negotiations, the proponent of a settlement seeks to demonstrate that it is generally in accord with the practice of states or principles of international law. The opposing side usually disputes this contention or attempts to make the case for a special arrangement.

There is still another objective in pursuing the give and take on the soundness, fairness, or reasonableness of the proposal. The effective negotiator uses it as a cover for probing the give in the other side's position. This aspect of the give and take may be likened to sparring in a boxing match as the fighters size each other up for the serious business that follows.

Once the dialogue gets down to the specifics of each issue under negotiation, however, the larger questions of fairness or reasonableness tend to fade into the background. For example, in a private negotiation involving a damage claim based upon negligence, the opening stages of the dialogue usually focus on the question of liability and damages, with each side adducing arguments in support of its position. As neither side will readily concede the issue to the other, the dialogue tends to be a sparring exercise until the first exchange on a settlement figure. Thereafter, the negotiation focuses on how much is needed to buy or sell the claim; it essentially becomes a sales transaction.[14] Similarly, in intraorganizational and international negotiations, the dialogue frequently starts with larger questions (e.g., corporate or governmental policy in the former; international law or practice in the latter) that serve as the backdrop for the ultimate movement toward specific settlement proposals. This preliminary focus is not mere ritual for the experienced side, which tries to use it as a probing vehicle to assess the give in the other side's position. If it is ascertained that the probing effort is not going well, the probing side should be disciplined enough to guard against making any disclosures that may be helpful to the other side. It may also be useful to try to redirect the probing to confuse the other side concerning the probing side's priority interests.

The relevance and importance of personal and positional credibility throughout the negotiation process cannot be overemphasized. Credibility should be viewed as the engine that powers the negotiation process. Once credibility is compromised or lost, the negotiating effort becomes stalled and, usually, dead in the water. Any effort to revive the dialogue under these circumstances entails such high start-up costs that it usually is not cost-effective. In theory, loss of the *personal credibility* of a negotiator may be salvagable by replacing him, but even here there may be accrued relationship costs that will prejudice continuation of the dialogue. In the case of loss of *positional credibility,* there can be no refuge behind the formal separateness of the principal-agent relationship (implied by replacing the negotiator) because, in effect, the consensus favored by the side that lost its positional credibility has become compromised. With this in mind, the effective negotiator carefully screens his procedural and substantive moves to make sure that his credibility story remains intact. In applying the continuing checklist, he treats as questionable and, perhaps, nonviable any move that detracts from his personal or positional credibility.

Probing

Probing throughout the dialogue is essential because it produces additional information concerning the sides, their special needs, and the positions they may be expected to pursue in the course of the dialogue. In this way it confirms, updates, and supplements the information developed during the preparation phase. For the effective negotiator, probing is an ongoing activity; he continually checks and cross-checks earlier perceptions of the other side's situation, goals, and objectives.

At the negotiating table, probing involves the exchange of amenities and information and other express and tacit communications and discussions relating to dialogue issues. Away from the table, it takes the form of small talk on a variety of related and seemingly unrelated subjects. For example, in a negotiation with an insurance adjuster, a nonthreatening question concerning his length of service with his carrier can serve a probing purpose, as an adjuster's settlement authority is usually related to experience and length of service.

Throughout the dialogue, the probing negotiator carefully sizes up the other side, its representation, and its negotiating goals and objectives. In terms of the other side's representation, he is interested in its negotiator's personality and negotiating style;[15] experience, authority, and principal control; and career concerns. In probing the position of the other side, the negotiator seeks information concerning goals, objectives, and perceptions related to the situation, including the burden of negotiation; consensus priorities; expectations; vulnerabilities; and procedural and substantive linkages. The take from the probing effort is factored into the negotiating game plan, which (having been conceived during the preparation phase) is then adjusted to reflect the results of that continuing effort. Without good probing, the negotiator cannot be effective. He needs a continuing source of reliable information to (1) keep the dialogue on course, and (2) exploit specific information and developments that affect the management and control of the dialogue.

Probing complements the operational aspects of the negotiation process. It provides an informational base for (1) managing and controlling the dialogue, including its maintenance, and (2) influencing the other side's negotiating effort. When the effective negotiator thinks of the give and take of negotiation, he does so in a professionally self-serving way. For him, the take connotes what he gets from probing to help him conduct the dialogue; the give means actively influencing the other side's perceptions, apprehension, uncertainty, and expectations by giving it information or reactions designed to impact negatively its conduct of the negotiation dialogue. The effort is to avoid contributing to the other side's probing effort and, if possible, to neutralize it with feints and thrusts that may blunt or confuse it.

As in many aspects of negotiation, the "think-negotiation" emphasis on advantage requires that probing be viewed in terms of offense and defense. For the effective negotiator, both give and take have offensive implications in that he seeks to get more than he gives in probing play. He can accomplish this by answering questions that are not asked, providing only half answers to some questions and no answers to others, or countering questions with other questions. Sometimes, a multifalse demand is used as a defensive measure to complicate probing for the other side; this creates confusion over goals and objectives, issue priorities, needs, and vulnerabilities. The main thrust of the defensive effort is to deprive the other side of any easy take and to burden it with the need to continually monitor and pursue the probing effort. The hope is that the other negotiator will tire of the pursuit of information because of its lack of productivity and potentially disruptive effect on the flow of the dialogue and, perhaps, the negotiating relationship.

In a mismatch of negotiators, the less effective one will suffer twofold from probing: His take will be small and his give damagingly large. The advice here is to "think negotiation" and focus on (1) seeking information related to personal and positional exposure, and (2) denying such information to the other side. The Soviets have good advice for any situation in which one can be prejudiced by unfocused slips of the tongue: "Learn from the fish—his moment of greatest danger is when his mouth is open!" This can be combined with another bit of Russian wisdom: "Measure nine times and cut once!" The net result approximates "thinking negotiation" in emphasizing the importance of an advantage/exposure focus in playing the probing game.

Tacit Communication

Sensitivity to, and active use of, tacit communication (verbal, physical, or other) are essential elements in effective negotiation. As a practical matter, every dialogue can be graphically represented:

_____express channel of communication
_____ tacit channel of communication

The effective negotiator makes use of both channels in managing and controlling the dialogue because he knows the great exploitative potential of full utilization (i.e., transmitting and receiving) of the tacit channel. Tacit communication is very important: One is not really negotiating if he does not transmit or, at the very least, receive on this channel.

The negotiator's use of tacit communication must be both offensive and defensive. He makes certain that all his transmissions on the tacit channel are intended and not slips of the tongue or other forms of undisciplined behavior. In receiving, he analyzes the communications from the other side for their express and tacit content. The starting point is to realize that communication is being effected. All types of signals, both substantive (e.g., hinting at a new proposal or possible avenue for exploration) as well as ploy (e.g., demonstrating a lack of interest in a proposal), can be transmitted tacitly. The popular ditty, "Your lips tell me 'no' but there's a 'yes, yes' in your eyes," gives the essence of tacit transmissions.

Communication can be nonverbal (by facial expression, gesture, or physical reaction) or verbal with a formulation (accompanied with or without special intonation) that has a dual or hidden meaning. The reaction to the substantive or ploy signal is the same as if it were an express communication.[16] As to nonverbal tacit communication, there is need to associate physical behavior with types of reactions and responses. As actions are communications, they must be coordinated with verbal ones to avoid the classic faux pas: to follow a stated position, which is announced to be final, with demonstration of an interest in, or a readiness to entertain, a counter from the other side. There must be consistency between behavior and dialogue.

The effective negotiator is always on the alert for nonverbal indications concerning the thinking of the other side. He observes carefully; he knows that the actions, mannerisms, gestures, and physical reactions of his opposite number may provide clues to his thinking, emotional state, and negotiating needs. Nervousness, a faltering voice, cold clammy hands, facial or other tics, flushing (blushing), and perspiration are noteworthy because they reflect some degree of stress or sensitivity. Just like the polygraph operator, the negotiator's alertness in this regard permits him to read the other side better and react appropriately.

The negotiator must assume that he is being similarly monitored and must guard his own reactions. For example, if he has a tendency to tap his pencil when he is impatient or annoyed, he should desist unless he wishes to use the tapping in an offensive move to convey his impatience or annoyance to the other side or any observing audience. If it is not intended or controlled, the tapping could betray the negotiator's (1) impatience and, perhaps, readiness to move more quickly to consensus, or (2) unhappiness with the negotiating relationship. Similarly, if a negotiator is aware that his hands get clammy when shaking hands, he should keep them in his pocket before greeting others in this way lest he convey his nervous reaction to a situation or issue. The negotiator seeking managed and controlled communications must discipline his nonverbal actions and reactions so that they can be harnessed to, and not betray, the negotiation effort.

In studying physical reactions for tacit communication, special attention should be paid to *watching the eyes* of the other side. Eyes are important because they mirror understanding, anxiety, happiness, disappointment, and a host of other reactions that are meaningful in reading the negotiating situation. As eyes are not easily controlled or disciplined, the reactions they reflect are frequently unintended and more meaningful. For example, if the start of a presentation on a particular issue brings the sunshine of joy to the other side's eyes, the flutter or blinking of anxiety or nervousness, or the cloud of nonunderstanding, anger, or disappointment, the presenting side may have the opportunity to adjust the presentation—and, if the negotiating situation permits, the position itself—to take advantage of its reading of the reaction of the other side.

Watching the eyes has a bonus effect because it is commonly considered a plus to look another person straight in the eye while engaging in serious discussion.[17] (Caveat: In some cultures, such as the Japanese, eye contact may be considered confrontational and a sign of disrespect. See later section on cross-cultural contacts.) By doing so, one avoids the opprobrium of the remark, "He could not even look me in the eye!" and, more important, enjoys a cover for watching for exploitable reactions. The effective negotiator, recognizing the communication potential of eyes, tries to effect an inscrutable poker face while listening to the other side. He then can change that expression to reflect the desired reaction. By consciously using facial expressions to react to a situation, he can better control his eyes because of their involvement in the facial reaction and thereby reduce the eye-watching take of the other side.

In the case of verbal tacit communication, one must carefully screen formulations for hidden or collateral messages. There must be sensitivity to nuances in formulation and tone and their potential implications for the

dialogue. For example, in a situation involving a request for financial assistance, a simple, unhesitating "no" would not leave any doubt. The situation might be considerably different if the reply were: "I cannot *give* you
that amount." The negotiator receiving on the tacit communication channel would be encouraged by such a reply; but his single-channel colleague
would be starting to look elsewhere for the financial assistance. Assuming
that the source of the reply is one whose past behavior indicates care in
the choice and tone of words, the reply could be interpreted as a signal
that there cannot be a gift (i.e., a loan may be possible) or that the amount
requested is too high. Intentional emphasis (on "give" or "amount") might
indicate which interpretation is correct. In any case, the reply potentially
opens up a whole new area of dialogue for exploration by the effective
negotiator.

Sometimes the express dialogue appears to involve trivialities, whereas
in fact it is a cover for serious procedural or substantive maneuvering. The
seemingly pointless, drawn-out discussions in Paris at the Vietnam peace
talks concerning table shapes are an excellent example. The thrust of that
dialogue from the U.S. point of view was to demonstrate to (1) the North
Vietnamese that the negotiation was to be hard-fought, and (2) its allies
and the rest of the world that the dialogue was not to be a cover for U.S.
surrender of its position in Vietnam. The best way to test tacit communications, verbal or written, is to carefully weigh the formulations used
and to analyze the unstated implications. These implications are key to
understanding hidden meanings or agendas. Questions such as the following are useful in uncovering intended or unintended communications: "Why
is this particular formulation being used? How else can the matter be stated?
If stated in other ways, what are the differences in meaning? Is intonation
a factor? What about the situational context, accompanying or related gestures, and physical reactions?"

As an example, consider some of the tacit-communication implications
of possible U.S. statements in reaction to the June 1989 massacre of pro-
democracy protestors in Tiananmen Square in Beijing. The absence of any
U.S. response could imply condonation of the events for political reasons
related to its relationship with the People's Republic of China—certainly,
not a courageous or politically cost-free option. A response deploring the
event in soft terms (e.g., the "tragedy" of Tiananmen Square) would imply
greater acceptability or acquiescence than one focusing on the nature of
the tragedy ("loss of life"), the action ("use of force," "massacre"), or the
actors ("Chinese military forces"). The negative tone of the response would
be appreciably escalated if it moved from "deploring" to "denouncing" and
"condemning" and described the event with formulations such as "brutal
force" or "unarmed, peaceful protestors."

This type of analysis should be practiced until it becomes second nature
to the would-be negotiator. Only in this way can he develop the sensitivity

to receive and react to tacit communications and hidden agendas, which would otherwise go unreceived and unexploited. Sensitivity and reaction to tacit communication logically are part of the "think-negotiation" mindset to seek and exploit advantage in the pursuit of interest.

The Tone of the Dialogue

As negotiation is basically an exercise in persuasion, the tone of the dialogue should be kept as friendly as circumstances will permit; it is more difficult to persuade someone who is angry. There is no point in burdening the process of persuasion by an antagonistic, argumentative approach. Hostility toward, or bad feelings for, the other side may result in posturing or other counterproductive responses that may adversely affect its desire or readiness to reach agreement. Experience shows that glaring sides seldom reach accommodative consensus quickly or at all.[18] Dialogue with a nonadversarial tone tends to disarm the other side and, in general, enhances the possibility of exploiting the situation's friendly persuasion potential.

Most commentators identify two negotiating approaches or styles: competitive (adversarial) and cooperative (problem-solving). Recent emphasis on win-win negotiation and the social responsibility of negotiators underscores the greater rationality of the cooperative approach. The effective negotiator, however, being preoccupied with pursuit of interest and advantage in an inherently adversarial process, is led by operational considerations to opt for a hybrid approach. This approach is adversarial in substance but problem-solving and cooperative in form and appearance. Under this approach, the friendly tone of the negotiating dialogue serves as a cover for the controlled, hardball pursuit of interest. The negotiating checklist items concerning viability and relationship maintenance ensure that the pursuit of interest remains under control.

The other side's perception of the quality of the negotiating relationship should be shaped or manipulated to facilitate persuasion. The effective negotiator must serve as a mood engineer to develop that perception. Essentially, he tries to disarm the other side by taking an approach that reflects a common interest in "working together" to resolve a shared problem. The goal is a negotiating relationship that is perceived to be based on cooperation and good will. Operationally, this is usually achievable because there is a natural tendency to prefer friendly, easy dialogue over one that is rancorous and hard-fought. The benefit, of course, is that the wooed side, lulled by the problem-solving cover of the dialogue, may become less vigilant and suspicious in reacting to the proposals of the wooing side. The result is a negotiating relationship that may be exploitable in the development of favorable consensus and, short of that, productive probing.

One's first approach in negotiation should be friendly and pleasant. Little is sacrificed by taking this initial approach, as the hard line can always be adopted later.[19] It also has the bonus effect of setting the stage for demonstrating provocation if the other side fails to respond to the softer, friendlier approach. Of course, some situations are inherently antagonistic; here, response in kind is necessary to keep from being overwhelmed or to convey a tacit message to interested audiences. For example, the peace negotiations in Paris concerning Vietnam were bitterly adversarial from the very start. It would have been fruitless (except to establish bona fides or play victim in order to court world public opinion) not to respond in kind lest a milder response be interpreted as a sign of weakness. The United States felt a need to reflect continued resolve to the world audience and, specifically, to the other states supporting South Vietnam (e.g., Korea, Australia, and New Zealand). Although they were not represented at the table, these states were affected by the results of the negotiation.

Playing victim can be a useful ploy, however distasteful that role may appear in the face of a hostile negotiating strategy on the part of the other side. In some situations, one can control the dialogue (and, perhaps, the representation and tactics of the other side) by playing the firm but unprovokable victim. As a result of this role-playing, the other side may instruct its negotiator to "ease up" or even replace him because of the lack of progress that can be attributed to his hostile and bellicose style. The negotiator playing victim cannot be considered the one at fault even though his own firmness has blocked progress. (Of course, the negotiator must explain the role playing to his principal lest he think his affairs should be put in stronger hands!) If a new negotiator is selected by the other side, he may be so impressed with the "failure" of his predecessor that he might be inhibited from, or instructed not to engage in, practices or techniques that strain the negotiating relationship. This inhibition or restraint may be exploitable in the course of the dialogue. However, there is a caveat: The replacement negotiator may be more difficult to deal with, and what is worse, more effective! The lesson is that the effective negotiator must consider all the worst-case scenarios as he adjusts the negotiating strategy of his game plan to the situation he faces.

Establishing the Haggle Zone

The presentation phase formally ends with establishment of the haggle zone. This usually occurs after the sparring over opening positions is completed and the dialogue progresses to the exchange of offers and counteroffers outlining the upper and lower limits of developing consensus. For example, in a dollars and cents negotiation the haggle zone is reached when the sides narrow the differences between their "not less than" or "more than" positions. The sides then refine the bargaining from this range to final consensus or closing.

Drawing the line of demarcation for the presentation phase at the haggle zone is somewhat artificial; in practice, presentational techniques continue during the final bargaining until closing and, thereafter, during implementation. It is also artificial to treat reaching the final agreement, including closing, as a separate phase because it follows naturally from the establishment of the haggle zone; the negotiating cost of backtracking at this point pressures the sides to close. There are, however, two justifications for the phase demarcation at the haggle zone: One is tactical and one instructional. Tactically speaking, this point in the negotiating process is worth separating out, as there is an exploitable tendency to ease up when "agreement is in sight" or "has been bracketed" or when "agreement in principle" has been reached. Negotiators who would ease up tend to underestimate the difficulty of the final bargaining (haggling) ahead. Also, many negotiators shy away from haggling because they (1) do not appreciate the contribution it can make to a favorable result, or (2) view it as somewhat demeaning. The effective negotiator's approach is based upon the "whatever-it-takes" mentality, consistent with the standard of prudence concerning professional and ethical behavior. The instructional justification for the demarcation is that it highlights the theory and manner of trading concessions and using bargaining chips effectively to reach final agreement.

It can be said that the presentation phase ends and the haggle zone begins when the sides have succeeded in narrowing their major differences. The side encouraged by the progress may feel that at this stage it can afford to relax somewhat and engage in looser bargaining-chip play in the interest of winding things up quickly. The effective negotiator can cultivate (and tries to exploit) this relaxed approach by stressing such things as the favorable "momentum" that has been achieved in the dialogue, the "basic groundwork" that has been laid for final consensus, and the need to "strain a little more" to close the matter. Of course, his chip play remains tightfisted because he views establishment of the haggle zone as an opportunity to exploit any impatience the other side might demonstrate, including the natural desire to wind up the negotiation. His tightfisted play is also helpful as a tacit signal that he is running out of negotiating room and is close to his final position.

Establishment of the haggle zone is frequently signalled by an announced agreement in principle, with the details on a given issue or issues remaining to be worked out. For the effective negotiator, agreement in principle signals the beginning of hard bargaining.[20] Too many novices look upon agreement in principle as the end of the negotiation process, with the details to flesh out the arrangement being a mere matter of mopping up. The holder of such a view will himself be the object of the mopping-up exercise. The effective negotiator carefully pursues his objectives through all the detailed arrangement making because he knows the cumulative importance of gaining little advantages in settling each detail. For him, "the devil is in the details." Ever alert to exploitable situations, he relishes the mopping-up role as he redoubles his efforts to make advantageous concession trades on the remaining details.

REACHING AGREEMENT PHASE

The effective negotiator plays his chips very carefully to obtain maximum mileage from them. As a practical matter, success in negotiation more frequently comes from getting a little more than one gives in making each concession than from a single grand stroke. It is essential, therefore, to focus on effective concession trading.

The Theory of Concessions

The basic principle is that "one never gives without getting, except when giving for effect." Concessions are traded, not simply made. The stated exception is apparent only because in giving for effect (e.g., to improve the negotiating atmosphere by demonstrating a forthcoming attitude), one actually gets something in return: the desired effect. This can be substantive or procedural. For example, bargaining over agenda and issue formulation is critical in many negotiations because of the desire to exploit, or defend against, loaded formulations. Also, there are tactical advantages in controlling the order in which issues are addressed and by which side.

A common concession ploy is the "good-faith" game. Each side tries to exploit the position that the other side is not negotiating in good faith. The play is to criticize the other side's failure to make a desired substantive or procedural concession as evidence that it is not negotiating in good faith. This shaming technique is seldom effective unless one is dealing with an inexperienced negotiator or one who cannot handle the imagined audience cost of rejection of the other side's attempt to get a cheap concession. A variation of this theme was evidenced by the effort of the Iranian government to get the United States to make some "gesture of good will" when two American hostages (Frank Reed and Robert Polhill) were released in the spring of 1990. The effort fell short of a pure good-faith play in that Iran could not credibly link U.S. inaction to a failure to negotiate in good faith. The play was flawed because the U.S. audience concern was to maintain its position that it does not negotiate for hostages; its concern was not the opprobrium of not being forthcoming in a negotiation for them.

A corollary to the principle of concession trading is that one tries to get more than is given in each exchange of concessions. This is usually accomplished by the false demand, exaggerating the importance of an issue, or some other bootstrapping technique that causes the other side to overestimate the value of the concession needed and, as a consequence, pay disproportionately for it. Bootstrapping is involved whenever a nonissue is introduced into the dialogue or a relatively minor issue is treated as a major one to increase its bargaining value.

In trading concessions, gradualism should be the operational rule lest the other side's expectations be unduly raised by the large size of, or ease in obtaining, concessions. Large concessions tend to stimulate greater demands because they suggest that the conceding side has a lot of room in its negotiating position or not much experience; rational concession trading is deemed to imply a careful expenditure of bargaining chips. Concessions should not come easily for the other side—it should be made to work hard for them, thereby obtaining the impression that there is not much give remaining in the conceding side's position. Keeping concessions small will have this effect. The impression can also be conveyed by verbal signals ("We might consider that a possibility if that is all that separates us") or by drawn-out, tenacious hard bargaining. However, one must be sensitive to the risk that tenacious bargaining may convey the impression of stonewalling, foot dragging, or not wishing to move toward final consensus, thereby putting dialogue maintenance and continuation in jeopardy.

Bootstrapping Issues

Bootstrapping takes two basic forms: (1) introducing a false demand, offer, or issue into the dialogue, or (2) treating as major an issue that is only of minor importance. In all environments, the false demand or offer is generally used to get negotiating mileage from a nonissue or a relatively unimportant, minor issue. It can also serve as a distraction or source of confusion for the other side to disrupt its conduct of the dialogue. The concession-take potential depends on (1) the other side's perception of the issue ploy as it relates to the location of the burden of negotiation, and (2) the ability of the exploiting side to get the other side to go for the bait. As a consequence, there must be credibility and consistency in manipulating the issue to obtain the desired perception and reaction. If it is hooked, the other side can be made to pay well for the experience.

Another bootstrapping technique is to introduce a subjective standard[21] or dimension to complicate the bargaining. For example, the following approaches are frequently used, depending on the negotiating environment: "It is a matter of principle for my client"; "My boss has a hang-up on this one"; "It is an emotional issue for our nation." The purpose is to introduce into the dialogue an intangible element that defies rational, objective probing and countering. The desired impact is the felt need of the other side to "buy" its way out of the potential impasse. Actually, the spectre of impasse produces the concession because the side that feels it has the burden of negotiation is ready to pay to keep the dialogue moving.

In some cases, bootstrapping may be possible as the windfall result of a misunderstanding. This can occur when the other side (1) misreads the situation and reacts as if there is an issue when none exists, or (2) treats as especially important one that, in fact, is not. The effective negotiator is always sensitive to these "failures of communication" and is ready to exploit them even when the negotiating game plan does not specifically call for bootstrapping. If it is decided to pursue exploitation, the game plan is modified accordingly. The modification may encourage and lead to other bootstrapping possibilities if the other side continues to reveal a manipulable sensitivity to impasse and the burden of negotiation, which are key elements in achieving success in bootstrapping. The focus on exposure analysis in the "think-negotiation" mindset provides defensive safeguards against the kind of perception manipulation that is at the heart of bootstrapping.

Packaging Deals

Packaging is an important element in the management and control of the dialogue. It has a general presentational role in enhancing position or proposal acceptability and a more specific application in the development of final consensus. Our earlier discussion covered the presentational role; here, the focus will be on the specific use of packaging as a closer to achieve final agreement where more than one issue remains to be resolved.

Actually, enhanced proposal acceptability is involved in both applications. What is different is the extent of reliance on substantive concessions in the packaging effort. In simple position or proposal enhancement, packaging tends to be more cosmetically oriented. When used as a closer, however, it involves concession trading because of the proximity of the sides to conclusion of the negotiation. The phrase "packaging deals," reflects the substantive nature of the effort. Packaging deals essentially involves the use of negotiating-chip flexibility to develop final consensus in a multi-issue situation on a "borrow-from-Peter-to-pay-Paul" basis. In effect, greater flexibility on one issue is used to make it attractive for the other side to settle on a twofer basis for less on another issue where the side pressuring for closing has less flexibility.

The first step is to distinguish the multi-issue from the single-issue situation. Where there is a single issue, there is nothing to package in the sense of trying to structure a deal by giving more on one issue to get a package consensus that includes another. As in other aspects of negotiation, however, the perception whether the situation is multi-issue is more important than the reality. Use of a false issue by bootstrapping or other false demand technique may create the impression that the situation is multi-issue, thereby lending itself to packaging deals. In such a case, the side that creates the impression will benefit greatly from any effort of the other side to package by using bargaining chips from the real issue to induce consensus on the nonissue. The reward for creativity will be reduced chip cost for consensus on the real issue.

Many multi-issue situations can be converted to single-issue by agreement to negotiate issues separately. This is the basic approach of the side that wishes to avoid giving up any part of the potential take on important issues. Unfortunately, it takes two to tango and packaging cannot always be avoided by going the agreement route. Moreover, in many cases issues are linked substantively (i.e., they are not severable or separable on the merits) or procedurally (i.e., there may be a requirement that all issues be negotiated as part of a single arrangement). In multi-issue situations where the issues can be negotiated separately, packaging should be considered a possible tactical option. The basic consideration is whether it is desirable to burden certain issues with the cost of obtaining agreement on others. If an issue is truly critical, having greater importance than the others involved in a possible package, the chip play to carry other issues may not be worth the potentially reduced take on the important issue. This value judgment should also take into account the potential utility of the packaging dialogue as a means of (1) probing the other side's issue priorities, position flexibility, and level of negotiating expertise, and (2) diverting attention from key issues and enhancing the apparent importance of others in a bootstrap maneuver to increase the bargaining value of lesser issues.

The basic technique to exploit packaging is the "suspend-and-move-on" approach to conducting the dialogue: All issues involved in the potential package are negotiated to a point to see what fallbacks are available and how much more may be needed to close the deal on the entire package. In this way, the effective negotiator is in a position to continuously review the situation and obtain some idea of what may be available and necessary to put together the consensus package. The progress made in moving toward agreement on all issues and the concomitant probing permit the effective negotiator to assess the continued desirability of packaging.

As in most cases of defense in negotiation, one starts with alertness to, and recognition of, the possibility of a packaging play. The mere presence of outstanding issues should trigger thinking about the possibility of deal packaging and its impact on the negotiating situation. If the decision is made to discourage packaging, the first line of defense is to insist on negotiating each issue, in isolation and to conclusion, before moving on to others. This effectively undermines the procedural basis for the packaging play. It can be justified by the need to make demonstrable progress toward final consensus. One can claim that the pauses involved in the suspend-and-move-on approach are, in fact, only delaying tactics. It also may be possible to increase the concession cost of the issues partially negotiated in order to defeat the packaging effort by reducing its cost benefit. For example, if progress on the carrier issue (i.e., the one with respect to which there is negotiating flexibility) becomes so costly that less is available to assist on the other issues in the package requiring support, the effort to package will collapse. In the process, the defending side may be able to increase its demand concerning the carrier issue: In playing the packaging game, the other side has signalled (by suspending the dialogue concerning that issue) that it has additional negotiating room, which was intended to be used to package the consensus including the other issues. This is the exposure inherent in the suspend-and-move-on packaging tactic. The exposure can be reduced, however, by a diversionary bootstrap effort that focuses attention on less critical issues by utilizing the same tactic in handling them.

Packaging deals is one of the most challenging aspects of the negotiation process because of the many considerations involved in the play and the cost of making a bad move during closing. Coming as it does during the crunch, packaging does not enjoy the forgiveness possibility of the correction of an error made earlier in the dialogue. The crunch, generally defined as "a decisive confrontation" or "a critical situation,"[22] relates to that moment in the dialogue when the sides put positions on the table in the area of their minimally acceptable consensus, with the attendant risk of dialogue breakdown should the bargaining not progress to closing.

The Crunch

In every negotiation comes the moment of truth, the so-called crunch, when the sides are close to final agreement. At this stage, the pressures to reach agreement are the strongest owing to the momentum built up during the movement toward consensus. Failure to recognize this moment[23] may cause the negotiation to break down, with consequent loss to the side that needs consensus most (i.e., the one with the burden of negotiation). That side must be especially sensitive to the onset of the crunch lest it continue to haggle rather than move toward final agreement. Continued haggling at this point becomes counterproductive and may push the other side into a break-off situation.[24] Thus, there is a point in every negotiation when haggling has to give way to the striking of a bargain, or closing. As its name implies, the reaching agreement phase involves the crunch, the last serious effort to close out the negotiation through a meaningful exchange of final concessions.

The effective negotiator senses the approach of the crunch as concession trades become more important and differences between the sides narrow. He knows that he must determine how much more can be gotten or how much more should be sought. If he needs the negotiated result more than the other side does, he cannot afford to be too demanding and frequently has to accept less than the maximum possible result. He may know that he probably could get one last concession but dares not risk it. On the other hand, if the other side is carrying the burden of negotiation, the effective negotiator can push for what the traffic can be made to bear. The operative principle here is the negotiating truism "if a side wants it bad, it gets it bad."

As the location of the burden of negotiation is critical, the effective negotiator tries to hide his own need, ascertain that of the other side, and create the impression that that side has the greater need. For him, location of the burden is an issue in every negotiation because it bears so heavily on the vulnerability of the sides and the results attainable in managing and controlling the dialogue. In whatever negotiating environment he finds himself, the effective negotiator tries to demonstrate in rather low key his side's readiness to forgo a negotiated result—for example, to sue (private); to have the issue decided by higher authority (intraorganizational); or to discontinue the dialogue at the present pace (i.e., by reducing the length of meetings, increasing the interval between them, or declaring a formal suspension) or entirely (international). At the same time, he seeks to impress the other side that failure to reach consensus through negotiation is contrary to its interests. In short, he tries to take the offensive by orchestrating, exploiting, and manipulating perceptions, apprehension, uncertainty, and expectations concerning the desirability of, or need for, a negotiated conclusion to the dialogue. In the process, he carefully assesses the reaction and responses of the other side to confirm (1) his original assessment concerning the location of the burden of negotiation, and (2) any success in shifting the burden to the other side.

Throughout the haggling, the effective negotiator must be alert to any signal that indicates the imminence of the crunch. He must also be sensitive to ploy play designed to simulate the crunch in order to create the perception that it has been reached (with the consequent need to make "final" concessions). In so doing, he must be prepared to cope with the false signals (e.g., "our last offer is") that he may expect to receive from the other side.[25] As there may be no real way of knowing whether the stated last offer is in fact the last one,[26] the effective negotiator usually leaves an avenue of retreat in the follow-up demand so that if "last" is, in fact, "last," he can still avail himself of the offer. The usual technique is to give an ambivalent response to the offer. Depending on the reaction of the other side, this may end up as "what my principal had hoped for" while accepting the original offer; if the other side caves, it may become a firm demand that is pushed for as the bargain closer. The negotiator's hedged response avoids a clear counterdemand that would reject the final offer and risk termination of the dialogue.

Experience shows that in wrapping up a deal the last word is not always said at the negotiating table. Even after "final" agreement is reached, a glitch sometimes develops and the consensus is in jeopardy. This is an inherent risk in the *ad referendum* process. For example, in a private negotiation, the client's cousin may know of a similar case in which the claimant got more; in an intraorganizational negotiation, a senior official may take a special interest in the matter and inject a new wrinkle at his level; in an international negotiation, the opposition political party may raise a question that could jeopardize internal approval of the negotiated arrangement. In all these examples, there is need for one last chip or other sweetener to guarantee that the deal stays closed. The contingent exposure to this need causes the effective negotiator to attempt to hold back some bargaining chips. The need for this kind of encore (i.e., closer) is frequent enough to warrant providing for it in the negotiating game plan as insurance against negotiation's version of Murphy's Law. Of course, if there is no such need, the chips that have been saved represent even greater success in the outcome of the negotiation; they also remain available for possible use during the implementation phase if postconsensus problems develop or during subsequent bargaining if the dialogue is ongoing. The effective negotiator is sensitive to the need to carefully handle the crunch, including the burden-of-negotiation issue, deal packaging, and the encore requirements of *ad referendum*.

Exploiting *Ad Referendum*

Every negotiator operates under his principal's instructions. All proposals that are not within the scope of those instructions can only be accepted *ad referendum* (i.e., they must be referred to the principal for acceptance). The other side, however, does not know the extent of those instructions; depending where the advantage lies, it can be led to believe that referral is or is not necessary. Unless otherwise agreed, the general understanding is that the principal's approval of proposals or counterproposals is required.

The *ad referendum* nature of the negotiation process facilitates exploitation of the process internal to negotiation. The effective negotiator determines the exploitation possibilities based upon his assessment of the situation and the anticipated reaction of the other side. Obviously, where there is strong representation on the other side, there will be reduced opportunity to exploit *ad referendum*. For example, the strong defender will seek assurances that the *ad referendum* process on the other side has been completed before accepting a proposal or counterproposal for submission to his principal.

In many situations, the negotiator is advantaged when the other side understands that all proposals must be submitted to his principal for approval. This permits some bargaining before submission, including, in the extreme case, attempted preliminary rejection on the basis that "I would lose a client, my job, or be recalled [as appropriate for the three environments] if I submitted this." The other side may react by favorably modifying the proposal to improve its acceptability. If it is not careful, the other side may, in effect, be accepting a two-stage approval procedure, which may become the pattern of the dialogue. The effective negotiator who can accomplish this gets for his principal an improved proposal without using a chip, thereby improving the bargaining situation by conserving chips. The counter to this technique is to insist that the proposal be submitted and, if personal career concerns are voiced by the negotiator for the other side, to state that the submitting side is prepared to send an accompanying communication that clearly spells out the firmness of its position in the face of strong attempts by the receiving side's negotiator to have it modified before submission.

There may be another advantage to having the other side believe that the situation is strictly *ad referendum*. The negotiator may be able, thereby, to insulate himself from the bitterness that may develop from a hard bargaining situation in the interest of preserving a good working relationship at the table. To be successful in this variation of the "good guy–bad guy" ploy, the negotiator demonstrates a readiness "to do all he can" to advance the dialogue. In demonstrating this cooperative spirit, he may be able to generate greater confidence on the part of the other side and be in a position to gain more insight into its negotiating position. Furthermore, by assuming an apparently detached role, he may be able to function as a surrogate mediator and influence the submission of proposals by expressing opinions or comments about the course of the negotiation in terms of his principal's probable reactions. In this mediator role, the effective negotiator is in a position to get modifications of a proposal without bargaining for them. For example, he may comment that his principal "would not go that far" or "needs a little more" or that the proposal would be counterproductive if submitted as suggested—all directed toward a follow-on modification of the proposal without having to bargain for it with chips.

There are other situations in which it is in the negotiator's interest to demonstrate that he has substantial authority and only in certain cases must refer back to his principal. As indicated earlier, this demonstration enhances the negotiator's position and permits him to accept a proposal on the spot and bind the other side. This is desirable because sometimes during *ad referendum* the proposing side has a change of heart and attempts to change its proposal before it is formally accepted. The belief that the deal has already been accepted by the negotiator may inhibit the proposing side from attempting to change or withdraw the proposal. To do so under the circumstances could constitute a breach of contract.

In addition, the negotiator who has demonstrated that he has full authority can exploit initial rejection of a proposal more effectively by countering that he has been instructed not to accept anything less than a larger figure. In such a situation, the other side is faced with the prospect of having to cope with the same two-stage approval procedure. The counter for that side, which is somewhat risky if the negotiator is actually conveying the substance of his instructions and the proposing side needs the negotiated result, is to insist that the proposal be submitted. The risk, of course, is that by pushing the "no," the proposing side may cause termination of the dialogue.

The *ad referendum* game cannot be played advantageously if principals are in personal contact with each other (e.g., in summitry) or otherwise actively participate in the formal dialogue. As a general rule, direct participation by the principal should be discouraged because of the loss of (1) the refuge of *ad referendum,* or (2) the possibility of making the surrogate-mediator play. (The problem in the first case is that although a negotiator's mistake can be corrected by "rejection" of the action by his principal, a principal's mistake is more difficult and costly to undo; for example, a contractual obligation may have to be broken.) As to the second, most principals are too closely involved with the substance of the dialogue to be disciplined, dispassionate negotiators, and they rarely bring to the bargaining table the negotiating mindset and skills of the effective negotiator.

There is also a career dimension to *ad referendum* play because it is an important element in the negotiator's dialogue to control his principal. For example, pressures are generated on the negotiator by having the principal as a witness to how the dialogue was handled and what actually occurred. As to the former, there is always the concern that the principal may get the impression that representation by his negotiator has fallen short of what was expected or desired—a factor that could inhibit strong negotiator pressure on the principal. The latter bears on any effort to pressure the principal to accept a proposal on the basis of the firmness of the other side's position or some other dialogue development affecting the negotiating situation. Thus, the vantage point of the principal's presence may dilute the pressures available to the negotiator, who, spurred on by his career concerns, may be a most ardent advocate of acceptance as he refers proposals to his principal. To assist in the negotiation with his principal, the effective negotiator prefers to be in a position to control and shape the reporting of dialogue developments. The hard-bargaining negotiator feels that reporting cables, memos of conversation, aide-memoires, and other reporting vehicles are best written by him, lest he suffer at the hand of a less cooperative or appreciative observer.

Drafting Consensus

The effective negotiator, always alert to exploitable situations, attaches great importance to controlling the drafting of negotiating documents. The ideal situation is to be the drafter, as the document can be made to favor the drafting side by the skills and art of its preparer. He believes firmly in the power of the pen and seeks to wield it as often as the situation[27] (including the relaxed vigilance, work habits, and inexperience of the other side) will permit. For example, he relishes the situation in which, agreement in principle having been reached, the other side relaxes because it considers the drafting to be merely a translation of the consensus into formal language. While the other side is resting and, perhaps, basking in the sunlight of the "good deal" it has made, the effective negotiator tries to improve it in his side's interest by continuing the negotiation through control of the drafting task. His first move is to offer to prepare the draft; if permitted to do so, he will make every effort to shape the text of the document to reflect the consensus in a way most favorable to the interests of his side. The key to success is to treat the drafting as a continuation of the negotiation process (i.e., to continue to seek advantage in the formulation of the draft text).

The approach to drafting applies to all stages of the negotiation. It is not limited to the final document. The effective negotiator knows, for example, that it is to his advantage at any and every stage of a negotiation involving a working document (e.g., the document from which the parties will negotiate) to draft it because the document can be slanted[28] to serve his side. He also is aware that control of the drafting will have a cumulative, positive effect on the quality of the final document, thereby gaining a "leg up." This leg-up possibility is the genesis of another contrived term of art, "leg-up drafting," which, in consonance with "thinking negotiation," implies purposeful, interest-oriented drafting techniques.

Effective drafting technique is a complex subject that is beyond the scope of a basic guide. The modest purpose here is to suggest a general approach to drafting and the kind of scrutiny that must be brought to bear when drafting and reviewing draft proposals.[29] The advantage of being the drafter is clear, principally because procedurally it puts him on the offense in structuring a favorable text. The nondrafting side is forced to defend by objecting specifically to particular formulations; by its very nature, the approach cannot produce a text to his complete liking. The drafter, on the other hand, enjoys the advantage of being able to slide things through, including the exploitation of favorable ambiguity, because he knows that the defending side will be inhibited from objecting to everything. The very process works against the nondrafter.

In leg-up drafting one should seek to employ the light and loaded approach. The objective is to cast favorably shaped or shaded (i.e., loaded in

one's favor) text in the "lightest" possible language and formulation structure. Avoiding complexity of language and structure tends to lessen scrutiny for hidden meanings; the text appears to be simple and straightforward. Juxtaposing of clauses can also be used to create special effects in
either expanding or limiting the effect of key operative language. For example, placement of a "subject to" condition at the beginning of a series
(e.g., an enumeration of authorized activities) has a much broader impact
than specifically relating it to one or more of the component elements.
This could be a type of lightning rod or false demand where the intention
to condition certain activities is covered by an open-ended formulation
that makes all activities subject to some condition. The formulation places
the burden on the defending side to uncover the loaded structure to protect its interests. In the process, that side will, at the very least, identify
for the drafting side what some of those interests are. Moreover, resistance of the drafting side to limiting the applicability of the "subject to"
formulation could result in the sacrifice of some of those interests or the
need to give more to have them excluded. The resulting bargaining advantage to the drafter illustrates again the plight of the defending side.

The lightning rod or false demand effects result from a technique known
as seeding, which is intended to generate bargaining chips in a bootstrapping play. The seeded formulations are used to gain acceptance of the
favorably shaded formulations or concessions on other issues. The lightning rod is intended to get the other side to focus on and question the
objectionable provisions and to finally "succeed" in "negotiating" them out
of the text while other formulations slip through in whole or in part. The
introduction of false issues adds to those that must be resolved before the
negotiation can be concluded and, thereby, increases the potential concession take for the seeding side. Seeding in the form of a subjective standard
(which is the trigger for the existence of a right for the drafting side and
a corresponding duty for the other) can be especially burdensome for the
defending side if the standard, although apparently keyed to an objective
event, in fact can be brought to pass at will by the drafting side.

For example, consider the negotiation of one of the U.S. status of forces
agreements that I handled. A proposal provided that the United States
would have the authority to exercise criminal jurisdiction over its military
personnel stationed in Country X if it were deemed necessary for the
good order and discipline of the U.S. armed forces. In that case the United
States expected, and was able, to get a big chip concerning operational
activities in return for modifying its position more in consonance with
standard international formulations on the sharing of criminal jurisdiction
(i.e., a formulation spelling out agreed limits on the exercise of U.S. criminal jurisdiction). It was possible to introduce such a one-sided proposal
and attempt to exploit it without prejudice because Country X had the
burden of negotiation. It badly wanted a status of forces agreement with

the United States to bolster its image as a respected member of the international system.

Where the other side is experienced, there will be difficulty in getting the drafting task or getting away with the more obvious leg-up techniques. On the former point, after bargaining back and forth as to who will draft, the logical compromise is to agree to share the drafting. In determining the drafting division of labor, the effective negotiator, thinking ahead and benefiting from having a negotiating game plan, knows which provisions or issues are of critical importance to his side. Only the fully prepared professional on the other side will have sufficiently thought the negotiation through to be in a position to oppose a sharing of tasks or exploit its potential. If he is, he will insist that the drafting of the critical provisions be shared. Even this exchange can be useful because it may show what is important to the other side. Certainly, it will include some issues that are critically important. Of course, cross-checking is needed to prevent the other side from using this exchange to bootstrap an issue (i.e., create the impression that it is an important issue) for bargaining advantage.

As to text scrutiny, every draft should be analyzed in terms of the specific language and formulations used and the juxtaposing of language. The eternal questions should be: "Why is this being said, formulated, or structured this way?" and "How else could it be said, formulated, or structured?" Specific alternate wording and positioning should then be analyzed to judge the substantive differences and effects. This type of scrutiny should be applied in studying the drafts prepared by the other side and in reviewing one's own drafts. The purpose is to make sure that one is not being "taken" by the other side, in the first case; and is getting maximum mileage out of the possibilities, and not inadvertently giving something away, in the second. For example, during preparation for the Baker-Aziz talks in Geneva in January 1991, the Iraqi foreign minister stated that his country would not "withdraw from Kuwait in accordance with the United Nations Security Council Resolution." The key portion of his formulation is the words "in accordance . . . Resolution." The next step, to analyze the resolution's conditions and develop an exploratory dialogue, would not have been necessary if the Iraqi position had ended at the word "Kuwait." To the disappointment of all observers involved in "thinking negotiation," the Iraqi text was not a seeded one. The talks failed because there was no intent to imply readiness to enter into a dialogue concerning withdrawal from Kuwait provided agreement could be reached on a modification of the Security Council's conditions.

In countering seeded drafts, one should isolate the key, exposure-laden language that has to be modified. There is much to be gained by retaining as much of the originally proposed language as possible; in effect, it constitutes a partial acceptance of the original proposal.[30] Also, the change may be saleable as a "minor one." It is also possible that the substance of the change may be overlooked by a careless reading of the new language because of its surface familiarity. In either case, the effort is directed at enhancing the possibility of a quick. but not careful, reaction on the part of the other side. Where the proposed language has to be drastically changed, there will be little chance of exploiting the "you snooze, you lose" principle. Instead, there will be a need to rely more upon the use of bargaining chips than clever drafting legerdemain.

THE IMPLEMENTATION PHASE

It is generally considered that the negotiation process ends with the reaching of final consensus. This is correct only when the consensus does not involve a follow-on implementation or other relationship connection. The most common example is the simple sales transaction between two individuals in which there is no question of warranty or other postconsensus responsibility or relationship. This is the true "done-deal" situation in that the negotiated arrangement is not subject to modification through adverse practice or relationship linkage (i.e., when other issues in the relationship are used to reopen the just-concluded negotiation). In the vast majority of negotiations, however, there is an implementation or other dialogue connection that is best viewed as a continuation of the negotiation process because the sides' interest in the negotiated result can be at risk.

The effective negotiator looks upon implementation as the final phase of the negotiation process. His view is that the negotiation continues during implementation because the negotiated arrangement is in play in the sense that it can be modified for better or worse by the conduct of the sides (i.e., through their practice under the agreement or attempts at modification by seeking a renegotiation of the arrangement based upon the linkage of a relationship connection). This section will focus on practice as a means of modifying the terms of a negotiated arrangement. Modification based upon linkage does not require special coverage, as it is a type of straightforward negotiation frequently encountered in continuing relationships when adjustments are desired.

The practice of the sides under a negotiated arrangement can affect its substance because the practice, in the absence of an objection to it, can become controlling with the passage of time. In effect, the establishment of practice constitutes a dialogue that should be managed and controlled in the pursuit of interest (i.e., it is negotiation). As a consequence, alertness to (or recognition of) the potential exploitability of practice in the postnegotiation phase is crucial.

The focus again is on exposure. The minimum goal is maintenance of the integrity of the arrangement as negotiated (i.e., defending against attempts by the other side to develop practice more favorable to it); the maximum goal is establishment of more favorable, self-serving practice (i.e., improving the negotiated consensus through substantive gains, including the favorable clarification of ambiguities). To achieve the minimum objective, the negotiator must be alert to practice that deviates in an unfavorable way from the negotiated result. When such practice is detected, the response should be to immediately call the other side's attention to the deviation and to demand that the agreed practice be followed. Quick and firm objection to the attempting side's play will deter other attempts at deviation because of the desire to avoid deterioration of the postnegotiation relationship (i.e., while the first deviation could be explained as a simple mistake, other attempts in the face of an earlier objection could be interpreted as bad-faith implementation or even a breach).

The decision to attempt to improve the negotiated result by creating more favorable practice depends on the perceived cost balance between the advantage to be gained and the risk of being caught. In most situations in which the other side is experienced, the potential risk and the consequent relationship cost (i.e., negative impact on the postnegotiation relationship) militate against the attempt because in all probability the maneuver will be detected, however artfully executed. Where in an appropriate case of acceptable risk it is decided to make the attempt, it must be done with the lowest exposure possible. The purpose is to provide a credible escape hatch to minimize the possibility of a counterproductive reaction that will adversely impact the relationship.

For example, assume that during a negotiation one side insisted that written notice be given by the other side a specified time before it takes certain action. Despite vigorous argumentation concerning the administrative and other problems of giving timely notice in writing, the demanding side held firm and the written notice requirement was included in the negotiated arrangement. Then, the side that unsuccessfully resisted the requirement decides that an attempt should be made to develop the practice of oral notice the first time the situation calling for written notice arises. If it is caught, the attempting side, seeking to preserve the continuing relationship by demonstrating good faith, disclaims any intent to breach the arrangement. It follows this by explaining its failure to give written notice on the same basis relied upon in unsuccessfully resisting the requirement during negotiation. In effect, the postnegotiation attempt is made to appear as "proof" of the burdensome or nonviable nature of the requirement. Two results are possible. (1) The other side remains adamant and reinforces the requirement by insisting that it be adhered to as a "done deal." (2) Having had "proved" to it that the requirement is burdensome and nonviable, it relents and acquiesces in a dialogue that invariably leads to some type of departure from, or attenuation of, the written notice requirement. The effect negotiator carefully watches the reaction of the defending side and views any hesitation in insisting upon written notice as an opening to present other reasons for changing the requirement (e.g., oral notice has been demonstrated to be just as effective as written). To prevent any perception of an opening, the defending side should avoid indicating a disposition to discuss the requirement beyond insistence upon compliance. The defensive move is essentially dialogue avoidance[31] because once a dialogue is opened, it will be difficult to avoid a negotiating cost in the form of some relaxation of the notice requirement as agreed.

During implementation, when the defending side fails to react to adverse practice, the attempting side reinforces it by repetition so that its consistency will be established. The other side may never react, and the practice is thereby "established." Even where there is a reaction after a period of time, the effective negotiator on the offense will be prepared to claim that his side relied on acquiescence in the practice and, in this way, attempt to renegotiate the issue. The side that has been sitting on its rights may find that it has to give something more to enjoy what it originally had when it left the negotiating table. In the previous example, suppose that, after a year of oral notice, the defending side complains. The effective negotiator's response might be along the following lines:

During the negotiation, we explained the many problems written notice would cause us. Although written notice was called for by the terms of the arrangement, we could not give it in timely fashion and thus gave oral notice. When your side failed to complain, we thought that, understanding our difficulty and seeing that oral notice was just as effective, your side waived the requirement in the interest of a smooth, trouble-free implementation. It is even more difficult for us now to give written notice; and we do not see why it was necessary in the first place, judging from the good results we have had with oral notice.

Faced with such an approach, sounding in victim play and estoppel and having implicit in it the apprehension-generating statement that implementation could be complicated by attempting to change the precise of oral notice, the defending side will be under great pressure to acquiesce in the practice. If it insists on reversing the practice, it probably can be pressured to make a concession (e.g., extend the period for notice or agree that it be less formal in all or certain cases). This concession would be the negotiating cost of insensitivity to the exposure potential of the implementation phase.

By adopting an artful, low-exposure approach, one can substantially reduce risk cost. If the other side insists that the requirement be observed as negotiated, the impact on the postconsensus relationship has been minimized by the disclaimer of intention to breach the arrangement. If the other side relents in the face of the proof of the unworkability of written notice as agreed, the arrangement has been favorably modified and a cost-free concession obtained. If the other side does not react at all to the substitution of oral for written notice, the side seeking modification may be on its way to establishing acquiescence in practice favorable to it. If an attempt is pursued in this manner, there is significant possibility of achieving some degree of success. The probability of success is substantially enhanced if the other side, being relaxed after the conclusion of the formal dialogue, is oblivious to the need to manage and control developing practice during the implementation phase.

THE CONTINUING CHECKLIST

Conceptualization of the negotiation process includes a continuing checklist that makes sure the dialogue is pursued in a productive, structured way. Items on the checklist represent the basic exposure concerns of the effective negotiator as he manages and controls the dialogue. They permit him to think in the most interest-oriented terms. They provide the cautionary, leavening considerations to ensure that he does not, by seeking too much or doing violence to the relationship, discourage desired dialogue or disrupt ongoing dialogue, which are the essential concerns in the management and control effort. Armed with this checklist, he will be able to pursue his goals and objectives in a way that is compatible with the operational needs of the negotiating situation. There will be no tendency to water down goals and objectives because of some generally stated precepts to make "wise agreements," defer to societal considerations, negotiative "creatively" to satisfy the other side's needs, or "forget about winning."[32] Correct use of the checklist permits entry into the dialogue at a point closer to the maximum-objectives end of the spectrum and, as a consequence, with increased negotiating room. Such an entry bodes well for a more favorable result in accordance with the negotiating truisms that openers are not closers and that the availability of more chips facilitates the bargaining to closing. To distinguish graphically the approach made possible by the checklist from those that defer to win-win harmony, it can be said that use of the list permits taking aim at the other side's jugular in setting goals and objectives, and that it thereby increases the possibility of attaining more of what the traffic can be made to bear. The list provides a means of "going for it" with built-in safeguards against reckless and counterproductive negotiating action.

The bargaining considerations are presented in checklist form as an instructional aid and to provide a disciplinary framework for the would-be negotiator. In effect, the checklist forces the user to focus on exposure, which is at the heart of the "think-negotiation" mindset. The checklist items involve promotion or realization of goals; viability of the proposed position, settlement, or arrangement; creation of a favorable basis for subsequent action; and effect on continuing relationships (i.e., between the parties or with others affected by the dialogue).

Goal Promotion or Realization

Goal promotion or realization is central. The negotiation dialogue is managed and controlled for the purpose of achieving desired goals and objectives in pursuit of interest. This item ensures continuous focus on interest, goals, and objectives as substantive positions and process-related strategies and tactics are formulated and implemented. It corrects a common failing in negotiation: a disjointed dialogue without the necessary substantive and procedural direction. For example, one cannot engage in effective concession trading without having a continuing focus on interest and maximum and minimum goals and objectives. The effective negotiator always he his eye on interest, goals, and objectives and stays aware of where he is on the spectrum of acceptable consensus. Such awareness is important because a common ploy in negotiation is to attempt to create a diversion to distract the other side's attention from its goals and objectives and, perhaps, confuse it, thereby reducing bargaining effectiveness.

Viability of the Position, Settlement, or Arrangement

The effective negotiator recognizes that a side can demand too much or get too much with counterproductive results. He knows that in many situations it is better to resist squeezing the other side to the utmost in the interest of viability of the negotiated result. He knows that it makes little sense to press for a result that will fall apart under anticipated postconsensus pressures. For example, "stealing a case" in a private negotiation can lead to judicial action to set aside a release and recover a much larger amount; "winning" a tough one in the intraorganizational environment can entail continuing-relationship costs in subsequent staff interactions; and "having one's way" with a friendly government in an international negotiation may result in weakening it or causing it to fall due to domestic opposition to the negotiated consensus. These are judgment calls for the negotiator as he assesses the situation, including the actors involved. No hard and fast rules can be provided. All that can be said is that while one should not easily give up a highly leveraged position, there is need to temper the exploitation of that leverage by the concern for viability and the continuing relationship. Failure to do so produces a high-exposure situation for the exploiting side, which may come back to haunt it after the negotiating coup. Viability is one of the principal exposure concerns in a situation involving unequal parties because the side with the clear negotiating advantage must resist the Gekko dictum on greed and exercise restraint in exploiting that advantage.

Favorable Basis for Subsequent Action

In all negotiating environments, there is a need to develop the documentary or other basis for subsequent action to enforce the negotiated result. This need varies from environment to environment and is a function of the type of follow-on or enforcement action that is foreseen. The basic issue for the negotiator with respect to the usual forms of enforcement—litigation (in private negotiations), executive decision (in intraorganizational negotiations), or diplomatic representation or protest[33] (in international negotiations)—is how much specificity is needed. Where there are no known or anticipated sensitivities on the other side, the effective negotiator seeks an unambiguous, clear record of the consensus as part of his effort to get the best negotiated result possible. He knows, however, that in some cases there may be issues of form that are difficult for the other side to handle. For example, that side may not want to publicly carry the burden of having made a specific, disadvantageous concession trade. The attendant sensitivity to image or political pressures may dictate a downplaying of specific negotiated results in favor of emphasizing the mutually beneficial nature of the negotiated arrangement. In all environments, these sensitivities manifest themselves as stated preferences for less specific, general language or, perhaps, a side or oral exchange external to the negotiated arrangement to cover the sensitive points.

As a means of conducting a bargaining-effective dialogue in such a situation, the negotiator has to determine his minimum needs for follow-on action so that he knows the lower limit of what he may have to settle for. In most cases, pushing for much more only raises his bargaining cost without commensurate substantive benefit or take. There is little point in insisting on a degree of specificity that, in light of the follow-on action that is actually contemplated or possible, would be unnecessarily costly[34] because of the other side's expressed sensitivities. The classic example is provided in the international negotiating environment where cosmetic concerns (born of domestic or international political considerations) frequently create pressures for more general language and avoidance of damagingly precise formulations. The concerns are cosmetic only, as there is a clear meeting of the minds on the consensus achieved and no attempt to paper over differences. In such a situation it is counterproductive to insist on so-called legal boilerplate at the cost of reduced acceptability and appeal of the consensus formulation. The effective negotiator knows that in the international environment the sides do not negotiate with a view to litigation and that most enforcement action will be in the form of a diplomatic representation or protest. Accordingly, he can afford to accept a general, more cosmetically acceptable formulation that is sufficiently precise to provide a peg for the diplomatic representation or protest. In the process he maximizes the concession take for his forthcomingness by avoiding unproductive bargaining and the need to expend chips for the unnecessary specificity.[35]

Many negotiators with legal training tend to lean toward legal precision and forget that precision, however comfortable and desirable, should not be pursued as an end in itself. The effective negotiator does not burden the dialogue with counterproductive demands for formulations that are cosmetically burdensome to the other side and are not necessary for follow-on action. Rather, after determining what he needs, he uses the chips saved from trying to get "more" to advance the dialogue on the other issues. In this way, he may be able to get substantive mileage out of his readiness to give with respect to form. It should be reemphasized, however, that if the other side does not have a credible cosmetic problem, the negotiator should get the most complete and precise formulation possible. Furthermore, whenever in his judgment the situation calls for less, he should fully explain this to his principal lest there be a misunderstanding (concerning the effectiveness of his representation in nailing down the consensus) that may come back to haunt him.

Effect on Continuing Relationships

Concern for continuing relationships is another cautionary element on the checklist. The purpose here is to avoid positions and strategies that will have a counterproductive effect on negotiating and other relationships. Relationships that go sour generally entail negotiating costs for the side that ignores the value of good relationship maintenance. This applies to the negotiating as well as the postnegotiation relationship; therefore, even in one-shot negotiations (i.e., where there is no postnegotiation, continuing relationship), the checklist item has relevance. The earlier suggestion that the negotiator's manner be as friendly as circumstances permit reflects the value attached to a good negotiating and postnegotiation relationship. A good relationship can be helpful and exploitable in effecting friendly and pressured persuasion. Furthermore, a side should carefully question the desirability of action that would embarrass the other side's negotiator and his principal because it might lead to the removal of the negotiator (or his principal in the intraorganizational and international environments). Lawyers (private negotiations); corporate or agency officials (intraorganizational negotiations); negotiators, officials, and even governments (international negotiations) may be replaced because of their failures in negotiation. At times it may be in one's interest to carry the other side on some points to achieve objectives of greater importance because of anticipated ease in negotiating them with that side, including its representatives.

There is also concern for continuing relationships in a broader, more general sense. Here the relationship being considered does not necessarily involve the other side in the negotiation; it may involve any nonparty that is affected or impacted by the negotiation. In this type of situation the cost concerns usually involve image and precedent. Consider an automobile warranty claim. The automobile manufacturer must weigh the impact of a settlement on the continuing relationship with the individual owner-

claimant and with the buying public at large. Publicity concerning unwill-
ingness to satisfy the individual's claim might be viewed by the manufacturer as harmful to its relationships with the individual and the buying
public. A settlement with the individual might seem desirable because it
would retain his good will and, possibly, his future patronage. It would
also project the positive image of a customer-friendly manufacturer. However, the manufacturer's cost-benefit analysis does not end there.

As in any judgement call, there must be a balancing of exposure costs
involved in the various decisional alternatives. The alternative not to pay
the claim may have redeeming merits to counter the obvious cost baggage
it carries. The manufacturer could easily conclude that the precedential
cost of the settlement would encourage many other claims, which would
result in unacceptable expense and notoriety, including the possibility of
a government-mandated recall program. To avoid this result, the manufacturer may have to sacrifice its relationship with the individual claimant and
its interest in projecting a positive image. Without the input for meaningful decisional analysis, we can only identify the nature of the analytical
process when exposure-cost concerns must be weighed incident to decision making.

The same exposure-weighing process applies to international negotiations. When a state is involved in a negotiation with another state concerning a relationship that is similar to one maintained with other states, a
change in the relationship under negotiation may have a costly domino
effect. The assessment actually involves choosing among lesser evils as the
negotiator must factor in the precedential costs of having to accord similar
treatment to the other states. The objective, of course, is to determine the
least costly resolution of the ongoing dialogue. "Thinking negotiation" requires a 360-degree approach to exposure concerns. It requires consideration of all the potential dialogue-and-attendant-relationship costs involved
in each possible resolution of the situation.

The continuing nature of the checklist arises from its applicability to all
phases of the negotiation process. The items on the checklist should be
used in question form to assess the desirability and feasibility of action
and reaction during every phase of the negotiation. For example, the question of goal promotion or realization should be asked at each phase as
follows:

Preparation Phase: Will the opening position promote goal realization?

Presentation Phase: Will the tactic, presentation, response, or reaction
                         promote goal realization?

Reaching Agreement Phase: Will the proposed concession trade promote goal
                         realization?

Implementation Phase: Will the practice that is developing under the ar-
                         rangement promote goal realization?

Similar questioning in relation to the other checklist items should provide the basis for informed judgments at each stage in managing and controlling the dialogue.

As a practical matter, the action or reaction being considered must pass muster with respect to all checklist items before being adopted as feasible. The go-signal is four yeas in response to the standard questions. A questionable response to any checklist item should be viewed as a yellow flag calling for careful consideration of all the exposure elements in the situation before pursuing the course of action. In most cases, one yellow flag will produce a negative decision concerning the course of action. For example, the attempt during implementation to develop against an effective negotiator a more favorable practice than is provided for in the arrangement should not be made because of the probable negative responses to questions relating to viability and the continuing relationship; although, strictly speaking, such an attempt could be said to promote goal realization and, if successful, provide a favorable basis for a modified arrangement. The attempt is deterred because of the failure to pass muster on the first two issues in light of the strong defense that can be anticipated.

Of course, in some situations, the negotiator has to "take a chance" because of the absence of other alternatives. Bluffing is a good example. The effective negotiator knows he is exposed in a bluff situation and usually seeks to avoid it. He may, however, have to resort to bluffing if he has no other way to pursue the dialogue, that is, if he has nothing to bargain with and the bluff represents an effort to gain some bargaining leverage. The credibility and other exposure of a failed bluff generally reduces it to an alternative of last resort. As in all high-risk negotiating situations, the effective negotiator makes a special effort to involve his principal as an understanding approver of the difficult decision.

The effective negotiator does not apply the checklist "by the numbers" as in the examples I have given. For him, implicit in goal promotion or realization are the elements of viability, adequate basis for subsequent action, and the continuing relationship. This is the case because he instinctively "thinks negotiation" and, in the process, combines all the elements of the continuing checklist as he attempts to manage and control the dialogue in his side's interest.

NOTES

1. To be an effective prober, the negotiator must be fully aware of the negotiating game plan; otherwise the probing effort will not be directed to serve all of its informational needs. The principal who seeks to exploit the limited authority approach by reducing the negotiator's knowledge of the plan (i.e., to benefit from the fact that a negotiator with limited knowledge is more credible when saying "no") will sacrifice the cross-check capability of a comprehensive probing effort.

2. A common ploy is the effort of one side to indicate through the use of a false break-off point that it is no longer in its interest to continue the dialogue if the other side persists in a particular demand (e.g., "In no case can I pay more than $200" when, in fact, the break-off point is $300). If the other side relents, it will be accepting a limit less than the original $300 break-off point set by the other side.

3. "Realistic" in this context implies resisting the temptation to seek what one hopes for or desires; instead, the criterion should be that which is feasibly negotiable. The effective negotiator looks upon negotiation as the art of achieving the possible and not a noncredible pursuit of dreams and idle hopes.

4. This is sometimes referred to as "the linchpin of consensus."

5. Negotiation begins only when both parties believe there is something to be gained from dealing or something to be lost by failing to deal. Unfortunately, many situations that should be resolved through negotiation founder because the dialogue never gets started. One cannot bring effective negotiating skills to manage or control a dialogue unless there is dialogue.

6, The principal purposes of a claim letter are to *advise* the addressee of a claim and to *demand* its satisfaction. The traditional approach is informational in the sense that the letter states the nature and basis of the claim and identifies the parties involved and the representational role of the writer. This may be denominated the "information-only" approach because it does not attempt to exploit the negotiating potential of the initial letter contact. The effective negotiator, "thinking negotiation" and seeking to exploit the opportunity presented by the letter to manipulate the perceptions, apprehension, uncertainty, and expectations of the recipient, uses it to launch the process of pressuring persuasion. In effect, he combines the information and negotiation functions by utilizing the letter as a negotiating contact. This is accomplished by including in the letter those known elements of the situation that can produce favorable perceptions, apprehension, uncertainty, and expectations. It requires analysis of the situation so that the included items reflect only the exposure and vulnerabilities of the other side. This approach is known as "information-plus," with the "plus" referring to the use of the letter to launch the negotiation.

For example, in a vehicular accident, the effective negotiator would include in his letter information relating to significant vehicle damage because it can influence impressions concerning the seriousness of injuries claimed. Similarly, any dramatic aspect of an injury (e.g., the head *striking* the windshield and *cracking* it) would be mentioned. The information should have only an outward cutting edge; there should be no exposure for the informing side. As to the information given in the example, the amount of damage to the car is easily established and does not change; all that is said about the injury is descriptive and not diagnostic. This approach can provide immediate positive results: A letter reflecting large claim potential will be given more attention because it communicates a serious situation with resultant impact on perceptions, apprehension, and expectations concerning the cost of disposing of it. This is most evident in the case of a casualty claim. Carriers can be influenced to set higher initial reserves on cases; this in turn changes the manner in which the files pertaining to those cases are handled within the organization, including the early involvement of senior officials with greater settlement authority.

Whether one uses the information or information-plus approach, there is a common need to write a letter that has professional credibility in terms of both the representative involved and the substance of the claim being pursued. Obviously, errors in grammar and spelling or a nonprofessional style and tone will detract from the personal credibility of the claimant's representative. This will reduce the usual apprehension (translatable into a perception of increased claim value) that accompanies attorney involvement. Similarly, slips or errors concerning substantive aspects of the claim will have a detracting impact. The point is that as credibility exposure is involved even when the information-only approach is used, it makes little sense to stop at the question of credibility when, with a little more "thinking negotiation," substantial negotiating benefits can be realized by using the claim letter as the opening salvo in the negotiating effort.

7. In cases involving property damage and no personal injury, I recommend that the claim letter be sent directly to the insured rather than his insurer. Most insureds are so concerned about policy cancellation and premium increases that they usually will make an attempt to settle the matter themselves. (Use of this routing is an example of the exploitation of process to enhance the claimant's bargaining position.) Readiness to contact the insurer is a chip that facilitates the management and control of any settlement dialogue that develops from the contact. If the insured does not attempt to settle, it can be expected that the original claim letter will be relayed to the insurer. Usually where there is personal injury the insured will be inclined to let the insurer handle the matter because of the greater financial exposure involved.

8. Attentive listening has an important substantive and presentational role in conducting the dialogue. Substantively, it ensures the alertness necessary to fully "receive" the express and tacit communications contained in the other side's responses or positions. Presentationally, it conveys an open-mindedness that reinforces the desired personal credibility image; that is, that the negotiator has come to the dialogue to resolve, fairly and on the merits, the matter under negotiation. A negotiator who does not listen and frequently interrupts will surely alienate his opposite number ("He would not even listen!") and may be depriving himself of useful probing take. Unfortunately, there are more than a few negotiators who "listen with an open mouth."

9. Nothing deflates a proposal as completely as a rejection out of hand.

10. Negotiating cost takes a variety of forms including political cost, image cost, precedent cost, monetary or other actual cost, chip cost, and relationship cost.

11. The prudent principal can best defend himself in the internal dialogue with his negotiator by recognizing that he is in the dialogue because of the career interests of the negotiator that may not be entirely compatible with his own. His demonstrated awareness of the career play by the negotiator will go a long way toward keeping the negotiator from pushing for too much control. If the negotiator cannot be inhibited from going too far, it may be wise to replace him because his demonstrated insensitivity to the awareness of the principal might reflect other professional deficiencies that will detract from the level of representation he can provide.

Although principals are not generally aware of their need to control the dialogue with their negotiators, they may protect themselves by action designed to counter other exposure aspects of the principal-negotiator relationship. The usual approach is to keep the negotiator under tight rein because of (1) apprehension over the potential exposure from the concept of *"apparent authority"* and (2) the desire to exploit the negotiator's limited authority in the interest of either conveying a hard line or preventing leakage of the side's position. In the case of the former, the principal wishes the other side to take nothing for granted insofar as the authority of the negotiator is concerned. It is his way of underscoring the *ad referendum* process so that only actual acceptance by him will be binding. The latter seeks to better protect a side's position on the theory that the negotiator cannot give away what he does not know and when he says "no" it is more convincing when he actually believes it to be so. The negotiator, chafing under the effort to limit his authority or role (not only because of the diminished control it gives him but also because of its impact on his professional image), might be able to get his principal to make him a party to the effort by demonstrating how he can enhance the effectiveness of the limiting action through supportive role playing. If he is successful, he may be able to position himself to exercise more control over the situation and, in the process, improve his own professional image.

12. A position without substantive credibility will tend to be discounted as a maneuver or ploy and not draw a serious response or reaction. This will adversely affect the effort to develop consensus and to probe the give in the other side's position.

13. The effort to establish personal and positional credibility is still another aspect of the mind-game essence of negotiation.

14. The view that the transaction becomes one of buy and sell is the basis for the jargon of some practitioners that the insurer is the "purchaser" whose unsettled claims constitute its "business" inventory. Such language reflects the requirement that carriers maintain cash reserves to cover their claim exposure.

15. For example, whether he is sharp, credible, trustworthy, emotional, lazy, or ill-tempered; and whether he is a bluffer, a hardball bargainer, or a smooth or marginal operator.

16. The response can be express or tacit. The signal may also be ignored as if the communication was not understood or received. The latter approach may be a ploy to (1) discourage further reliance on the tacit channel, which may interfere with desired audience play, or (2) mislead the other side by conveying the impression of a lower level of negotiating experience on the receiving side.

17. See Judy Licht, "Eye Contact and Attitudes," *Health Journal of Medicine, Washington Post,* July 9, 1991, p. 9.

18. Generally, it is said that impasse results when parties lock themselves into unalterable "principled positions" and substitute posturing for negotiation. Talleyrand noted in this regard that "negotiations are more fruitful when based on fact rather than principle."

19. It is far more difficult, and potentially costly, to start with the adversarial approach and change to problem solving and cooperation. For example, the change may be interpreted as a movement to the defense that is usually associated with a weakened position. Furthermore, any benefit from the improved relationship will be slow in coming because the first impression will be remembered until the changed attitude is confirmed by subsequent negotiating behavior.

20. Ken Adelman, "Out of Place in a Skewed Summit," *Washington Times,* May 23, 1990, p. F1. "And for good reason, George Marshall once said, 'Don't ask me to agree in principle, that just means that we haven't agreed yet.' "

21. A common sales bait, "No *reasonable* offer will be refused," highlights the subjectivity of the formulation and the consequent lack of exposure when it is used as a ploy to stimulate a lower offer than might otherwise have been made.

22. *The American Heritage Dictionary,* 2d college ed. (Boston: Houghton Mifflin, 1982), 345.

23. Failure to close when a good deal is offered is a common cause of dialogue breakdown. Recognition of a good deal is a function of good preparation because it involves considerations of goals and objectives, interests, and vulnerabilities as they relate to realistic consensus expectations.

24. Once the other side has broken off the negotiation, any attempt at resumption will entail high negotiating cost for the pressing side. If the dialogue is to be resumed, the side that broke it off will be in the driver's seat, having demonstrated a readiness to forgo a negotiated result (i.e., that it does not have the burden of negotiation).

25. Another technique is to deliberately slow down the concession-trading process by diminishing the size of the concessions or by spacing them out. The intended effect is to herald the onset of the final, hard bargaining of the crunch.

26. "This is our final offer" is as credible in practice as "The check is in the mail." To enhance the credibility of a statement of finality, one should distinguish it from others by tone, formal solemnity (e.g., in written form), or collateral actions (e.g., demonstrated readiness to leave the negotiation site).

27. In some cases the negotiator can ensure that he is the drafter and reap the benefits of that role by taking negotiating initiatives that involve written documents. Examples that come to mind are the use of (1) claims letters to launch the pursuit of claims, (2) settlement brochures to support proposals for resolving claims, and (3) litigation briefs slanted to encourage or promote settlement by the parties or by judicial intervention. He can also practice *anticipatory drafting* by preparing documents as if they were already, or would be, challenged and providing for their defense by seeding them with a supporting rationale and evidentiary materials. For example, I usually recommend that federal tax returns be prepared as if they had to withstand the scrutiny of an Internal Revenue Service audit. With this in mind, the drafter should seed the return with supporting documentation to counter anticipated challenges in the areas of "creative" compliance and, of course, with general indications of the taxpayer's honesty and effort to be law-abiding. A return having such surface credibility will tend to be passed over as a nonproductive audit candidate in a process that, because of its limited capability to check many returns, has to be most selective.

28. Slanting the text in favor of one's side increases the probability that if the document has to pass the test of third-party interpretation, it will reflect and support the favorable bias crafted into it.

29. One should be especially alert when the other side insists that it do the drafting or that its language cover a particular point or issue because it indicates the experience level of the negotiator for that side and, perhaps, the importance of the point or issue. "Perhaps" reflects the caution of the effective negotiator in accepting "as gospel" the signals he receives from the other side.

30. Certainly, the proposing side would be hard pressed to reject out of hand the counter containing a good bit of its original proposal on the basis that its position was ignored or that no attempt was made to meet it halfway.

31. As seen elsewhere in the Guide, dialogue avoidance is an essential part of dialogue management and control.

32. Robert W. Goddard, "Negotiation: How to Win by Forgetting about Winning," *Training,* March 1984, pp. 33–34 and 37, at p. 33.

33. A diplomatic representation or protest is used by a nation-state to advise another state about some objectionable condition or situation in the receiving state. A representation is the weaker of the two because it essentially is advisory; the protest is a formal objection to state inaction or action concerning the condition or situation.

34. The cost may involve disruption of the dialogue, delay in concluding it, or deterioration in the negotiating or postnegotiation relationship.

35. This can also be true of the other environments, which are more remedy-oriented. For example, the readiness to accept a handshake on certain aspects of consensus may be a very successful, disarming tactic—provided, of course, that the negotiator (1) has ascertained that there is a good probability that this symbol of agreement will hold up; (2) has limited it to a peripheral issue in order to exploit the symbolism with reduced risk; or (3) has otherwise protected his principal with sufficient collateral specificity in usable form for enforcement or other follow-on action.

5

Specific Applications of the
Universality Principle

GENERAL

Under the universality principle, every dialogue involving competitive interests presents negotiating considerations and possibilities. The omnipresence of interest-oriented dialogues and the effectiveness of negotiation concepts and techniques in managing and controlling them implies the broader applicability of negotiation. Many situations that are not considered to involve negotiation in the sense of a formal, structured dialogue can be viewed as negotiation because they do, in fact, involve consensus development through interest-competitive dialogues. This section is intended to demonstrate that the presence of dialogue and interests suggests negotiation as a managing and controlling tool.

The sections that follow cover some situations that are not usually viewed as involving the pursuit of interest and consensus development. Areas other than lawyering, management, decision making,[1] and interpersonal relationships could have been included. For example, selling and lobbying[2] readily come to mind, as do rule making, counseling, and interviewing.[3] Actually, whether the setting is commercial, managerial, or social, the related dialogues invite application of negotiation concepts and techniques because they provide the best means for interest pursuit and realization.

In some situations the dialogue and clash of interest are no greater than the desire to influence relationship behavior. In this feature of interpersonal relationships, there is a potential clash of interest to the extent that there may be resistance to the behavior that is sought. This same interest is present in most social relationships and contacts where the relationship structure and objectives are even less specific. For example, the everyday effort to control behavior through "winning friends and influencing people" can be enhanced by utilizing negotiation concepts and techniques as analytical (to better understand personal motivation and behavior) and operational (to improve control over, and management of, the behavior) tools. Experience demonstrates that the effort to influence the behavior of others is best handled as a form of negotiation because it is more effective to combine friendly with pressured persuasion.[4]

In still other situations the dialogue and interest clash may be rather passive, being no more intense than the desire to protect one's self against the real or intangible cost of negative reactions to personal behavior, including decision making. The other side in this type of situation is any potentially hostile audience (i.e., anyone with standing to question or criticize, with consequent cost or prejudice, the behavior). Thus, protection of one's personal reputation can involve interest-oriented dialogues to which negotiation concepts and techniques are usefully applicable.

LAWYERING

In accordance with the universality principle, the omnipresence of dialogues for the resolution of competitive interests calls for (1) applying negotiation concepts and techniques, and (2) involving every individual as a potential negotiator. However, the individual's involvement is sporadic and not on a continuing, workaday basis—as is the case with a variety of professionals, including lawyers. Unfortunately, lawyers tend to underestimate their role as negotiators and the potential benefit that can be realized from effective negotiation. They do not fully realize that lawyering involves negotiation.[5]

As an advocate, a lawyer is involved on a daily basis in persuasion-generating dialogues on behalf of his client-principals. In handling transactions, the lawyer is usually involved in structuring (i.e., "selling") favorable consensus; even if he is given only a drafting task, he must artfully record and conserve the fruits of the bargain and sell the draft. In these situations, selling involves persuading the other side that the transaction is mutually beneficial or that the draft fairly reflects the consensus reached. When representing a client in a controversy, the lawyer pursues the claim or interest to a successful conclusion in a most competitive situation. The nonnegotiation-oriented lawyer is preoccupied with finding a forum for litigating the controversy rather than mounting an effort to resolve it in-house through negotiation, including the orchestration of litigation as part of the negotiation effort.

A lawyer who is too litigation-minded fails to realize that in most cases the economics of his practice are better served by negotiation than litigation. Furthermore, in his contacts with opposing attorneys he may be insensitive to negotiating overtures and signals and not exploit the negotiating potential of the litigation process. Actually, a lawsuit should be viewed as an adjunct to negotiation or a negotiating context, with every stage relevant to the development of favorable consensus. The threat of a lawsuit and its actual commencement are apprehension-creating and credibility-substantiating actions. Demonstrated will to litigate reflects seriousness of purpose, confidence in one's case, and little concern for the burden of negotiation, which tends to be shifted to the other side by the litigation action. Preparation for, and conduct of, the trial should likewise have a negotiation-related orientation, as it is not unusual for the parties to settle after the actual trial commences and before the case goes to judgment.[6] For example, discovery incident to trial preparation makes it possible to probe the other side's needs, concerns, and objectives while providing the opportunity to educate it concerning its vulnerabilities on the merits and other reasons for seeking a negotiated result. In effect, discovery can be used to orient the other side toward a decision to substitute a settlement dialogue for litigation and may influence the court to request that the parties attempt to settle the case. The negotiation-oriented lawyer will be especially effective in handling his client's interests in a settlement dialogue or mediation conducted by the court or under its auspices.

The lawyer's advocacy also extends to his relationship with his clients. His principal interest here is to persuade clients that he is an effective representative whose advice and services should be sought when interests are at risk. Client reliance on his representation permits the lawyer to establish control over his clients when setting case goals and objectives. (At times, this advocacy must even be used to resolve intraside disputes among clients with competing interests.) Control over his clients enables the lawyer to get more doable tasks and, in the process, an enhanced capability for successfully concluding the purpose of his representation (i.e., delivering what his client has "tasked" him to get)—the ultimate objective of successful lawyering. When the situation does not lend itself to a "win," the lawyer can use his control to persuade his client that he has been an effective representative who "did the best possible under the circumstances," the only other career-enhancing perception of a lawyering effort.

Thus, whatever dialogue he pursues on behalf of (or with) clients, the lawyer is involved in negotiation and it behooves him to acquire effective negotiating skills.[7] The value of improved negotiation skills for lawyers has been recognized, but by some only in the limited context of a specialty in lawyering. "Most legal problems are not settled through legislative or judicial action but by negotiation. All lawyers negotiate, but few of us have either a conceptual understanding of the process or particular skill in it. It is time to recognize negotiation as a field for specialization."[8] The extent of the practitioner's involvement in negotiation requires that it be part of the professional representation he can provide on a daily basis. The client should be able to have a single source of representation in pursuing his interests. Lawyers specializing in negotiation[9] should be retained only for difficult and complex cases, as is done in other areas of the law when a benefit is perceived from having more specialized representation.

A MANAGEMENT TOOL

Even those who are less committed than I am to the universality principle will appreciate the relevance and applicability of negotiation concepts and techniques to the tasks of management. Traditionally, a manager is expected to achieve organizational goals and objectives through leadership; problem analysis and resolution; rational decision making; and planning and implementation based on the cost-effective use of available resources. The management role (which is keyed to and driven by organizational goals and objectives—denominated Management by Objective, or MBO—and which utilizes dialogue as the principal implementing tool) essentially involves persuasion in pursuit of interest, a process most compatible with the basic thrust of negotiation. This inherent compatibility provides the basis for the operational link between negotiation and management and the conclusion that effective negotiation can facilitate and improve the performance of the operational tasks of management.

The tasks of the manager involve a series of interest-oriented dialogues with staff members, colleagues and others operating at his level, and superiors. The mark of the manager's success is reflected in his ability to manage and control these dialogues to influence and motivate others to support or accept courses of action or positions desired for organizational or personal reasons. The manager who achieves this is said to be a leader or to have leadership qualities. The Dale Carnegie Leadership Institute describes as successful those who "have the ability to communicate, influence and motivate others. They get their ideas across, make friends easily, arouse enthusiasm and win people to their way of thinking." [10]

There can be little quarrel with the proposition that the task of leading (i.e., motivating or persuading) is immeasurably facilitated by generating rapport or, in "think-negotiation" terms, by nurturing the continuing relationship. Nevertheless, more should be and can be done to reconcile, in the leader's interest, the issues involved in management dialogues. The effective negotiator recognizes the importance of rapport and a generally friendly approach in effecting persuasion. The demands of his service, however, require that he use more than friendly persuasion to achieve goal realization for himself and his principal (organization). Effective negotiation meets that requirement by combining friendly persuasion with pressured persuasion, with the former being reinforced by the latter in a more complete and effective approach. Thus, negotiation can provide the manager a multifaceted approach to producing the desired support or motivation (i.e., consensus) from his workplace relationships. In effect, it is suggested that he embrace the value of a "rapport-plus" approach, with the plus being application of the concepts and techniques of effective negotiation. The manager will benefit from the negotiation approach because it emphasizes consensus development to manage and control people, not just winning their friendship or exerting friendly influence over them.

In looking more closely at the dialogues in which the manager is involved, we can easily conclude that those *inter pares* (i.e., with other managers and colleagues) and with superiors constitute negotiation because they are, in effect, competitive dialogues generated by the MBO process. Competitive interests with respect to other managers and colleagues involve excelling in the achievement of desired organizational objectives; with respect to superiors, selling career-enhancing advice and suggestions relating to the adoption of organizational objectives and expectations concerning their realization. In such a highly competitive setting, it is difficult for the manager to succeed if he relies only upon rapport or friendship as the operational approach. Furthermore, in his relationship with superiors he has to contend with the negative control potential of the relationship, which has a built-in bias (because of performance evaluations and other methods of rewarding and penalizing personnel) toward compliance with, and support for, the superior's views in accordance with the bureaucratic wisdom, "go along to get along". Only artful, pressured-persuasion–oriented negotiation can bridge the interest gap between competing managers and between managers and their superiors. Of course, rapport generation can be helpful by providing a congenial tone to cover the pressuring effort.

Even in his relations with staff members, the manager/leader can usefully employ negotiation techniques to maintain and improve continuing support and motivation. For example, through effective communication and probing he can better understand the needs of his people and how to motivate them or, at the very least, identify the resistance factors that have to be muted if motivation is to be enhanced. The exercise is essentially one of dialogue management and control. It can be facilitated by full utilization of the exploitative potential of his supervisory position; essentially, this is the available process to stimulate positive subordinate response (i.e., in negotiating terms, the structured system of rewards and penalties that can be used to motivate or to create apprehension and uncertainty and control expectations). If exploitation of the supervisory relationship advantage is muted or cloaked by the presentational and rapport-generating techniques of effective negotiation, the leader can manipulate his staff with a very light touch that is barely distinguishable from the "nice guy," rapport-only approach. The result is effective, low relationship cost control, which can be reinforced by greater use of the system of tangible rewards for productivity and other indicators of staff support for management's objectives. The reinforced approach may even produce an aura of charisma, which characterizes an advanced stage of leadership.[11]

The other tasks of management (problem analysis and resolution, decision making, and planning and implementation) parallel those involved in negotiation. This further suggests the applicability of concepts and techniques of negotiation. Both by work habit and approach, the effective negotiator is positioned to succeed in the management role. For example, the "think-negotiation" mindset and the continuing checklist prompt him to factor in critical concerns such as career and organizational interests, personal and organizational exposure, impact on continuing relationships, and solution rationality and viability in all the management tasks he may undertake. He is also accustomed to situational analysis, identification of issues, formulation of objectives, dialogue planning and orchestration, decision making in accordance with dialogue developments, and careful conservation of bargaining chips—all utilizing a balancing of interests/costs approach.

The tasks of management essentially involve the same process as negotiation, and their execution would benefit from the experience and discipline of the effective negotiator. One can arrive very quickly at the conclusion that the concepts and techniques of effective negotiation can be a useful tool to achieve enhanced managerial results.

DECISION MAKING

Organizations suffer when decisionmakers are so concerned about career risk and personal exposure that they are inhibited from timely, quality decision making. Many decisionmakers cannot handle having to choose among lesser evils: a situation inherently loaded with inhibiting personal risk and exposure. Inhibited decisionmakers tend to (1) avoid making decisions (failure to decide constitutes a decision to go with the status quo and forgo the opportunity to control the situation through decisional action); (2) delay making decisions (procrastination disrupts the flow of organizational activity); (3) involve others to spread the risk (such involvement distorts the structure and process of the organization); or (4) otherwise play it safe (e.g., choosing the safest, but not necessarily the most potentially productive, option). All four of these actions deprive the organization of the sound decision making it is paying for.

At the other end of the spectrum of organizational pain is the hyperactive decisionmaker who tends to act precipitously before an issue or problem is ripe for settlement. The experienced decisionmaker avails himself of the happy possibility that by waiting for the appropriate decisional moment the problem or issue may resolve itself, in which case he has avoided unnecessary personal exposure and use of organizational process for a decision that did not have to be made. It is clear that the organizational need is for objective decision making minimally tainted by the paralysis of the decisionmaker who fears making a poor decision or any decision at all. He can overcome this paralysis and become a confident decisionmaker if he harnesses the tools of effective negotiation to decision making.

The pursuit-of-interest and preoccupation-with-advantage thrusts of the negotiation process can facilitate decision making for those who are responsible for it as well as those who are participants in the decisional process. Whatever the role of the decisionmaker, he can benefit from the sharper focus that negotiating concepts and techniques provide. The key to enjoying the negotiator's edge is to view the decision-making process as a dialogue or series of dialogues, which can be better managed and controlled by the concepts and techniques of effective negotiation.

Decisions can be made individually or can result from a group decisional or problem-solving dialogue. In both cases there are dialogues, albeit informal in many respects, that should be controlled in the decisionmaker's interest through negotiation. Even though the image of individual decision making connotes the loneliness of the single decider, there are in fact a series of dialogues with those involved in, and affected by, the decisional process. At the very least, there is dialogue with staff members and others who are charged with acquiring data, analyzing issues and decisional options, and recommending solutions. There is also dialogue with others who can be expected to react to the decision by implementing it or taking action to contest or impede it. It is in the decisionmaker's interest to be successful in all these dialogues to ensure the proper degree of staff assistance and support during the process and to minimize opposition, negative feedback, and other criticism of his effort after the decision is made.

In dialogues with staff members and other supporting personnel, the decisionmaker cannot be successful if he is working with flawed data or analysis. His sensitivity to the need to stimulate complete staff support will enable him to ferret out the shaky providers as well as the flawed results of their efforts—one of his principal exposures as decisionmaker. In this way, the decisionmaker as a good manager can position himself to have the data and analysis for a sound decision. Furthermore, in the dialogue with those who are otherwise involved or affected by the decision, he must be concerned about structuring consensus on the issues and objectives (i.e., the decision to be made and goal to be served); the process (including its fairness, soundness, timeliness, and the involvement of key players); and the substance of the decision (i.e., what was decided.) The consensus is designed to enhance the acceptability of the decision and facilitate its successful implementation—understandable career concerns of the decisionmaker who seeks to minimize the risk of failing (e.g., reversal from above or other discrediting of the decision) or being the object of criticism or controversy in this most important management task.

In group decision making or decision by committee—the alleged gene-sis of the camel when the decisional task was a horse—the participant seeking to be the decisionmaker must gain control of the process in order to be able to move the group to the decision or solution that serves his personal and professional interests. This can best be accomplished by fol-lowing Mr. Inside's negotiation techniques in structuring desired consen-sus in multilateral intraorganizational dialogues (i.e., shaping the decision proposal to attract support for it). This task is facilitated when the group decision making is done in accordance with a prescribed process that iden-tifies the participants and their roles and interests. Such identification en-ables the decisionmaker to focus his pressuring effort on key or lead play-ers and to do it less obtrusively by blending it into the procedural flow. Where the process is not prescribed and there is flexibility regarding the level of the decisionmaker's participation, he may have to participate more actively and openly to better control the dialogue through the shaped-position, search-for-allies approach. The more open involvement of the decisionmaker in managing or controlling the dialogue may have the neg-ative effect of stimulating bloc or other group resistance to his effort.

Having control over the dialogues involved in decision making sets the procedural stage for a good decision. There is, however, the critical judg-mental phase in selecting among recommended options and alternative courses of action. This phase requires a focus on objectives, risks (expo-sure), and consequences (costs) in terms of personal and professional in-terests. While good judgment cannot be blueprinted, it is possible to iden-tify helpful considerations to make sure that interest-wise judgment has been applied to the relevant issues. The "think-negotiation" mindset and the continuing checklist are especially helpful in this regard. The former ensures continuing focus on interest (objectives) and advantage (benefit); the latter refines the focus by scrutinizing the objective-serving, viability, continuing-relationship (including "audience") impacts and the procedural-adequacy (enforcement and implementation) aspects of the options. Se-lecting options on the basis of these considerations can only enhance the rationality of the decision, with resultant benefit going to the decision-maker and the organization he serves.

INTERPERSONAL RELATIONS

Dale Carnegie is best known for suggesting the importance of making friends and influencing people through relationship development and cul-tivation. Interpersonal relations, consisting of continuing dialogues with individuals and groups, can be further improved through the management and control techniques of negotiation. The key distinction between the Carnegie and negotiation approaches is that negotiation offers specific techniques (additional to relationship development and cultivation) to influence behavior.

Use of negotiation as a tool to improve the manager-staff interface in the workplace has been covered in the preceding discussion. The focus here is on management and control of interpersonal relationships in comparatively relaxed settings both within and outside the workplace where the competition and interest involvement are not as intense and do not involve the usual considerations of careerism and parochialism. Notwithstanding the reduced intensity, there are behavioral preferences and quality-of-life considerations that indicate the desirability of dialogue management and control to pursue interest and otherwise derive benefit from interpersonal relationships.

It makes sense to view interpersonal relationships from the standpoint of interest realization. Few relationships with individuals are interest-neutral in the sense that no advantage or benefit can be derived from managing and controlling them. Being subjected to an unproductive or unsatisfactory relationship can be most burdensome in terms of time, effort, and, at times, stress. There is no point in entering into personal relationships that may be prejudicial per se or not provide any benefit in the broadest sense, including the pleasure of association. The reason, of course, is that interpersonal relations that go deeper than a passing acquaintanceship require servicing and attention (i.e., they carry a maintenance cost).

The natural tendency is to assume that one can always walk away from a relationship. But this may not be a cost-free option. For example, certain relationships should be avoided altogether in consonance with the wisdom that "you are judged by the company you keep"; others require a long courtship before a relationship decision should be made—the Italians claim that "it takes eating a ton of salt together before one really knows a person." In both cases, the prejudice or cost attaches once the relationship or association is initiated. Although most ongoing relationships can be dropped if one is prepared to suffer the attendant cost, some may have to be endured because of the interest stake in maintaining them. Negotiating concepts and techniques provide (1) the analytical tools for balancing interest considerations in making a decision in all such cases, and (2) the operational method for managing and controlling the relationship to maintain the interest benefit at acceptable cost levels.

If one accepts the desirability of managing and controlling interpersonal relationship dialogues, attention must be focused on starting, maintaining, changing, and exploiting relationships. The threshold question is whether a particular relationship can be beneficial and, therefore, worth the effort. In striking a balance between cost and benefit, the effective negotiator must consider all the start-up and maintenance costs and compare them with the real and intangible benefits that can reasonably be anticipated from the relationship. The possible exposure to a costly or burdensome relationship must be evaluated in light of the personality, position, and relationship involvements (e.g., "connections") of the relationship candidate and the monetary, emotional, and other consequences of passing up the relationship. Theoretically, this question applies to all interpersonal relationships; but some, such as relationships with coworkers, neighbors, and relatives, have a heavy built-in cost burden if a relationship is passed up. Although it is not unusual to find coworkers, neighbors, and relatives without a personal relationship, the effective negotiator does not accept the viability or desirability of noninvolvement in relationships such as these which, on balance, are better managed than avoided. (Noninvolvement in a relationship is a decision to leave the interface to chance, as it is the relationship dialogue that provides the vehicle for potential control.) For example, coworkers can be stimulated through a managed dialogue to pull their weight, thereby avoiding the need to shoulder the burden of laziness on their part; neighbors can be persuaded to be cooperative because of their interdependence and the benefits of reciprocity; and relatives can be sensitized to the need to contribute to harmony in the family. In each case, the effective negotiator seeks the dialogue approach that will produce the benefit of making the relationship worthwhile and viable.[12]

Once initiated, personal relationships must be properly monitored to ensure interest-oriented maintenance. Management of the tone of the dialogue, both express and tacit, can ensure its maintenance without undesired deterioration or improvement. Negotiation concepts and techniques permit the monitoring of dialogue quality and any early adjustments that may be necessary to maintain the desired degree of closeness and commitment. The temperature of the dialogue (i.e., warmth of the relationship) can be maintained, raised, or lowered through the more careful communication and action techniques implied by negotiation. For example, carefully worded and delivered praise, rebukes, or barbs; considerate attention, studied neglect, or indifference; warm or subdued, correct cordiality; and other controlled relationship conduct are useful in fine-tuning or otherwise adjusting relationships.

As to control of commitment, most relationships can be managed to guard against any surprise or unwanted demands. Commitment avoidance can be achieved without relationship cost: One can appear to be interested and solicitous but always in the context that personal or professional responsibilities preclude involvement greater than the sympathetic ear. Emphasis on personal or professional responsibilities keeps expectations under control and usually discourages requests for favors or assistance that might otherwise have to be turned down (with consequent cost to the relationship). Should the other side attempt to exploit the relationship, the defending side must be prepared to say "no" if other attempts to discourage the request fail. For example, discouragement could take the form of (1) feigned embarrassment that one cannot help a friend in need, and

(2) an expression of doubt concerning the value of the relationship to the requesting party. Of course, one is not precluded from (1) being generous and conferring a benefit that is not fully reciprocated, or, moving to the offense, (2) seeking an unreciprocated benefit from a nondefense-minded relationship partner.

Monitoring the relationship dialogue also permits reading the other side's regard for, and interest in, relationship maintenance as well as a continuing assessment of personal credibility and trustworthiness. Being jilted at the altar is no more painful than discovering that unwarranted reliance has been placed on what was thought to be an interest-worthy or beneficial relationship.

Personal relationships can be exploited (and some may be cultivated for that very purpose) to take advantage of the position, reputation, or means (including "connections") of the other party. To enhance and set the stage for exploitability, reciprocity should be the stated operational principle for the relationship, with emphasis placed on the concept "do unto me as I *would do* unto thee" rather than "return the favors already extended." The former is more exploitable than the straight quid-pro-quo relationship implied by the latter formulation (i.e., the "you-owe-me" factor) which could interfere with getting without first giving. If the relationship does not provide the benefit sought, it should not be maintained. To do so might invite attempts at exploitative relationships by others.

There may, of course, be reasons for desiring to maintain an unequal relationship. For example, one may simply enjoy the relationship despite its exploitability. Or, in a more calculating approach, one may wish to impress special audiences that one's relationships with individuals who have the position or means to be helpful are not exploited, but rather are entered into for friendship's sake. This may be a useful way of covering one's exploitation of a relationship. It may also help in developing exploitative relationships with members of that audience. Whatever personal interest is deferred to is not as important as thinking in terms of interest when making decisions about relationships.

Participation in group activity should be given an interest focus for a variety of reasons (e.g., political, business, and pleasure-oriented). The value of the participation can be calculated using "think-negotiation" analysis to include assessment of the leadership situation within the group, the existence of cliques and interest blocs, and other considerations related to the potential for influencing consensus and group behavior. One can also effectively utilize the probing techniques of negotiation to sound out group receptivity to proposals for organizational or policy changes. Once it is determined that the group is a worthwhile and workable target, its behavior can be effectively influenced through Mr. Inside's technique of searching for allies through rapport and position shaping in the intraorganizational environment.

Mr. Inside's technique is especially effective in unstructured-group relationships away from the workplace because it is very unlikely that the concerted effort implied by the technique will be undertaken by another member of the group. For one thing, there will be no need to contend with others for control of the dialogue, which will fall by default to the one in the group with a plan, method, or reason for managing and controlling consensus development. Moreover, in an unstructured group the volunteer is generally welcomed because that person takes the burden off other group members. Furthermore, suspicions concerning motive or interest are not aroused, as most members do not view the social grouping as an arena for its pursuit.

The efficacy of the blueprint for "getting one's way at the PTA" results from a conscious effort to exploit the control potential of an interest-oriented actor with a technique for handling consensus development in a group of individuals who may not feel their interests are significantly engaged. The involvement of members of the group, being more relaxed and casual and lacking an interest focus, facilitates snowballing a consensus; competing positions usually will not attract strong commitment, as visible "participation by voting" tends to be more important than the specific stand taken on issues. In this process- rather than interest-oriented participation by members of the group, the early proponent of a position will usually be able to carry the day before any opposition can develop. The interest-driven negotiator can be successful in controlling group decisions or action because he usually has the field to himself.

NOTES

1. Negotiation actually provides on-the-job training for decision making because the same operational analysis and tasks are common to both.
2. Jeffrey H. Birnbaum, "Latest in Lobbying—Business Group Uses Professors, Not Cash, To Influence Congress," *Wall Street Journal,* June 25, 1990. pp. A1, A4. "One of the tests is to look at the other person's eyes, and as soon as they start to glaze over, back off" (p. A4).
3. See Robert M. Bastress and Joseph D. Harbaugh, *Interviewing, Counseling, and Negotiating Skills for Effective Representation* (Boston, Toronto, and London: Little Brown and Co., 1990).
4. The negotiation approach to dialogue exploitation is more comprehensive than conventional friendly persuasion, which suffers from comparison because it does not include the additional techniques available to pressure persuasion.
5. Growing recognition of the relationship between lawyering and negotiation is reflected in the increasing number of works devoted to "legal negotiation" (see Selected Bibliography). It is estimated that 90 percent of a lawyer's practice involves negotiation (Bastress and Harbaugh, *Interviewing, Counseling, and Negotiating,* p. 259).
6. Once trial has commenced it is more difficult to settle the case because the

parties have incurred the expenses, and have emotionally prepared themselves, for litigation. Thereafter, settlements usually depend on trial developments and disclosures that impact its probable outcome.

7. There is a hilarious dowry negotiation scene in the stage play, Gigi. In the song "The Contract," the inadequate negotiating skills of Gaston Lachailles's attorney are revealed. When bargaining with Gigi's Aunt Alicia stalls, Attorney Dufresne, fearful that he will not be able to fulfill his commission to return from the meeting with a dowry agreement, encourages further dialogue with Aunt Alicia. He confesses that "I am known in my profession by my inclination toward concession." This amusing example of ineffective representation does point up the serious problem of the primacy of the representative's career concerns, as well as other negotiating realities. The scene is recommended as an enjoyable, sometimes instructive spoof of lawyering and the negotiation process.

8. Roger Fisher, "What about Negotiation as a Specialty," *American Bar Association Journal,* September 1983, pp. 1220–1224.

9. As a lawyer's lawyer, I provide a broad range of negotiation services that include consultation, representation, planning, training, and instruction.

10. "Success Is No Accident," advertisement in *Washington Post,* February 18, 1988, p. B2.

11. Charisma: "1. A rare quality or power attributed to those persons who have demonstrated an exceptional ability for leadership and for securing the devotion of large numbers of people." (*The American Heritage Dictionary,* New College Ed., p. 227.)

12. In writing this section I have specifically not included engagement, marriage, or cohabitation, the most personal relationships of all with the greatest potential for benefit as well as high cost. The section's principles are, in my opinion, generally applicable to all these relationships; the problem is that a guide on negotiation is hardly the place to cover the many considerations involved in personal decisions relating to marriage, divorce, separation, and palimony. My sensitivity to personal exposure keeps me out of the substantive territory of the marriage counselor; I can go no further than to state generally the aspects of the negotiation process that may be relevant in the decision making and dialogues related to these relationships.

6

Negotiating Tactics and Ploys

GENERAL

As indicated at the outset of this Guide, much of the literature on negotiation reflects by-rote approaches in the form of lists of the basic "do's"
and "don'ts" of negotiation. For the most part, these approaches do not
provide a rationale for a negotiating game plan that can carry the would-
be negotiator over the gaps in the lists and serve as a general, across-the-
board guide to dialogue management and control.

This Guide suggests effective negotiation as a user-friendly approach
for this purpose. It is based on the premise that negotiation is a mind
game[1] requiring an understanding of the negotiation process and an
interest-oriented, conceptual framework and mindset that position the negotiator to know what to do next: basically, some form of friendly or pressured persuasion to desired consensus. There is no need to rely on a list
or other mechanical approach to reacting to dialogue developments. There
is no faltering because guidance is provided by the negotiating game plan,
which reflects that understanding and the "think-negotiation" mindset.
Notwithstanding the fact that lists do not constitute the material out of
which negotiating game plans can be fashioned, they should not be ignored. They are, in essence, enumerations of frequently encountered tactics and ploys, knowledge of which can be most useful to would-be negotiators.

The dynamics of the negotiation process as it relates to tactics and ploys
involve either offense or defense, depending upon the situation and the
interests of the sides. Knowledge of tactics and ploys is essential because
it permits the negotiator to react quickly to a play in the dialogue (e.g.,
the early opportunity to exploit, or defend against, a tactic or ploy). Early

recognition is important because it provides a head start in a situation calling for a decision. In all aspects of negotiation, early recognition, whether of the existence of the dialogue itself or of developments in it, constitutes an advantage for the alert side because it provides additional time for decision making, preparation, and orchestration.

Tactics and ploys are important tools of negotiation because they constitute the plays used to implement the strategy of the dialogue as reflected in the game plan. Actually, there is a complementary interaction: Tactics and ploys become more meaningful when they are placed in the larger context of an approach to negotiation based upon an understanding and conceptualization of process. To emphasize this point, I have placed the discussion of tactics and ploys at the end of this Guide following discussion of the effective negotiation approach to dialogue management and control.

Tactics and ploys are so closely related that they should be treated together. In many cases tactics and ploys are indistinguishable because, essentially, a ploy is a tactic with a twist. *Webster's* defines ploy as "a tactic intended to embarrass or frustrate an opponent."[2] The twist is that a ploy usually involves a conscious effort to mislead, divert, or otherwise frustrate the other side. For example, playing victim is both a tactic and a ploy. To the extent that the purpose is to cause the other side to make "being fair" a part of its negotiating game plan or distract it from that plan, victim play is a ploy; it is, of course, also a tactical effort to gain advantage. The same may be said of the decision to personally involve one's principal in the dialogue. This can be a tactic to (1) exploit the advantage of any superior negotiating skills he may possess, something not usually expected of principals, and (2) demonstrate the passion of his commitment to a key dialogue issue. If the latter is feigned to distract or mislead the other side, we are dealing with a ploy. Common to both examples is seeking advantage, the nexus between tactics and ploys.

It is difficult to present an exhaustive listing of tactics and ploys because the possibilities and combinations are almost endless. There is also overlapping; some tactics and ploys can be included under several headings. Moreover, as the effective negotiator develops his own style, he tends to personalize the tactics and ploys he uses. He does this quite naturally as part of the "think-negotiation" mindset, which pushes him toward devising new ways to gain an edge in conducting the dialogue. Thus, probably no two negotiators would have the same list although common features would be apparent.[3] The following discussion is intended to cover the basic negotiating tactics and ploys in the form they are most commonly encountered. To enhance understanding of their effective use, I emphasize the substance of each tactic and ploy and the procedural considerations[4] relating to offense and defense.

THE TACTICS AND PLOYS

The Ethical Issue

The ethical issue in negotiation involves the extent to which one goes in representing his principal and pursuing his interests. The realities of negotiation are such that it would be ostrich-like to prescribe (as some writers do) that in negotiation one should "always be fair and ethical."[5] It is more realistic to state the prescription in terms of the importance of giving the impression that one is fair and ethical.

Puffing, exaggerating, misleading the other side, and even lying[6] are frequently encountered in the behavior of negotiators.[7] Heavy emphasis on the importance of the clever use of ploys in conducting negotiations implies, at the very least, approval of the effort to distract, if not mislead, the other side. (Such behavior is sometimes euphemistically referred to as good "advocacy" or "salesmanship.") This Guide would be remiss if it failed to note the low level of morality that may be encountered at the bargaining table. It would create a gap in the preparation of the would-be negotiator and leave him exposed in an arena where ends sometimes justify and dictate the means.

There are many reasons why negotiators depart from the "always be fair and ethical" precept. The motivations cannot be neatly catalogued; they vary from individual to individual and situation to situation. Careerism, of course, is a major factor. Gekko's greed is another. It is enough for a guide to state the problem and provide cautionary advice. It cannot and should not attempt to prescribe standards of personal conduct. Accordingly, the most helpful approach is to provide a means for determining what one *can* do on his principal's behalf, leaving it for each individual to determine what he *should* do (i.e., let him decide the ethical question) in the light of his personal situation and preferences.

To assist in determining what one can do, a standard of prudence has been developed for the would-be negotiator's guidance. As a practical matter, the standard is a checklist that indicates what one can get by with; it is not intended to prescribe an ethical standard. For example, applying the standard of prudence may indicate that certain sharp conduct can be indulged in with little or no prejudice or risk. The negotiator then has to engage in a little introspection to decide what he should do under the circumstances. The final decision is a personal one reflecting a host of individual and situational considerations. One generalization does pertain, however: If the would-be negotiator comes to the conclusion that he should never be anything but fair and ethical, he may find his ethical standard to be a burden in conducting negotiations, as he will be severely limiting his tactical and other options. He may be "too good" to represent his principal in some negotiations that take on the character of street fights because of the ethical level on which the other side attempts to operate.

The foregoing discussion may be graphically represented as follows:

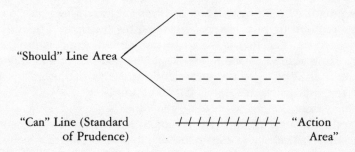

"Should" Line Area

"Can" Line (Standard of Prudence)   "Action Area"

The "can" line represents that which is obtained from applying the standard of prudence; the "should" line area represents the personal ethical decision. If one were to superimpose the "action area" (i.e., the area of general negotiating activity), one would find that negotiating action is conducted in the general area of the "can" line. Therefore, the would-be negotiator who feels he must operate considerably above the "can" line may be removing himself ethically from the action area. The point is not that negotiators must be scoundrels to be successful; rather, they must at the very least be prepared, and know how, to fight fire with fire.

The standard of prudence—devised because most negotiations tend to be conducted at the lower end of the ethical scale—represents the point beyond which the prudent negotiator should not go for his principal. Essentially, it involves three considerations: (1) effect on the continuing relationship, (2) exposure to disciplinary or other unfavorable, career-related action, and (3) impact on one's credibility or reputation as a negotiator. As with the continuing checklist, a course of conduct must pass muster on all counts. The go-signal here is three yeas. For example, the testing process should involve the following questions:

1. Will the proposed conduct alienate the other side or one's principal (both aspects of the negotiating relationship)?

2. Will the proposed conduct expose the negotiator to possible disciplinary action, such as dismissal by client or professional censure (private negotiating environment), loss of position or reassignment of representational function (intraorganizational negotiating environment), or recall as governmental representative (international negotiating environment)?

3. Will the proposed conduct adversely impact the credibility or professional reputation of the negotiator?

Obviously, where the other side consists of a principal who represents himself in a one-shot transaction, he will be the least inhibited by considerations involved in the standard of prudence that are oriented toward the career concerns of the professional negotiator. There is, therefore, a greater potential for unethical practice in a situation not involving a professional negotiator.[8] Where there is professional representation, an effort should be made to ascertain the negotiator's reputation for ethical behavior. This can generally be accomplished by informally checking with colleagues or by other investigative means if the importance of the negotiation warrants it. The effective negotiator takes into account the possible exposure to unethical conduct by the other side and his own approach to the ethical question as part of his vulnerability analysis during the preparation phase.

Dealing with Irrational Parties

Dealing with irrational parties may appear to be a mission-impossible situation, because the entire approach to pressured persuasion is premised on the competence of the other side to react rationally to decisional choices. Theoretically, there is no known negotiating approach to influence the behavior of the truly irrational or mad decisionmaker; in reality, however, there are relatively few situations of that type.

The word "truly" is key. It is frequently made to appear that a position or demand is nonnegotiable because it is based on a deep commitment to a principle, ideal, or cause (e.g., God's will, martyrdom, or jihad). This ploy play is directed at conveying a hopelessness in attempting to negotiate down from that position. The best defense and only way to handle the situation is to continue to negotiate because the stated commitment to a principle, ideal, or cause should at the very least be verified by probing. If there is real commitment and not just a ploy play, it should be viewed as any other substantive position that is amenable to reconsideration or modification based upon greater interest or need considerations, which can be uncovered and manipulated as part of the dialogue management and control effort.

The dialogue barrier that is truly not negotiable is procedural in the sense that the decisionmaker does not have the competence or capability to focus on a cost-benefit analysis or decisional choice. For example, the surface irrationality of the terrorist or hostage taker who is willing to die for his principle, ideal, or cause should not be viewed as presenting a hopelessly nonnegotiable situation. The dialogue should be pursued even though it is more difficult because it requires, usually against time and other stressful constraints, a great deal of patience to probe the real interests and needs that may be exploitable in resolving the situation. Dialogue may show that there are other interests or needs (e.g., the desire for publicity or release of other terrorists) that can be used in the bargaining effort, which should then focus on probing to see what consensus may be possible or desirable. The point is that most situations are negotiable, however intractable or insensitive the other side may appear to be, principally because there is no remedy or other alternative to negotiation. Once the dialogue ends, the show is over for both sides, literally and figuratively.

If probing produces a resolution price, the effective negotiator must evaluate it in the light of his principal's interests and react accordingly. If the price is deemed unacceptable and further negotiation appears fruitless, consideration must be given to combining dialogue with recourse to self-help and other active measures in a talk-and-fight effort to increase the cost burden of the other side (i.e., raise the ante) with a view toward stimulating more fruitful, additional dialogue. The high-stakes nature of these dialogues and their inherent fragility and unpredictability rank them among the most difficult to handle.

Cross-cultural Considerations

Cross-cultural considerations arise in all environmental contexts, although they are usually associated with international negotiations. For example, in a multicultural society such as the United States, one can expect to encounter dialogues with foreign nationals and foreign corporations in the private negotiating environment. In preparing for negotiation one must take account of cultural differences and national practices of the other side as part of factoring into the negotiating game plan all operationally relevant information about that side.

Once cultural differences are encountered, the effective negotiator seeks information concerning national customs, practices, and amenities, as well as negotiating styles and techniques. He can acquire this information from travel handbooks and guides, memoir accounts of international negotiators, discussions with negotiators actively involved in crosscultural dialogues, and library reference material. The purpose is to be in a position to exploit this information to (1) establish rapport and other elements of a good, personalized negotiating relationship, (2) adapt pressuring persuasion to cultural caveats or weaknesses, and (3) better read the other side's reaction to dialogue developments. Whether responding to a bow or *abrazo;* following toasting practice and protocol at a luncheon or dinner; reciprocating traditional gift giving or reacting to pro forma, national reserve, hostility, or negativism; the effective negotiator seeks to project the appearance of being knowledgeable, comfortable, and confident.[9] This appearance, sharply departing from that of the "ugly American" with a penchant for cultural imperialism, will generate respect and appreciation. Impressed by the well-prepared negotiator's knowledge and professionalism, the other side will take him and the principal he represents seriously.

This constitutes the essential starting point for dialogues involving cross-cultural interface.

Preparation should also include some effort to master at least a few expressions in the foreign tongue as another sign of the respect accorded the other side's cultural heritage. One cannot be expected to go much further in language mastery, but the usual verbal and nonverbal methods of expressing positive or negative reactions should be included in the cram-language preparation. The effective negotiator should be able to understand the meaning of reactions such as the positive thumbs-up signal or applause; the negative rolling of eyes and upward head movement toward one's maker; and the noncommittal, frozen half-smile correctness. Anger, of course, speaks for itself!

Should the effective negotiator be in the happy position of knowing the foreign language involved in the dialogue, he should limit reliance on it to simple, rapport-building amenities. He should not convey such depth of knowledge that would put the other side on guard from carelessly conducting intraside discussions in his presence. The inexperienced foreign negotiator may view the language barrier literally and conduct his discussion with colleagues openly. The capability to (1) eavesdrop on the intraside exchanges of the other side, especially those about the side's positions, and (2) monitor the precision of the translation of positions and proposals by one's own interpreters, represent the best operational use of the negotiator's linguistic skills.

As for the use of interpreters, it is recommended that only rarely should the negotiator rely on his own linguistic skills in conducting the dialogue. The career risk is too great in that any postdialogue dispute concerning the agreed resolution of contentious issues may be laid to a misunderstanding owing to the negotiator's linguistic deficiencies. Moreover, not using an interpreter deprives a side of the benefits of (1) hearing a proposal made by the other side and its translation by the interpreter (with the corrective or clarifying comments of the making side), and (2) hearing the proposal twice, once when it is conveyed in the foreign tongue to the receiving side's interpreter, and again in translation with corrective, clarifying exchanges between the interpreters of the respective sides.

Great care should be utilized in selecting interpreters. Usually, they are native speakers who are trained to handle general consecutive or simultaneous translation tasks. It is rare to find one whose skills extend to nuance and other differentiation associated with legal or semantic analysis. There may also be difficulties associated with the technical nature of the subject matter. As a consequence, monitoring by the effective negotiator with a linguistic capability is very significant. In the absence of that possibility, the negotiator should review and check key translations to see how they can be rendered to best preserve the nuance or special meaning. One may recall that a poor translation, which was not subject to prior staff monitoring, embarrassed President Carter during his arrival statement in Poland. What was heralded as a historic visit became an embarrassingly memorable one because of the unintended sexual overtones of his arrival statement.

The ideal preparation for cross-cultural dialogues may seem too demanding, given the usual time constraints. Obviously, more preparation is better than less; nevertheless, some basic tools will enable the effective negotiator to get by even with reduced preparation. These tools have a universal currency that can assist in bridging cultural or other differences. The principal ones are the ability to convey friendship, sincerity, and good will; respect for the other side and its position; seriousness of purpose and commitment to the dialogue; and professionalism with use of humor in appropriate situations. The bottom line is respect and professionalism, the attitudinal and operational elements, respectively.

Situs Arrangements

Situs arrangements should be classified as ploys because they are usually used to distract or inhibit a side's representation. The basic consideration is to create conditions that are not conducive to the physical comfort and mental well-being of a negotiator so that he will be distracted or otherwise burdened in conducting the dialogue. Obviously, if he is seated where there is a source of discomfort or distraction (e.g., the sun in his eyes—an arranged situation that happened to me when I was negotiating a last-minute change to the draft Defense Treaty in the 1964–1967 round of United States–Panama negotiations), he will be less alert. Similarly, seating arrangements or working conditions that are inferior to those of the negotiators for the other side can be unsettling and distracting.

During the cease-fire negotiations at Panmunjom, Korea, the chairs of the U.S. negotiators were shortened or otherwise arranged so that the Chinese and North Korean negotiators were seated higher. The U.S. negotiators had to look up to them. Another variation of this technique is to hold the negotiations in the impressive office or other facilities of the senior official of one side to demonstrate to the other his importance and, derivatively, lack of patience and time for haggling or unnecessary dialogue. Subjecting negotiating teams to the intimidation of demonstrations (e.g., "meetings of the people") in support of positions can be effectively exploited and orchestrated in connection with the dialogue and, in the process, interfere with the rest and well-being of the individual negotiators. The counter for this type of harassment is to object quickly and refuse to negotiate under such conditions, assuming the burden of negotiation does not weigh too heavily. If the dialogue must be maintained, the sites of the dialogue sessions should be alternated so that retaliation will be possible if corrective action is not taken.

The situs of the negotiation itself can become an issue because of its symbolism and considerations of tactical advantage. Audience scrutiny may make it symbolically important for one or both sides to select one side's turf, neutral turf, or a system of alternating between respective turfs. The larger side might wish to defer to the smaller side's turf preference to demonstrate to an important audience that it intends to be fair and forthcoming or that the smaller side has won this "concession." Of course, an effort should be made to get a chip from the smaller side in return for the favor. This follows the basic rule concerning concessions (i.e., to get more when giving), as the deferring side actually does incur a negotiating cost warranting the chip payment. The rationale for the chip is that negotiating on one's own turf carries many advantages of convenience (e.g., proximity to staff support and resources, security, and physical and mental well-being), which the deferring side forgoes. The effort to get a chip for deferring should be pursued with some vigor even though the side making the concession did so in pursuit of its own interest in an audience play.[10]

Boulwarism

Boulwarism is the "one-price" approach to negotiation. In its best form, it represents an effort to shorten the negotiation process: After a discussion of the issues and mutual interests, an offer is made for a reasonable settlement on a "This-is-it!" basis. In effect, there is no opening position followed by discussion and haggling; the opener is the closer. At its worst, boulwarism can be ultimatum, not negotiation.[11]

There are several reasons why boulwarism may be a counterproductive tactic.[12] The greatest difficulty is that it is seldom used; the general expectation is that the first stated position is not the last, however it may be presented. It is most difficult to make the other side believe that the stated position is not negotiable (i.e., that boulwarism is being practiced) because the effect is to forgo any attempt on its part to improve the proposal. In essence, it constitutes a procedurally oriented loaded agenda (i.e., to accept the boulwarism approach is to acquiesce in limited bargaining). Added to that is the practical problem of getting the other side's negotiator to convey this message convincingly to his principal, since it really means that there is reduced need for his services because no bargaining will follow the initial exchange of positions and views. Therefore, attempting boulwarism without the other side fully comprehending and accepting the seriousness of the attempt can result in breakdown of the dialogue.

For boulwarism to work, the other side must be carefully prepared so that the position, when stated, will be considered the only offer or proposal that will be made. Without this preparation, there is the danger of miscalculation on the part of the receiving side. It may think that boulwarism is not being practiced and that counterproposals can be made without disrupting the dialogue. During the Sadat-Begin negotiations in 1977–

1978 the dialogue broke down because the Israeli side failed to make clear to Sadat that a proposal was final and not subject to the usual countering; in effect, it was a boulwarism play. The Egyptian counter triggered the breakdown of the dialogue, which was not resumed until the Camp David talks mediated by President Carter in September 1978.

There are other problems with boulwarism. Its ultimatum-like character runs counter to the natural desire to participate in fashioning consensus. Moreover, it may expose the practitioner to the charge of not negotiating in good faith and thereby adversely affect the negotiating relationship. Boulwarism can also negatively impact the postnegotiation relationship because the adjustments and difficulties that invariably arise in the course of implementation can be attributed to the "imposed" result. For all these reasons, boulwarism should not be resorted to or accepted as the negotiating regime except in the most special of circumstances.

The defense against boulwarism is to reject, as a matter of principle, involvement in a diktat situation or nonnegotiable dialogue. If the defending side has the burden of negotiation, it may have to appeal (with consequent embarrassment for the side attempting a boulwarism play) to an important audience for relief from the refusal to negotiate a resolution of the situation.

Win-Win

Win-win can be a tactic or ploy depending on whether it is respected by both sides (tactic) or is an effort by one side to exploit the commitment of the other to win-win consensus (ploy). In the former case both sides recognize the importance of consensus, which serves the common, win-win purpose of a mutually beneficial result. This is similar to boulwarism in that both sides must respect a bargaining constraint that defeats the negotiating scheme if it is not observed.

The effort of one side to exploit the other's commitment to win-win can best be described as the "win-win with a wink" ploy. Just as in boulwarism, uncertainty concerning whether both sides will play win-win may result in guarded commitment to it by the side sensitive to the exposure inherent in the ploy. For this reason, win-win operates best when a continuing relationship provides a common interest basis for the level of cooperation necessary for a win-win dialogue. As a practical matter, the relationship also provides a forum[13] for policing both sides' commitment to win-win. Viewed as a negotiation compact, win-win cannot be utilized in openly hostile or highly competitive dialogues where there is no basis, either actual or implied, for ensuring that the sides will substitute common goals for the hardball pursuit of interest. In view of the possible limitations on win-win (generally related to the quality of the continuing relationship), it is difficult to consider it an all-encompassing approach to negotiation. It can and should be recognized as a desirable approach that has situational limitations.[14]

Treating win-win as a universal approach can lead to unfounded expectations concerning the nonadversarial character of the negotiation process and consequent prejudice to the believing side. The Gekko dictum may be an operational limitation on win-win until the enlightened negotiator overcomes his love affair with greed and self-interest. The failure of other efforts to improve mankind (e.g., the Communist experience in attempting to develop the new Soviet man) does not portend near-term, across-the-board commitment to the win-win approach.

The effective negotiator's technique in conducting the dialogue positions him to participate in and benefit from win-win negotiation. He encourages a friendly, cooperative dialogue as a ploy to encourage the desired consensus. This exploitative approach reflects the practical need to defer to continuing relationship maintenance. At the same time, it can be used to convey the perception of participation in win-win. It actually is an effort to have one's cake and eat it too.

The effective negotiator is not an enthusiast of win-win because of his preoccupation with interest-oriented advantage and dialogue-constraint avoidance. At best, he can be described as a very careful participant in win-win, motivated more by the conventional desire to serve continuing relationship needs than any interest in developing a more enlightened, socially productive approach to negotiation. Operationally speaking, his tendency is to view win-win as a tactic or ploy with all that is implied in terms of offense and defense.

Summitry

Summitry involves getting the principals together to resolve the outstanding issues. It can take place in all negotiating environments and can include meetings of all types. It can involve direct participation of both principals in a negotiating session (private), direct dialogue between corporate or agency heads (intraorganizational), and discussions between heads of state or senior foreign ministry officials (international). In effect, summitry removes the insulation of the principal from the negotiator interface and all the substantive and procedural flexibility related to negotiating under instructions and *ad referendum.*

Unless a side is blessed with a principal who can function as an effective negotiator and who will do his homework and prepare adequately for the meeting, summitry is a dangerous game. The possibilities for the compromise of negotiating positions and strategy are vast, and errors cannot be retrieved without negotiating cost. It is not surprising, therefore, to hear effective negotiators wryly state that at the summit even the burps are substantive and costly. Although the negotiator generally opposes his reduced role in the dialogue, he can still serve his principal well in advising him whether to engage in summitry and briefing him for it.

Summitry tends to be the tactic of the weaker side. It attempts to exploit, with publicity and other means of audience involvement, either (1) the meeting (the results or lack thereof) if it is held, or (2) the rejection of the proposal for the meeting. In short, the side proposing the summit meeting attempts to get negotiating mileage from the mere proposal, however it is received. Being aware of this, the defending negotiator should try to head off such proposals by first demonstrating (*not* with chips, but with a stated readiness to explore meeting possibilities) that there is no need, insofar as progress in the dialogue is concerned, for the principals to meet. He may also attempt to appeal to the other negotiator's professional concerns and express fears that as negotiators they risk muddying the negotiation waters once their principals get directly involved. If he is unsuccessful, the defending negotiator could attempt to drag out the dialogue concerning purpose, agenda, timing, place, and other details with a view to discouraging the other side from pursuing the proposal (i.e., by trying to demonstrate that it will delay the dialogue without guaranteeing progress at the summit when it is held). If in doing this he detects that time is an important factor for the other side, he might intensify the delaying tactics by linking it to the difficulty of finding time on his busy principal's schedule. The impression that the request for a summit meeting inconveniences or pushes a principal who is preoccupied with other issues can be used to detract from its attractiveness; a meeting under such circumstances could be portrayed as potentially unproductive or even counterproductive. The too-busy-principal ploy might also be exploitable to reflect the lesser interest of the principal in the negotiation and, thereby, in its results—with attendant impact on the perception concerning which side has the burden of negotiation.

If the meeting cannot be avoided, the defending side's principal must be thoroughly briefed and schooled on all aspects of the negotiation. He must be sensitized to the continuing exposure of every contact, social and other, with his opposite number. The problem is that all contingencies cannot be foreseen and even the best-briefed principal constitutes an exposure hazard to his own cause. Moreover, principals of the larger, usually defending sides are frequently neither accessible enough, nor willing or able, to devote sufficient time for proper briefing and preparation. Unfortunately, there is no quick process for preparing a principal for negotiation.

Team versus Individual Negotiator

Team versus individual negotiator is a choice that must be made by the principal in selecting his representation. The advantages of having a team are that it brings greater expertise to bear, permits better (collective) reading of the other side's intentions and positions, and provides additional witnesses to what actually transpired. In terms of ploys, a team approach permits "good people–bad people" play (i.e., fragmenting the team along good guy–bad guy lines for presentational advantage) and development of an in-team *ad referendum* step (i.e., the claimed need to get the views or approval of key team members). The disadvantages are related to maintaining discipline[15] in pursuing positions, controlling inadvertent tacit communications, and neutralizing the greater susceptibility to divide-and-conquer tactics of the other side. These disadvantages stem from the difficulty of putting together a competent negotiating team (e.g., a specialist may not be an effective negotiator) and the fact that competing approaches to the substance and process of the negotiation may manifest themselves in exploitable parochial and career rivalries among team members.

In view of these difficulties, the effective negotiator prefers to avoid the team approach. Furthermore, in terms of his career concerns, use of a team dilutes his control of process as he faces the other side and as he negotiates with his principal. He does not appreciate the audience exposure of team involvement. By its very nature, it provides a "witness" presence that tends to constrain his negotiating style.

Divide and Conquer

Divide and conquer involves an attempt to exploit personality or substantive differences on a negotiating side or in a voting bloc to compromise its position or otherwise gain negotiating advantage. This tactic is used in all environments. The presence of exploitable differences is a vulnerability that is carefully considered during preparation of the negotiating game plan. The play can take many forms, including exploiting differences between the negotiator and his principal, between members of a negotiating team, and among members of a voting bloc.

An example of the first situation occurs when principal and negotiator disagree on the desirability of accepting a quick settlement. Career or other considerations pressuring the negotiator (e.g., the desire to conclude the negotiation because of its impact on promotion opportunities or the need for the negotiator's fee) may dispose him to recommend quick acceptance of an improved counter offer of the other side. If the negotiator's eagerness is known to the other side, it may be able to conclude the negotiation with a lower counter than it would otherwise have offered, and probably more quickly than anticipated.

The more common situation lending itself to divide and conquer involves the panel negotiating team. Here personality differences, competing career objectives, and differing substantive views may present exploitable opportunities. People being what they are, it is a rare grouping that does not contain at least one weak link who may (1) be dissatisfied because he does not have a larger role in the negotiation, (2) have different views on how to resolve the issues or conduct the negotiation, (3) otherwise be in conflict with the panel leader, or (4) simply lack professionalism or experience. Watching the eyes and facial expressions during the dialogue is most important in identifying the weak link and the source of the differences. Once these are known, an exploitation-oriented probing and cultivation operation can be undertaken. Frequently, merely cultivating such a person by deferring to him and giving him an opportunity to talk will evoke a response that provides insight into the other side's solidarity and its vulnerability to divide and conquer. If he is inexperienced, the task is that much easier.

In the case of a voting bloc, the success or failure of divide and conquer depends on the strength of the bloc bond, which is a function of the relationship and its issue sensitivity. In intraorganizational negotiations, entity solidarity tends to be very issue sensitive and, therefore, easily penetrated. In the international environment, there are examples of blocs that are and are not issue sensitive. During the Cold War, the Socialist Bloc under the leadership of the Soviet Union tended to take a common stand on most issues; on the other hand, the Organization of Petroleum Exporting Countries and the developing countries in the North-South dialogue tend to be less cohesive and more easily fragmentable depending on the issues.

The defense to divide and conquer in the first situation (i.e., negotiator and his principal) is nonexistent in the sense that the prime defender, the negotiator, is so personally engaged and involved that he tends not to be defense-minded. He cannot provide the solution because he is the problem! In the second situation, the panel leader must see to it that the requisite level of discipline is maintained and that discordant panel members are controlled or removed. The leader should be sensitive to personality clashes or disagreements among panel members as well as special attention paid by the other side to individual panel members. He should caution panel members to refrain from showing personal reactions to developments at the negotiating table and to protect the security of negotiating positions and documents. Inexperienced panel members should be given special attention. In the voting bloc situation, there may not be a defense if there is solid bloc opposition to the minimum position acceptable to the defending organization.

Search for Allies

The search for allies is the basic technique for developing consensus in multilateral situations[16] in all negotiating environments. As was discussed in detail in connection with the activities and role of Mr. Inside in the intraorganizational environment, the technique essentially involves ascertaining (usually informally) dialogue participant interests and then shaping a position so that it takes account of one's organization's needs and, at the same time, attracts the support of as many participants as possible. In effect, the search for allies is a way of structuring an ad hoc voting bloc.

In the multiparty situation, one should be aware that group neutrality is not the general rule. Actually, groups with competing interests emerge as the focal point of what becomes a bloc-voting situation; individuals tend to prefer a low-profile posture and are content to participate through group action and following a "leader."[17] Furthermore, some participants may have limited interest in the issue while others have an overriding interest in its disposition. The shaping effort must take account of such varying levels of involvement and interest. It must defer to participants who tend to be the leaders and those who have a major interest in the dialogue. Divergent interests among the participants may make the search for allies difficult and require compromising one's own position in the effort to identify a support level that is attractive to the bloc being courted. The bottom line, however, is that the compromise position must still serve the basic interests of the shaper's organization. This is no small task. It requires careful assessment of interests and artful position shaping.

The distinction between issue-sensitive and nonissue-sensitive blocs may be useful here. The former, representing a less cohesive and looser grouping, can be more easily reached through position shaping because there is a better chance that portions of the bloc can be made allies. With the latter, position shaping appeals either to the whole bloc or not at all. In a sense, this all-or-nothing approach facilitates the search for allies. If support of the bloc is deemed unattainable because of its inherent solidarity in opposition, there is no need to waste time or bargaining chips in a futile shaping effort.

The manifestation of the search for allies in the bilateral context is the traditional balance-of-power play. This play seeks to balance a relationship through alliance or supporting relationship with another or other actors. The current formulation involves having a "card" to play to redress a balance. Its currency became widespread during the Nixon Administration when an attempt was made to exploit trilateral diplomacy (between Washington, Beijing, and Moscow) in the détente effort with the Soviet Union. Playing the China card was supposed to be the ace in the hole for the United States. During the actual normalization of the United States–Peoples Republic of China relationship under the Carter Administration in 1975, it was not clear whether the United States had played the Chinese card or vice versa. Its manifestation in the private and intraorganizational negotiating environments is the old-fashioned tactic of playing one side off against another. In this respect, the card play has some features in common with whipsawing.

Standard Ploy Signals and Responses

Some standard ploy signals and responses are utilized to mislead or confuse the other side and disrupt its conduct of the dialogue. For example, false optimism and encouragement may be signalled (e.g., "We are really getting close") to stimulate higher offers, including the need for "just one more concession" as a closing tactic. To improve the probing take, a signal may be conveyed that the other side has the inside track on a deal and should solidify its position by facilitating the approval process through the provision of greater particulars and details.

Ploy reactions or responses include (1) pretending to ignore a tacit communication or not reacting to a trial balloon or hypothetical question, thereby forcing the other side to expressly state or formally table a position; (b) feigning surprise over, or lack of understanding of, a position, thereby evoking a fuller explanation that may facilitate or advantage the probing effort; (3) stating, for the same purpose, that one is uninstructed on an issue and requesting the fullest possible explanation for reporting to one's principal (another form of exploiting *ad referendum*); (4) noting the difficulty in gaining, or expressing doubt about, acceptance of a proposal by one's principal; (5) treating a proposal as having been made in jest because of its clearly unacceptable character (e.g., "What a moon shot!"); (6) rejecting a proposal out of hand, or ignoring one, without stating a rationale or with the invocation of a higher principle to underscore its unacceptability (e.g., "This is preposterous" or "Too unreasonable or unfair to consider"); (7) countering an unacceptable proposal with a position known to be equally unacceptable or unreasonable to the other side; and (8) expressing hurt feelings or anger, with concomitant cost risk to the negotiating relationship (e.g., "This offer is insulting" or "Your explanation is an insult to my intelligence").

The main purposes behind these signals, reactions, and responses are to force the proposing side to (1) have to work and, perhaps, pay to get an issue into the dialogue, which tests its resolve and attitude toward the importance of the issue; (2) divulge the maximum amount of information concerning the position or issue; or (3) inhibit further pursuit of an issue. The proponent's counter is to (1) persevere and not be deterred, and (2) watch his substantive exposure in giving additional information concerning the position or issue. The felt need to explain should not contribute imprudently or unnecessarily to the probing take of the other side. The best advice, as always, is to stay focused on exposure as part of "thinking negotiation."

Personalizing the Relationship

Effective negotiators understand the importance of maintaining a good negotiating relationship and therefore try to keep the tone of their dialogues friendly. They work at developing that relationship by finding out during the preparation phase all the idiosyncrasies of the individuals on the other side, avoiding these and other irritants during the dialogue, and developing a level of trust by following through on commitments and otherwise being a reliable dialogue partner. These ongoing activities are frequently accompanied by outwardly friendly or "reduce-hostility" maneuvers such as hand shakes, bear hugs, and back pats. I myself have had success with exploiting the "family" ploy in contexts such as "since I feel we are like family, I can divulge . . ." (potential set-up) and "I thought we had a family relationship and am shocked. . . " (a shaming maneuver to inhibit or induce action). The appropriateness of using approaches such as these depends on the personal, cultural, and other characteristics of the other side.

A good relationship facilitates conduct of the dialogue in many ways (e.g., it may permit off-the-record trial ballooning and generate "only-for-you" confidences, which of course should be double-checked for a possible set-up), and portends a good postnegotiation relationship. Moreover, principals are usually impressed by the generation of a high level of rapport at the negotiating level because they correctly believe it will facilitate the persuasion process. It is not unusual, therefore, for negotiators to try to be on a first-name basis with their counterparts. They consider the personalization process especially useful when dealing with a less-experienced negotiator because it can be utilized as an exploitative device. Personalization may dull "think-negotiation" alertness and develop a confidence factor ("You can trust me") that can be exploited to gain greater insight into the thinking of the other side, including (perhaps) its negotiating needs and objectives. Thus, for a variety of reasons related to their external (with the other side) and internal (with their principals) dialogues, effective negotiators seek to cultivate good negotiating relationships.

The effective negotiator is never off-stage. He is busy orchestrating the effort both at the negotiating table and away from it. Accordingly, social meetings at lunch, cocktail parties, and elsewhere provide an opportunity to interact with the other side when it is relaxed and likely to err in responding to negotiation-related trial balloons, tacit communications, and other tactics and ploys. Essentially, the play is either a probing or planting (the seed of an idea or perception) operation. Humor can be very helpful in probing or planting because it contributes to the informality and off-the-record, nonofficial character of the meeting, thereby enhancing its exploitative potential. Apart from contributing to a good atmosphere, humor implies an "I was only kidding" string on a position that can reduce the negotiating cost of an unanticipated negative reaction. The probe or plant should, of course, be skillfully woven into the fabric of the conversation so that it does not stick out like a sore thumb.

Talk and Fight

Talk and fight is the ultimate in pressured persuasion in that the strongest possible leveraging action is undertaken to complement and reinforce a continuing dialogue. In effect, self-help or other strong recourse action is used to parallel and impact an ongoing dialogue. Based upon Karl von Clausewitz's concept that war is an extension of the political dialogue,[18] it became the principal tactic (i.e., protracted conflict) of the forces of socialism in waging the international class conflict (including revolutionary struggle) during the Cold War. It was also very visible during the Persian Gulf crisis when unheeded Coalition Force ultimatums were complemented by (1) the massing of force, and (2) its application during the air and ground battle phases of the successful effort to destroy Iraqi military power.[19] The key element in the talk-and-fight tactic is the continuing nexus between dialogue and pressuring action, be it self-help or recourse to an available remedy. It is not a sequential relationship (e.g., failed dialogue resulting in self-help action).

Application of talk and fight is not limited to international negotiations. It has less dramatic but conceptually similar applications in the other environments as well. For example, the use of litigation as a parallel action to pressure the settling of a claim under negotiation in the private environment has the same elements of pressuring action in support of dialogue. Another is a work action by labor (e.g., strike) or a management response (e.g., lockout) during labor negotiations.[20] The same type of parallel action is frequently encountered in the intraorganizational environment when staffing exercises reflecting organizational rivalries are paralleled by overt action to resolve them by contrary practice or executive or legislative action. For example, an ongoing dialogue among the military services concerning military roles and missions is paralleled by one service's preemptive assumption of the disputed mission or role or by its lobbying to get executive or legislative approval for it.

Parallel and Other Covered Dialogues

The covered dialogue is a ploy that seeks to exploit the lack of the target side's awareness that the pressuring persuasion of negotiation is in progress. The lack of awareness may result from the tacit or masked character of the communication or its being directed to others. The effort is to lower resistance to the creation and manipulation of a favorable perception of a negotiating situation without the defensiveness encountered in open, direct dialogue. The ploy essentially involves catching the other side off guard by accessing its attention and ear in a nonthreatening setting that appears to be free of any interest or dialogue involvement.

Covered dialogues can take a variety of forms, the essence of which is the use of masked, indirect communication to influence a target side. Audience play is the most common form of covered dialogue.[21] While it actually parallels the principal negotiating dialogue, it benefits from not having the appearance of parallel dialogue. Several years ago, I enjoyed great success in organizing as a covered, parallel dialogue a labor-management seminar on contemporary management problems in the railroad industry. This was done to (1) make management's case, and (2) influence subsequent negotiation with the union in which some of the seminar participants were key actors. The more conventional parallel dialogue involves direct dialogue conducted by one party with a view to its relevance and impact on an ongoing or imminent dialogue with another party, the principal target. A prime example is the 1990 dialogue of President Gorbachev with Lithuania concerning secession and independence, which influenced the same dialogues with other Soviet republics.

The defense to covered dialogues is sensitivity to dialogue awareness, which is part of the negotiator's alertness under the concept of "thinking negotiation." Communications (and actions) of those who are involved in extant or developing relationships should be screened for relevant dialogue content. Thus, defense starts with dialogue recognition and continues with analysis of the perception or impact potential of the communication. Thereafter, defense involves conveying signals or otherwise demonstrating that the communication is not being received or that the desired perception or impact is not achievable. If the other side is influenced by the defense, it may be possible to move to the offense and convey self-serving perceptions to reverse the intended effect of the covered dialogue and to use it as a supporting part of the defending side's dialogue.

Agenda Plays

The use of a formal agenda can be exploited. The agenda dialogue can serve as an excellent vehicle for gaining bargaining advantage and for probing positional priorities and parameters. A *loaded agenda* frames an issue in such a way that agreement to the formulation concedes its basic substance, leaving for negotiation only the procedural aspects of the issue. The "think-negotiation" emphasis on distinguishing between substance and process is helpful in coping with the loaded agenda play. For example, if the issue to be negotiated is whether the U.S. flag may be flown in a given area in a foreign country, a loaded formulation of the negotiating task would be "to negotiate conditions governing the flying of the U.S. flag in area A of Country X." If the formulation is accepted, the right to fly the U.S. flag in the area mentioned is conceded, as the issue for negotiation is limited to conditions under which the flag may be flown.

The extreme nature of this example should not be taken as assurance that the loading ploy can be easily detected. A defensive rule of thumb is to be alert to loading whenever the other side expresses the need to define or formulate an agenda or agenda issues. One should subject any agenda formulation to the standard drafting scrutiny of alternate wording and juxtaposing of language (see the Drafting Consensus section in Chapter 4). There are many artful and subtle lighting-rod formulations that include double and triple loading; uncovering or correcting one aspect still leaves a prejudicial element in the formulation.

A general approach to defending against the loaded agenda (where the defending side has no intention to employ the loading tactic itself) is to get prior agreement that either side may address any issue at any time during the dialogue. This approach reduces the concession exposure of initially accepting a particular agenda formulation. On the offense, all consequences of a loading attempt should be carefully thought through before resorting to it. Loading is usually most effective—principally because it is less easily detected—if it is used to gain a little edge rather than to deal the other side a wipe-out stroke. Against competent representation it is highly likely that only a "scratch hit" is possible; a home run, almost never. The problem with getting caught in a loading play is that (1) the other side may have a better view of the loading side's issue priorities, and (2) thereafter, all the drafts of that side will be treated as suspect and subjected to more careful scrutiny.

Another defense is to substitute a short, general formulation for a detailed, loaded one that is seeded with all sorts of traps. For example, the highly loaded agenda formulation, "the timing of the withdrawal of U.S. troops to the eighteenth parallel" (i.e., loaded both as to the principle and extent of the withdrawal) can be countered by a less threatening formulation, "withdrawal of forces," which is both simple and reciprocal. The proposing side cannot defend its original formulation without compromising its loaded character. It certainly cannot claim that the general formulation does not get the basic issue on the agenda, nor can it otherwise attack its patent evenhandedness.

Apart from formulation loading, a formal agenda can be used to gain advantage if it is structured as a *shaped agenda*. Here the agenda, though not loaded in the technical sense,[22] is shaped to gain procedural and substantive advantage. For example, it may be procedurally advantageous to specify a certain order for the discussion of issues. (One might want to discuss first those with respect to which a side has considerable flexibility. This will launch the dialogue on a positive, forthcoming note. Conversely, one might want to handle first those on which there is little give. This will convey a tough bargaining stance.) On the substantive side, pressing for agreement on definition of the issues for negotiation can serve to keep out of the dialogue, or minimize the involvement of, issues that a side wishes to avoid or downplay. That agenda play can also be utilized to uncover and manipulate the importance and priority attached to issues (i.e., bootstrap them). Moreover, the side resisting issue definition may be made to give something to keep an issue in the dialogue.

Because there are so many and varied favorable shaping possibilities, careful consideration should be given to the ploy possibilities of a formal agenda. Most negotiators tend to overlook it, or minimize its importance, when traditional loading is not involved. After checking the agenda for a loading play, negotiators usually make very little effort to check for prejudicial shaping.

Timing

Timing considerations are critically important in dialogue management and control. Timing can be used as (1) part of an improved orchestration effort that coordinates the timing of proposals and other actions with related and significant developments in the dialogue, (2) a sweetener to enhance proposal or consensus acceptability, or (3) a lever to pressure persuasion and consensus. These three roles—to orchestrate, facilitate, and pressure consensus—have substantive and procedural dimensions that should be understood if one is to handle well the timing opportunities encountered in conducting the dialogue. Two procedural applications, delaying actions and establishing deadlines, are discussed in the sections that follow. The focus here will be primarily on the substantive exploitation of timing considerations.

Timing needs of the other side are probed during all phases of the negotiation dialogue. Where the other side has an actual timing need or can be made to believe that it has one, it can usually be brought to the dotted line by some effort to defer to that need. In some cases it may be made more costly for the side with the real or believed need if the other side, seeking greater exploitation of the situation's timing potential, claims to have a conflicting need that raises the cost of any accommodation of the original need. The bootstrapping of a reciprocal need is simply a ploy plan to increase the bargaining take.

In all timing plays, the effort is to stimulate and exploit the "brass-ring" mentality[23] that one must seize a quickly vanishing opportunity. It is a way of getting the other side to react quickly and positively to a "favorable" situation that has a narrow window of accessibility in terms of time. It seeks to reverse the standard wisdom of looking before you leap. For example, in a labor negotiation a poor earning report can be used by management to pressure quick acceptance of the wage offer on the table that "is sure to be reconsidered in the light of this unexpected development."

As a sweetener, timing games can take the following forms: "If you buy two widgets now, you will receive a third one without cost" or "You can make a special deal with us today during our lost-our-lease, clearance sale." In the latter formulation, the sweetener is broadened to reflect that both sides have timing needs: the seller, to sell during the liquidation period; the buyer, to enjoy the favorable, short-term price situation.

When used as a lever, timing can be most compelling as a closer. Examples are: "You had better accept my offer now, because (1) I am planning to file for bankruptcy next week. . . (2) my assets are being sequestered for back payment of alimony and child support." Timing can be effectively exploited because it constitutes a critical element of situational control; the side with an actual or perceived timing need related to the dialogue has a vulnerability as weighty as the burden of negotiation. Accordingly, timing plays are frequently most effective as closing tactics or ploys, with the actual or contrived nature of the need distinguishing the tactic from the ploy.

Timing considerations can also be used creatively to facilitate consensus. The technique that comes to mind is known as *loose linkage:* One side demands the immediate resolution of an issue and the other side, unable to accept this approach, suggests a present commitment in principle with deferred implementation as an acceptable alternative. During the Persian Gulf crisis the Iraqi position was deemed to be considerably softened by its substitution of a Coalition Powers' commitment to *address* the issue of Israeli occupation of the West Bank and Gaza Strip for its original demand that there be an *actual Israeli withdrawal* from the territories as the price of an Iraqi withdrawal from Kuwait.[24] A similar approach was reflected in the Japanese proposal for the April 1991 summit with President Gorbachev that the Soviets recognize Japanese sovereignty over all the disputed northern islands, with the immediate return of only two as the condition precedent to any dialogue concerning aid to the Soviet economy. The original Japanese demand was that all four islands be returned. Again, creative use of the timing possibilities made it possible to be forthcoming in an effort to advance the dialogue.[25]

The defense to a timing play is, as in the case of the burden of negotiation, an effort to hide the need or create the impression that the other side has a greater need. The best way to hide it is to extend the probing dialogue and not show haste in movement toward resolution of a specific issue. The defending side may also be able to project a waning interest in the dialogue by proposing recesses and other delays in an effort to show that the dialogue is losing its importance to it. The problem with all the greater-need defensive ploys is that they may not meet the real needs of the defending side. If they do not, they cannot be continued because, in the final analysis, the side with the burden must ultimately deal with it as a matter of self-interest.

Delaying Action

Delay tactics are frequently encountered in a variety of forms. They range from the abused and overused, "The check is in the mail" or "I haven't had a chance to discuss the matter with my principal" to more sophisticated approaches involving attempts to obfuscate issues or to shift dialogue focus to the burdensome process. The former, which are more common, can best be described as *simple delays.* They are intended to gain time either for the convenience of the delaying side or as a means of testing the other side's commitment to pursue the dialogue or available remedies. They can be brought to an end by persistent demands for movement or progress in the dialogue. Usually, failure of the delaying side to act will result in dialogue termination and resort to available remedies. Except where the delay is useful for a special purpose (e.g., to exploit the other side's need for a quick settlement—delay may cause it to settle for less; or to await a special favorable development relevant to consensus), the simple delay tactic has limited utility to produce a win. It is quite risky because, by its very nature, it usually leads to confrontation over dialogue continuation. However, one can exploit simple delays to advantage if the risk factor is minimized by readiness to promptly renew the dialogue upon demand.

If the defending side fails to challenge the delay play, it may signal its pursuit of a frivolous dialogue or the onus of the burden of negotiation (1) because there is no remedy, or (2) because the remedy that is available is perceived to be not practically available in the negotiating sense. This may lay the basis for the delaying side to take the offensive and terminate the dialogue, if frivolous, or if not, push for a favorable settlement based upon the defending side's exposed dependence on a negotiated settlement.

Delay tactics can also be used to confuse the issues under negotiation and otherwise complicate the process so that the defending side questions whether the entire effort is worthwhile. This type of *complicating delay* usually takes the form of hyperactive responsiveness to the tempo and demands of the dialogue. There is no impression of delay because the delaying side seems to be committed to, and actively participating in, the dialogue. The complicating delay tactic is intended to impress the other side that the dialogue will be long and burdensome and to make it appear that the deal, if consummated, may not be worth the investment of time and other resources necessary for its resolution to the desired point.

A good example is the tactic of the overcooperative taxpayer in an Internal Revenue Service audit. Aware of the career pressures on the auditor to conduct productive dialogues, the taxpayer draws out the audit by raising questions concerning tax law and requesting more time to submit his records. The purpose is to demonstrate, however slowly, that he is cooperative; can substantiate that he has complied with the requirements of the tax laws once they are clarified for him; and will contest the audit at each stage, including the resolution of any and all collateral issues and the use of all available process. The auditor, mindful of the time burden, will seek ways of extricating himself from it (e.g., quick settlement of the tax liability at a low attractive level for the taxpayer) so that he can move on to more productive involvements. This tactic works best when the taxpayer's total exposure is small because, as in all complicating delay situations, continued involvement in a dialogue made to appear endless is measured against the ultimate benefit of staying the course.

Other examples can demonstrate how the will of the other side to continue the dialogue can be challenged. In purchases of goods, one can involve the time of the seller in describing features of the product, demonstrating it, answering detailed questions, and haggling over price. After a period of time, the seller may be amenable to consummating the sale on a more favorable basis because of the amount of time he has already invested and his desire to avoid further dialogue. The counter is to "defend" by threatening termination of the dialogue on the basis that "I'm spending too much time on this deal. At this price it's not worth it!" The short answer is, "OK, we've both invested a lot of time in this. The time is already in; let's not waste that; I'm ready to close the deal for X dollars." This is a variation of the diminishing asset ploy.[26] Its success is dependent upon the perception concerning the benefit of closing the deal for the amount offered. The exposure here is great; either a deal is struck or the dialogue is terminated because the defending side has no interest in prolonging the dialogue by countering.

A related situation involves the use of details as a delay technique to weaken the other side's interest in continued dialogue in an effort to improve the current state of the bidding. The side on the offensive seeks to shift the dialogue to details of the transaction, thereby bogging down the dialogue. The offensive effort, essentially to cross every "t" and dot every "i," can usually be exploited against an impatient side, which can be frustrated into seeking an early end to the dialogue at the lower price. The defense is to press for early deal consummation at a price just below the current level and to charge that the focus on details is a dilatory tactic. In an appropriate situation this delay tactic can be used to weaken the other side's resolve to continue the dialogue to a certain point or at all. The possibility of successful exploitation depends on the locus and nature of the burden of negotiation and the amount at stake.

The bottom line here is that delay is frequently encountered in negotiation and one must assess its potential use as a negotiating tactic or ploy on the offense or defense. Obviously, its use to discourage further dialogue should indicate its limitations when the stakes are so high that the parties can be expected to stay the course. Even in this case, the effective negotiator's "think-negotiation" mindset will dictate the desirability of continued monitoring of the situation. Because of changed circumstances, such monitoring may reveal a different attitude toward early termination of the dialogue. The best example occurs when original parties are replaced by heirs or other representatives whose principal interest may be a quick settlement and termination of the dialogue without trying to get the most out of it. In effect, delay tactics cannot be expected to be effective against those who by nature or interest involvement (e.g., burden of negotiation) remain committed to goal realization.

Establishing a Deadline

Establishing a deadline involves getting agreement expressly or by acquiescence that the negotiation must be concluded by a certain time. As with the burden of negotiation, the side with the actual time need is under the greater pressure to be forthcoming and avoid running past the deadline. This pressure provides negotiating leverage for the other side, which can push for concessions to meet the agreed time limit. Any attempt to hold to a position can be attacked as bad faith or a breach of the agreement to expedite the negotiation.[27]

The effective negotiator is amenable to establishing a deadline where the time constraints burden the other side and can be exploited. Where he has the burden of time, he seeks to mask it and avoid agreement on a deadline. If pressed on a deadline, his first line of defense is to go no further than giving assurances that his side's responses and reactions will be timely because it too wants an early conclusion of the dialogue. The keys to this defense are (1) the substitution of assurances for an agreed deadline and (2) the fact that the assurances relate to responses and reactions, not to the reaching of consensus. At the same time, the impression of a shared interest in expeditious negotiation is conveyed. This helps in the masking effort and in resisting further efforts to obtain agreement to a deadline. Should the other side keep pushing for a deadline, the effective negotiator resists on the basis that he is not aware of any need for one. He requests an explanation why one is necessary when both sides have expressed an interest in an expedited dialogue. The purpose here is to reinforce the impression that time is not of the essence for him while probing the actual time needs of the other side by seeking its justification for a deadline.

Audience Play

Audience play has already been discussed in a variety of contexts (e.g., privacy of negotiation and covered dialogues). Essentially, it is an attempt to create external pressure on the other side or its negotiator to impact favorably, by inhibiting or otherwise, the course of the negotiation. The basic tactic is to search for allies among the elements of a relevant audience by playing to their interests or prejudices and using their support to pressure the other side. One of the most frequently encountered techniques to reach audiences is to arrange press coverage of the negotiation either through a leak (where there is an understanding that developments in the negotiations will not be publicized) or through a press conference or other open contact (where there is no such understanding).

Whatever the form of audience play, it cannot be ignored without cost. It must either be stopped or countered by a defensive effort directed at winning over or neutralizing the audience. Where audience play by the other side portends substantive or procedural prejudice, a strong response must be made lest further resort to unacceptable audience play be encouraged. The defense is to claim bad faith because of the attempt to negotiate through pressure tactics rather than on the merits. Depending on the defending side's need for a negotiated result, the claim may be reinforced by an express or implied suggestion that continuation of the dialogue is at risk. The sense of that risk can be heightened by stiffening negotiating positions or spacing out scheduled meetings to demonstrate the counterproductive effect of resort to this play. In negotiation, as elsewhere, bad behavior should be penalized; if not, it will become a continuing feature of the relationship.

There are situations, however, in which the best defense is to counter the other side's effort rather than attempt to terminate it. For example, the audience whose attention has been attracted may be so important to the defending side that it feels the need to state its case. In this situation, the defense involves a competing play for audience support. In cases in which audience interest or scrutiny can be anticipated, a preemptive defense may be indicated even though the other side has not yet made a move to involve the audience.

In any case, defending against audience play requires position formulations that address the specific issues of the dialogue and those related to the audience dimension. For example, in responding to a warranty claim arising from dissatisfaction with its systems for controlling vehicular pollution, General Motors may feel audience pressure because (1) it has been invoked by the other side, or (2) it is anticipated because of heightened public interest in clean air developments. The impact of this dual exposure (i.e., to the claimant and the audience) requires a response that addresses the specific claim and the audience interest. An appropriate response for General Motors would be a formulation that stresses the quality of its technology and its readiness to keep it under warranty as a feature of its policy to be a good, socially responsible, corporate citizen. Furthermore, its position might strongly support the goal of promoting cleaner air while lamenting the limitations of the current state of the art to achieve it. This exercise in minimizing specific and audience exposure requires measured or balanced responses that usually include lip service to a larger principle combined with reference to an exculpating situational condition. The result is a finesse of the apparent two-front, exposure dilemma.

Victim Play

One of the most commonly encountered tactics and ploys is the attempt to exploit weakness and to develop bargaining strength through victim role playing. This is practically feasible only where (1) there is an audience to play to, and (2) the other side is sensitive to the scrutiny (i.e., opinion or reaction) of that audience. (It is a rare negotiating situation in which one can use victim play to touch the heart—and purse—strings of the other side. That would be a windfall of wondrous proportions!) The key for the role player is to gain enough notoriety so that the requisite audience pressure can be generated and brought to bear. The objective is to get the other side to perceive the need to lean over backwards to demonstrate that it is fair and to cause "being fair" to become one of its negotiating objectives, a distraction from full attention to goal realization. That side may reflect this by adopting a more conciliatory negotiating style and making concessions to demonstrate fairness. At the very least, the victim seeks to disrupt the negotiating rhythm and play of the other (defending) side by making it overly sensitive to the fairness issue.

The counter to the victim play is to demonstrate (to the victim) little sensitivity to audience scrutiny while exploiting every opportunity to show (to the audience) fairness and reasonableness in handling the victim. A kindly approach and credible concern for the victim can go a long way toward (1) undermining the play to the audience, and (2) avoiding compensatory concession making, which is usually counterproductive because it tends to encourage further victim role playing.

Embarrassment of Power (Shaming)

Embarrassment of power (shaming) is generally encountered in a negotiating situation in which the sides are unequal. Actually, it is a form of victim play. The weaker side attempts to inhibit the stronger from exploiting its strength by making direct references to that strength intended to produce concessions or forbearance based on shame. The weaker side also uses as a deterrent its readiness to bring to the attention of audiences to which the stronger side is sensitive any instances of overreaching or other use of that strength. Once the stronger side shows a sensitivity to this type of pressure, it will thereby encourage greater use of the embarrassment ploy.[28]

The best defense is not to overreact to its use and to try to reverse the tactic by insisting that the other side negotiate the merits of the matter and not introduce extraneous issues. A form of reverse victim play can be utilized as follows: "Here I am taking the time to meet and resolve this issue on the merits and all I hear is that I am bigger than he is. This has become a hopeless waste of my time." The implication that a breakoff is being considered may deter further embarrassment play. The credibility of this defense depends on the perception of where the burden of negotiation lies. If the stronger side clearly has the onus, this defense will not be effective in the long run.

Good Guy–Bad Guy

Good guy–bad guy is one of the most widely used ploys. It is designed to fragment the negotiating side into the understanding, cooperative negotiator, on the one hand; and the difficult principal, on the other. Examples by negotiating environment are: "My client will just not be reasonable" (private); "My boss has shotgun vision on this issue" (intraorganizational); and "The government, the Congress, the military, the people . . . will not buy this arrangement" (international). The purpose is to develop a friendly relationship at the negotiating level in the form of a potentially exploitable common effort to work out an arrangement that will be acceptable to the difficult principal. A desirable result is to have the negotiator mediate the dialogue between the other side and his principal and, thereby, be in a position to (1) probe more easily the other side's goal and objectives, and (2) create a two-stage approval process that will increase the concession cost to the other side. (See the Exploiting *Ad Referendum* section in Chapter 4.)

Inhibiting

Inhibiting is a basic tactic of negotiation.[29] It involves efforts to deter the other side from proposing or taking action that would be prejudicial to the inhibiting side's interests. Through the creation of (1) low expectations concerning the success of a proposal or course of action, or (2) apprehension and uncertainty concerning its counterproductive impact, the side seeking to inhibit tries to steer the other side away from that proposal or action. If this is successful, the inhibiting side avoids the need to react, thereby saving bargaining chips if a concession would have had to be made, or avoiding an express rejection or other action that might negatively impact the negotiating relationship.

The classic inhibiting action is to deter negotiation or haggling by claiming that it is not necessary or even appropriate because fair and reasonable positions will be encountered (i.e., the basic implication of "round-table" discussions and the thrust of boulwarism). Many automobile dealers take this approach during left-over-model sell-offs or other difficult times. They claim self-servingly that their "cut-to-the-bone" prices obviate the need for negotiation because the fat has already been removed. They underestimate the moxie of their buyers in using a "no-need-to-negotiate" slogan as a come-on.

During the vulnerability analysis in the preparation phase, the weaknesses in both sides' positions are identified and possible inhibiting efforts are considered. The undertaking of, or defensive response to, an inhibiting effort is structured into the negotiating game plan. The usual offensive technique is to signal to the other side that some proposal or action would have undesirable or counterproductive negotiating consequences—essentially an apprehension-creating exercise. The inhibiting effort is most easily worked and most successful where the burden of negotiation is on the other side, because its need for a negotiated result makes it more cautious and therefore more easily inhibitable from conducting the negotiation in a way that might be perceived by the other side as counterproductive.

The defense to an inhibiting effort is to lead the other side to believe that inhibiting is not possible. This can be done by (1) apparently ignoring the signals meant to inhibit, and (2) raising the subject of the proposal or action to be inhibited (without formally proposing or taking it) and using discussion[30] of it as a probing device. Such defense involves low exposure; there is no formal action (only a *discussion* of it) that could trigger the undesirable consequences signalled by the side attempting to inhibit (i.e., as no *action* has been taken, the threatened counteraction should not follow). If the side attempting to inhibit is really sensitive to the issue, it will be demonstrated in its reaction to the defensive feint. It may then be possible for the defending side to develop a bootstrapping situation (i.e., the issue's importance, if not central to the defending side's position, can be exaggerated by it and the inhibiting side may be worked to make larger concessions in negotiating it). In addition, the defending side may be advantaged by creating the perception that it is not so wedded to a negotiated result as to be deterred from taking risks. As a result, the side attempting to inhibit may forgo further attempts to exploit the burden of negotiation against the defending side.

Bluffing

Bluffing should be sparingly used because it can destroy credibility. As a matter of "thinking negotiation," one must assume that the other side has prepared well for the negotiation and will be in a position to uncover a bluff. A bluff called and uncovered results in a loss of credibility and potential negotiating cost. The cost factor is inflated because the credibility loss is both personal and positional. From then on, all positions and statements of the side that attempted the bluff will be suspect and subjected to greater scrutiny. The effect will be to sharpen the alertness on the other side and eliminate the possibility of lulling it into a less alert, error-prone posture.

Threats

Threats are most effective when they are low-key and injected into the dialogue tacitly. Concern for the negotiating and postnegotiation relationship requires that the other side be made to feel that it is not under duress as consensus is developed. Furthermore, nonviable use of leverage or crass exploitation of the other side's weakness may generate undesired audience exposure. The audience to which the sides are playing may become aware of the strong-arm tactics as part of the weaker side's defensive action or because the negotiation cannot be kept completely private. Of course, where the negotiating game plan is based upon a hard line, either because of the desire to punish the other side or to make an example of it to deter others from initiating negotiation on the same or related issues, threats should be clearly conveyed to achieve the special impact that is desired.

Whether tacit or express, threats involve the credibility of the making side. Failure to follow through on a threat lessens the effectiveness of future threats because they will be perceived as a bluff. In fact, it may encourage the other side to disregard or ignore subsequent threats. The result may be the need to take the second threatened action because of the desire to restore credibility.[31] Taking that action will certainly strain the relationship and may either terminate or contribute to the termination of the negotiation dialogue. This possible consequence is a serious matter for both sides, as presumably they are in dialogue because they believe their respective needs can be satisfied through negotiation. For the side with the burden of negotiation, the result is especially damaging.

For all of the reasons just given, the effective negotiator usually employs the "hint-of-the-hops" technique in exploiting the leverage or other advantage his side enjoys in a negotiation. He usually tries to avoid direct threats, preferring instead a lighter, indirect approach because it involves less risk to the relationship. It also reduces the credibility cost of a failure to follow through on an ignored threat.

Brinkmanship

The same considerations that are applicable to bluffing and threats apply to brinkmanship. Generally, brinkmanship is a procedural play involving a bluff or threat to resort to some remedial action, including self-help (e.g., suing; kicking the problem upstairs; breaking off talks)—all directed toward suspension or termination of the dialogue. The tactic seeks to exploit the burden of negotiation against a side that perceives that it has the burden.

The counter is victim and image play (to an appropriate audience) stressing the other side's hard-line approach and lack of a serious effort to negotiate the issues and respect the negotiating relationship.

Packaging

Packaging involves concern for enhancing the acceptability of proposals or reactions to proposals in the interest of relationship maintenance. It focuses attention on the cosmetic or other appeal of positions and ways of structuring them for greater presentability and acceptability. It suggests the use of cosmetic and, at times, substantive sweeteners whenever it is deemed necessary to protect the relationship from a potentially counterproductive proposal or reaction. Of course, if there is no relationship concern (i.e., if one side either desires to put the other down or does not feel that any prejudice will result from a negative response), there is no need to employ a sweetener. Avoidance of the unnecessary use of substantive sweeteners is part of the continuing effort to avoid giving without getting something in return.

A sweetener can be cosmetic (a semantic improvement in a presentation to make it more attractive) or substantive (the linking of positive to negative positions so that the appeal of the former will carry the latter). Consider the following example of semantic sweetening: X requests a loan of $5,000 from Y. Y cannot lend the money but is concerned about the impact of a negative response on the continuing relationship with X. In responding to X, he might employ as a cosmetic sweetener a detailed, sympathy-evoking tale of his financial straits as a means of making the negative response more palatable. Just making the effort to explain the "no" reflects deference to the relationship. If the concern for the relationship warrants more, Y might add such substantive (i.e., involving an undertaking or commitment) sweeteners as, "If you want me to, I will try to borrow it for you," or, "All I can scrape up for you is $250." The latter is slightly more exposure laden than the former, which is little more than a best-effort undertaking; the latter risks the possibility that X may accept the $250. If it turns out that Y was correct in assuming the $250 would not be accepted, this sweetener will prove to be the most cost-effective protector of the relationship; it will portray Y as being prepared to do something very concrete to meet X's needs. Again, the concern for exposure and careful chip play must be involved in opting among the possible sweeteners.

The substantive linking of positions to produce an attractive formulation must be distinguished from deal packaging in multi-issue situations (see the Packaging Deals section in Chapter 4). In the former, the packaging is used to produce a positive effect by providing attractive cosmetic formulations to soften the impact of a negative presentation or a turndown. In

effect, attractive and not-so-attractive formulations are combined so that
positions not acceptable separately become so because of their association
with attractive ones. After all, a bitter pill can be swallowed more easily
when it is sugar-coated. The common preference is not to use substantive
chips to facilitate swallowing; these are usually reserved for deal making.

Bootstrapping

Bootstrapping has already been discussed in connection with the reaching agreement phase. It involves either (1) a false demand or offer, or (2)
exaggeration of the importance of an issue to improve one's bargaining
position. This is accomplished by creating the perception that the cost of
compromise to the other side will be high, thereby increasing the mileage
that can be gained from chips the bootstrapper has for concession trading.

Lack of Interest

Lack of interest is frequently used to signal the other side that a proposal must be made more attractive if it is to be considered or accepted.
Actually, it is the reverse of the exaggeration of interest used in bootstrapping; it is yet another way of getting more than one gives in concession
trading. The effort is to stimulate a substantive sweetener (i.e., to get a
bargaining chip) to overcome the demonstrated lack of interest in the original proposal. The play may come before the formal dialogue is joined or
during an ongoing dialogue. In either case, the burden of action is on the
side seeking dialogue or its continuation.

If the proposing side suspects that the lack of interest is a ploy, it can
defend against it by delaying a specific proposal on the basis that the other
side is apparently not interested. If the other side returns to the subject
or otherwise indicates continuing interest, the suspicion is confirmed and
the proposing side should not be inhibited from making or sticking with
the original proposal. If the other side does not react to the defensive
counter and continues to exhibit lack of interest, nothing has been lost by
resorting to the counter; the proposal can always be made more attractive
in accordance with the bargaining needs of the proposing side.

The Silent Treatment and Eliminating the Negative

The silent treatment and eliminating the negative constitute a way of
reacting or responding negatively to proposals made by the other side
while protecting the negotiating relationship. In some cases it may even
enhance bargaining power. For example, the effective negotiator knows
that a delay in response is sometimes interpreted as a rejection by the
impatient and inexperienced negotiator, who may then proceed to im-

prove the proposal by presenting a fallback position. If this proves to be the case, one has gotten a concession without giving. Thus, unless there is a need to (1) grab and "run with a good deal," or (2) reject immediately for effect, it usually pays to remain silent after a proposal is made.

Nothing is lost because one is expected to consider and analyze a proposal carefully before responding. In fact, silence, giving the appearance of such consideration and analysis, is good for the negotiating relationship. It demonstrates a readiness to seriously consider the other side's proposals. If the silence does not produce the desired happy effect, one can always respond on the merits. Thus, the initial rejection by silence is used to give the other side an opportunity to make a mistake. It is very similar to a football quarterback using a long count in a short-yardage situation to get an opposing lineman to jump offside.

The effective negotiator is sensitive to the negotiating cost of continuously rejecting proposals made by the other side. A string of negative reactions can burden the negotiating relationship and may be exploitable by the other side; it may demand some positive evidence that the negotiation is being conducted in good faith. This would amount to an attempt by the other side to "shame" a concession out of the "negative" side for the sake of the negotiating relationship. To avoid this, the effective negotiator tries to reduce the number of consecutive noes; he spaces them out by diverting the dialogue to areas where he can be more forthcoming. Of course, where the strategy is to be hard-line, the cost to the negotiating relationship is of reduced importance and the bargaining table can be covered with noes back-to-back.

The Innocent Question

The innocent question is one of the most widely used tools of negotiation. It can serve many purposes. Its use in probing the other side's position is obvious. Perhaps not as obvious is its use to get an issue on the table that the questioning side does not wish to raise formally (e.g., "Do you think that option A has any possibilities? Let's take a look at it").[32] It may also be used in rhetorical form as a tacit means of conveying a negative response or reaction to a proposal, or at least great difficulty with it: "How could I ever explain that to my principal! What possible rationale could I use?" The other purpose is to probe by causing the other side to "explain" how to present the matter to the principal. The explanation might indicate a line of thinking that suggests a fallback acceptable to the proposing side. Moreover, using a question to prepare the other side for a rejection helps to eliminate negative language from the dialogue (consistent with the concern for reducing the number of noes). Furthermore, the innocent question is not as abrasive as a more direct challenge ("I cannot believe that!") and has the bonus effect of conveying a readiness to listen and hear out the other side, thereby contributing to a good negotiating relationship.

Whipsawing

Whipsawing involves playing off one party against another when both are competing for a transaction with the whipsawer. The sales situation comes quickly to mind as a prime example. Here, either on the buy or sell side, the interest of other parties is used to create apprehension on the part of each to improve the terms of the transaction for the whipsawer. If there actually is multiparty interest, the playing-off process is continued until the resistance point is reached and then the highest bidder gets the deal. In many respects, whipsawing can be said to introduce auction bidding into negotiation through "shopping the deal" with all interested parties. Frequently encountered formulations are: "I can get it cheaper at Jones's"; "I have already turned down an offer for more than that"; or "Jones really wants it."

In a real whipsawing situation (i.e., where there is actual multiparty interest), some of the parties involved in the dialogue are actually being used as unwilling shills by the whipsawer and the play can become very rough. I myself was exposed to some of this in Eastern Europe where competitors were invited for negotiations at the same time and were put up in the same hotel so that all could feel the full pressure of the competition for the deal. In other cases, the greater need of the weaker competitor was exploited by the whipsawer to get an important concession, which was then used to bait the preferred competitor to match the deal. One possible defensive ploy, therefore, is to confront the whipsawer with his lack of good faith and try to "jawbone" him away from the whipsawing play by indicating that it is not in his interest to get the reputation of being one who negotiates this way. This, of course, may have limited effectiveness if (1) the transaction has no continuing-relationship feature, or (2), standard operating procedure involves such whipsawing, which was the case in the former command economies of Eastern Europe.

There is another possible defensive ploy. The side being whipsawed can (1) stress the benefits of concluding the deal with it (e.g., claiming to be a more credit-worthy party or a party with a better reputation for quality performance and trustworthiness) as compared with the other interested parties, and then can (2) try to create apprehension by indicating readiness to walk away from the deal because of the tactics being used. That side can also contact the other known parties to the whipsawing and advise them how they are being used by the whipsawer. This may cause some of them to lose interest in the dialogue; the consequent reduction in number of interested parties may cause the whipsawer to change his tactics for fear of not being able to close a deal with anyone. Apprehension, however, cuts both ways. If the defending side really needs to consummate the transaction, it will be inhibited from objecting to the manner in which the dialogue is being conducted because objection may result in elimination from the group of contenders for the deal.

It is possible to have whipsawing even when there is no interested other party or parties. In such a contrived situation, the party against whom the whipsawing is being used is led to believe that there is other interest as part of the apprehension-creation effort. If that party bites, the whipsawing scenario can be followed. Obviously, if the multiparty interest is contrived, the whipsawer has a vulnerability that can be exploited. He is ploy playing; if he is caught at it, he can be made to pay for his play, usually by an offer from the other side to conclude the dialogue at or below the current state of the bargaining.

The defending side focuses its probing on whether there is actual multiparty interest. The tone of the whipsawer in claiming that interest and his reaction to indications that the defending side does not wish to be involved in this type of dialogue should be carefully scrutinized to determine whether the claimed interest really exists. One can confirm this by threatening to terminate the dialogue. A less exposed approach would be to stand pat and not continue chip play in the face of a claim that a better bargain can be struck with someone else. The worst thing the defending side can do is to "chase the deal." If the whipsawer does not get a chip from the defending side and still continues the dialogue with that side, there probably is no other interested party. One should be especially alert to statements relating to why, despite other interest, the whipsawer wishes to favor the defending side by giving it the deal. Where deal making is involved, being personable, having nice manners, and enjoying the reputation as a good person to deal with are not the usual substitutes for a better offer. That approach should be viewed with the same suspicion as the proverbial free lunch.[33]

Layering

Layering involves the use in hierarchical fashion of negotiators with differing degrees of negotiating authority in an effort to increase bargaining power. It seeks negotiating advantage by exploiting a structured organization with limited bureaucratic authority at various levels. The classic example is the negotiation with a large organization[34] in which each negotiator has a superior with whom additional and "final" authority rests. The game plan in layering is to get the other side to use bargaining chips to alleviate the impasse that develops at each layer as negotiating authority is exhausted. The effort is directed at getting concessions to move up the ladder of authority. When it works, layering provides an excellent means for getting more than a side gives because of the concession mismatch that is created (i.e., the need to give a *substantive* chip for a *procedural* move to the next negotiating level).

Layering is difficult to defend against because the limits of negotiating authority at each level are not readily known. Even when they are known, the usual approach of the layering side is to insist on getting something— at the very least, a demonstrated willingness or commitment to move from the impasse position—to justify involving busy, important superiors in the dialogue. The following scenario is quite typical:

The parties trade concessions and, after much give and take, the layering side's negotiator becomes intractable. After several attempts at obtaining a breakthrough concession from the other side, the negotiator for the layering side admits flat out that the situation is beyond his authority. In response to the request that the negotiation be turned over to a superior with the requisite authority, a demand is made for "something" or "some indication" that progress would result from getting the "very busy" senior official involved.

In this scenario, the layering side hopes to gain disproportionately during the intractability phase and the "bargaining" to get the senior official involved. At the very least, layering provides an excellent opportunity to probe negotiating objectives.

Another difficulty in defending against the layering technique stems from the inequality of the parties and the fact that the pressure for progress (i.e., the burden of negotiation) is usually on the smaller side. The best defense is to adhere to the basic principle that one does not give without getting and, when stiffening is felt on the other side, to stop negotiating in the sense of attempting to work out breakthrough concessions. At that point, the smaller side should use the negotiator for the other side only as a channel of communication to the superior (i.e., negotiating in accordance with the globality principle). In this way, the defending side can continue to work on apprehension, expectations, and uncertainties without wasting bargaining chips. The readiness to explore hypothetical or other possibilities, rather than offers of concessions or other commitments, should be the sweetener used by the defending side to get the superior engaged in the dialogue. If this doesn't work, the defending side may attempt to challenge the layering tactic as dilatory; thereby testing the extent of the larger side's interest in continued dialogue.

In any negotiating involvement with a large, structured organization, the smaller side should be alert to the layering possibility and attempt to defend against it early in the dialogue. Initial discussions with the first negotiator encountered should involve discreet probing of the procedures that will have to be followed in resolving the matter. If it is ascertained that a superior's approval or other involvement is necessary, the point can be made that the superior should participate from the very beginning "to save time for all concerned." This approach may evoke some indications of the limits of the authority of the first negotiator, which will be helpful in determining how far to go in attempting concessions with him. There is a problem, however, in that this approach can cut the other way as well. In demonstrating that he has X authority and therefore can handle the negotiation, the negotiator is working on the expectations of the defending side by indicating that that is the layering side's view of the upper limit of the transaction. To negotiate with this representative would be a tactical error; this is a subtle loaded-agenda situation in which commencement of negotiation with knowledge of the representative's limited authority could be viewed (and, perhaps, later claimed) by the layering side as acquiescence in its view of the value parameters of the deal (i.e., establishment of the haggle zone). In accordance with the dictum that negotiation in the narrow, nonglobal sense of concession trading should be conducted only with those who have authority, the defensive counter should be communication with the representative coupled with a continuing demand to get the superior involved. This defense may enhance the apprehension of the layering side concerning the size of the claim, the expertise of the defending negotiator, or the lack of success (and even counterproductiveness) of the layering technique. The counter to the counter could be a slowdown game on the part of the layering side to smoke out any special need that the defending side may have for quick resolution of the matter.

"Take Me to Your Leader" or "Up the Ladder"

"Take me to your leader" or "Up the ladder" is a tactical variation of layering. In a sense it is a reversal of the layering tactic because it is used as a tool of the smaller side in its effort to cope with the bureaucracy. In regular layering, the smaller, defending side is forced to climb the ladder of authority to achieve its negotiating objectives. In the leader tactic, the ladder of authority is invoked to combat the inertia and timidity of the bureaucracy at the lower levels. It is a very effective tactic to relieve the frustration generated by clerks who easily say "no" because they are unwilling to expend the effort required to get to "yes," do not know how to do it, or are wedded to following the safe, routine course. This bureaucratic lethargy can be jolted by seeking the involvement of supervisors and other higher officials to resolve the situation.

Frequently, it is enough to ask to speak to a clerk's supervisor or the organization's customer-relations office. The career concerns generated by the request tend to provide some motivation to reconsider the ever-ready "no." If not, the next step is to pursue the chain of command until the matter is resolved.

Experience reveals that there is greater solidarity with the "no" at the lower level of organizations. This requires patience in climbing the ladder to the decisional level where career timidity is subordinated to organizational interest in its policy of relationship maintenance with the clientele. The presence of customer-friendship or consumer-relations offices in large organizations indicates the extent of the problem and management's awareness of it. Recognition of the organizational interest in attempting to implement a more friendly, customer-relations approach should encourage use of the "take-me-to-your-leader" tactic to reverse a preliminary, bureaucratic "no." The absence of a designated organizational office for this type of recourse should not deter climbing the ladder. You can build it as you climb!

Baby Steps

Baby steps is a tactic used either at the beginning of a difficult negotiation or at a definitive stage in it when strongly held positions separate the sides. It can be used to convey both positive and negative signals. On the positive side, it can demonstrate the feasibility of, and generate some momentum toward, a negotiated result by reaching consensus on peripheral issues (i.e., to start with baby steps toward final consensus). Some negotiators refer to this as the building-blocks approach. The theory is that a forthcoming attitude on these issues and the consequent movement will have a positive, spillover effect on the difficult issues separating the sides and the overall negotiating relationship.

On the offense, the effort is directed at stimulating some movement toward consensus on the difficult issues or, failing that, at least their identification as such in a position-probing effort. Thus, the effective negotiator using the baby-steps approach seeks to exploit the other side's effort to be forthcoming through reciprocation by seeing if (1) momentum toward consensus can be stimulated, (2) desirable concessions can be picked up cheaply, or (3) the play will serve to improve the probing take. The effectiveness of the tactic depends on the experience level of the defending side.

The defense essentially is to recognize what the other side is up to and attempt to turn the tables by letting that side use its bargaining chips to create the atmosphere of movement (i.e., to give without getting) and, perhaps, divulge its real priorities and needs concerning the issues. In effect, the play is turned off by lack of reciprocation for the chip expenditure, which is enjoyed until the side on offense realizes that desired movement on the difficult issues will not be achieved by expanding "baby" chips.

The use of baby steps as a negative signal takes the form of a dilatory ploy to slow down rather than promote the move toward consensus. In this variation, the intent is to signal, with a view toward perception creation, the onset of tough bargaining or the crunch by reducing the size and frequency of the concessions being made. (See the section on Delaying Action earlier in this chapter.)

Advantage through Characterization

Advantage through characterization is a subtle way of influencing expectations and consequent reactions through self-serving characterization or negative or belittling comment concerning the dialogue. The downside of this ploy is that it may have a negative impact on the negotiating relationship. Nevertheless, the ploy is frequently used to (1) lull the other side into a false sense of security concerning dialogue involvement, or (2) put that side on the defensive with respect to the dialogue.

The classic formulation to convey the impression that a dialogue is non-adversarial (i.e., that is a round-table discussion) is an example of the former because it masks the adversarial reality of the dialogue and the globality principle that all *contacts*[35] potentially involve negotiation. As to its use to put the other side on the defensive, the following examples by negotiating environment convey what is meant: "Let's see if we can dispose of this *minor* matter today." "How much is this? It looks like *old stock.*" "You are being *unfair.*" (private); "The boss will never buy this." "You are being too *legalistic.*" "We do not do things *that way.*" (intraorganizational); "Your position is a *violation* of international law." "You are trying to *exploit* us." "This is an *unequal* arrangement." (international). The side on the offensive seeks to produce an inhibiting reaction (either in the substantive position or the negotiating approach) by creating the perception that the product, service, position, or approach has a defect or reduced value that affects its desirability and, therefore, its negotiability. Some other examples known to professionals who render services include "Doc, take a *peek* at my throat," (not *"examine* my throat") and "Counselor, *scan this document quickly* and give me an *off-the-cuff, horse-back reaction"* (not "your *opinion."*) Again, the purpose is to inhibit any or a full charge for the service requested.

The defense is to ignore the attempt at disparagement and not be inhibited in setting positions or otherwise pursuing the dialogue, including billing in the situations just noted. The defense essentially is to not reward the disparaging side. Of course, if that side persists, account must be taken of the characterization because it may reflect its actual view of the situation; it may not be just a ploy play. If the former is the case, serious consideration should be given to terminating the dialogue, as it probably will not produce an acceptable result. If the defending side is locked into the dialogue by the onus of the burden of negotiation, it can expect a difficult salvage operation.

To conclude, the sampling of tactics and ploys is a necessary part of the training of the would-be negotiator. He should understand their basic elements and purposes. It should be apparent that distracting the negotiator, pressuring persuasion, inhibiting action, enhancing position acceptability and appeal, manipulating perception creation, and maximizing bargaining power and probing are the usual purposes served by tactics and ploys. When they are properly integrated into the negotiating game plan, they can effectively support the overall dialogue management and control effort.

Knowledge of tactics and ploys and their effective integration in the negotiating game plan do not necessarily ensure success. In many situations they will not work to their full potential. Much depends on the skill and experience level of the sides. The most that can be realistically expected from the knowledge and effective use of tactics and ploys is an edge in conducting the dialogue; at the very least, the ability to defend against their use by the other side. Defending against tactics and ploys points up the important nexus between awareness and defense. Awareness is an essential precondition for effective defense because it jumpstarts the effort to initiate defensive or countering action. Timing can make the difference. It certainly contributes to the negotiator's edge, which is what this Guide is all about!

NOTES

1. World Chess Champion Gary Kasparov has observed that "those of us who play chess know that tactics not mated to strategy lead to unintended consequences." ("The Lingering-and-Fatal Gorbachev Illusion," *Wall Street Journal,* January 30, 1991, p. A10.)

2. *Webster's Seventh New Collegiate Dictionary* (Springfield, Mass.: G. & C. Merriam Co., 1967), 652.

3. For example, Dr. Chester L. Karrass identifies twelve major categories: authority tactics, demand and offer tactics, time tactics, decoy tactics, credibility tactics, association tactics, indirect fact-finding tactics, initiative tactics, direct fact-finding tactics, concession tactics, tension relievers, and closing tactics. (Chester L. Karrass, "Negotiation—The Pyramid of Planning," *Government Executive,* October 1977, pp. 15–16, at p. 16.) In the distinction between tactics and ploys, the decoy tactic would appear to be a misnomer because its decoy nature places it in the ploy category.

4. I relish each opportunity to restate the substance-process dichotomy as key to critical understanding and analysis of negotiating situations.

5. Victor H. Pooler, Jr., "Developing the Negotiating Skills of the Buyer," *American Management Association, Management Bulletin #50,* 1964.

6. Henry Fairlie, "An Ambassador Must Be Free To Lie," *Washington Post,* August 19, 1979, p. E8, quoting the well-known quip, "An ambassador is an honest man who is sent to lie abroad for the good of his country."

7. In a *Wall Street Journal* editorial. "Ethicsgate," "ethic absolutism" is stated to be an unrealistic ideal. "The point is that there is a kind of ethic absolutism that no human and no human institution can sustain. It is not necessary to abandon

ethics to recognize that the real world will always be full of cut corners and uneasy compromises." (*Wall Street Journal,* July 15, 1983, p. 18.) Perhaps this is best reflected in our language distinctions concerning degrees of lying. For example, fib is defined as "an inconsequential lie" (*The American Heritage Dictionary,* New College Ed., p. 500); prevarication, "an evasion of the truth" (p. 982); and, of course, white lie, "a diplomatic or well-intentioned untruth" (p. 1379); but, as of this writing, no *fiblet!*

8. One can facetiously argue that a negotiator contemplating retirement offers an increased risk because he may not be deterred by the last two elements of the standard of prudence.

9. There are, of course, limits. For example, Soviets and Romanians frequently exchange kisses when greeting official counterparts. During a ministerial visit that I arranged on behalf of the U.S. government, the enthusiasm of the U.S. counterpart extended the kissing to every encounter, well beyond the usual initial greeting and farewell. The Romanian minister dutifully reciprocated in good form, never betraying his surprise at how affectionate U.S. officials can be.

10. Negotiating is like fishing. Many times the line is thrown out just to see what may be catchable and, especially, who is biting.

11. See Harry T. Edwards and James J. White, *The Lawyer As A Negotiator* (St. Paul, Minn.: West Publishing Co., 1977), 268.

12. It cannot be used as a play to get the other side to forgo bargaining because it has no general credibility as a viable approach to negotiation. The same is not the case with win-win, which is credible and fashionable enough to be exploitable by one of the sides.

13. There are actually two forums, the ongoing relationship and the dialogue itself. If it appears that one side is not practicing win-win, the other side can retaliate by reverting to a more aggressive, pursuit-of-interest approach in both forums.

14. Even the international environment, potentially the most congenial for win-win because of the common interest of nation-states in having a dependable dispute-resolution process as an underpinning of a stable international system, cannot be expected to reflect win-win in political controversies that have traditionally eluded acceptance of constraints on the egoistic pursuit of national interest.

15. The negotiating team is inherently exposure-laden because of the level of group discipline required to protect positions from compromise both at the bargaining table and away from it. The very mechanics of panel team operations contribute to the security problem in preventing position compromise (e.g., notes are passed, whispers are exchanged, and copies of negotiating documents are in the hands of the panel members). The intercept, eavesdropping, and other methods of breaching security procedures are utilized in all environments, with the extent and the methods used being a function of the importance of the negotiation. In all negotiations, careless handling of negotiating documents and information will be exploited. Use of a negotiating panel rather than an individual negotiator facilitates the breaching and exploitational effort of the other side.

16. Included would be RBN (regulation by negotiation) situations in which interested parties are brought into the regulation formulation process. The theory is that the reconciliation of competing interests through negotiation during the formulation process will reduce the amount of controversy and litigation after the regulations are promulgated.

17. In government and corporate bureaucrats, it is known as the short-neck syndrome.

18. According to Karl von Clausewitz, "war is nothing but the continuation of political intercourse, with the admixture of different means." See "Clausewitz, Karl von," *Encyclopedia Britannica* Vol. 5 (1965), pp. 887–888, at p. 888.

19. A more recent example occurred on May 26, 1991, when rebel forces occupied positions around Addis Ababa on the eve of peace talks in London between the Ethiopian government and the rebel forces. (Jennifer Parmelee, "Insurgents Make Gains in Ethiopia," *Washington Post,* May 27, 1991, pp. A1 and A28.)

20. On April 29, 1991, the Supreme Court agreed to decide whether employers can cut wages or change working conditions during contract negotiations. (Stephen Wermiel, "Justices to Decide Whether Employers Can Cut Salaries during Contract Talks," *Wall Street Journal,* April 30, 1991, p. B2.)

21. Another common form is the round-table discussion, which has the connotation of being a nonadversarial forum (because of its side-less table configuration). The formulation is also an example of advantage through characterization.

22. Loading can take the form of seeding with a "lightning rod" to draw attention away from a shaped agenda.

23. This mentality, which can be related to joyful rides on a carousel, is the basis for most telemarketing scams and sting operations.

24. Richard Cohen, "Signals Out of Baghdad," *Washington Post,* January 5, 1991, p. 23.

25. Urban C. Lehner, "Japan Softens on Reaching Pact with Soviets on Disputed Islands," *Wall Street Journal,* March 25, 1991, p. A6.

26. This ploy is usually directed at reducing the perceived value of the other side's asset so that it will take less for it. For example, the shopper in the antique shop delights in pointing out defects or questioning authenticity of an item that, in fact, is highly desired. This is also an example of the advantage-through-characterization ploy: "This piece is a reproduction!"

27. In Eastern Europe, de facto time constraints were exploited in negotiations with foreign negotiators. State trading organizations, working closely with state transportation agencies, were able to orchestrate proposals and reactions with the known scheduled times of departure of the foreign representatives. The state monopoly position in the economy made it possible to achieve the "deadline" effect without the need to develop an agreement. A similar technique is encountered in the bureaucracy when staffing proposals are made with a short, Friday-afternoon response deadline. The action officer ("Charlie Friday") does this to encourage and pressure a quick concurrence by participants who do not relish working over the weekend. To stop continued use of this tactic, participants must combine to complain to their supervisors that Charlie's cheap tactic is not conducive to the orderly staffing of organizational business. If this does not correct the situation, they should be prepared to work several weekends at a *deliberate* pace to show Charlie that the tactic does not work. Deliberate consideration of the action on weekends could reverse the heat on Charlie, who has the ultimate responsibility for staffing a timely organizational response. Turnabout is the fairest of plays!

28. The ploy is sometimes referred to as the "mobilization of shame."

29. Inhibition is another mind-game feature of dialogue management and control. Others include the creation of perceptions, apprehension, and uncertainty,

and the control of expectations, concerning the negotiating situation. A display of lack of interest is another.

30. The discussion approach is an excellent device to get something on the table without the exposure or cost of having to table it formally. The exposure and cost come from being the formal proponent of a proposal.

31. "Few things are more dangerous to a nation than an international reputation for blustering and backing down. Yet that is what the United States has done repeatedly in the Middle East, as well as in Central America." (Thomas Sowell, "The Panama Predicament," *San Juan Star,* December 29, 1989, p. 20.)

32. The counter to all efforts to get issues on the table without formally tabling them is dialogue avoidance. It takes two to have a dialogue, and whenever it takes two, both have vetoes over the situation.

33. The observation that "there is no such thing as a free lunch" is stated to be a "universal truth." (Thomas L. Koziol, "Fishing by Phone; Telemarketing Scams," *The Retired Officers Magazine,* February 1991, pp. 45–48, at p. 48.)

34. Layering was frequently encountered in the negotiation of foreign trade transactions with the state trading organizations of the socialist countries before the Gorbachev-inspired reforms led to direct end-user involvement in such negotiations.

35. Under the universality principle, all *dialogues* are potentially negotiation, depending on the existence of an interest dimension.

The Closer

The competitive, "negotiation-is-everywhere" reality of human relationships suggests the need for a user-friendly, how-to guide devoted to negotiation. This Guide attempts to fill that niche by elaborating a single approach to negotiation that is effective in the private, intraorganizational, and international environments, which constitute the principal negotiating arenas. Furthermore, it includes the operational concept of dialogue recognition, management, and control. This extends the application of negotiation concepts and techniques to any situation involving dialogue with an interest or competitive implication. The result is an approach that enhances the handling of all situations implied by the universality, "everywhere" principle.

This Guide is about effective negotiation, a concept and technique that permits the realization of interest-oriented objectives in formal and informal dialogues. The ability to cope with these dialogues is an important factor in the quality of our professional and personal lives. It behooves all of us, from professional negotiator to individual trying to cope with life's dialogues, to become familiar with the negotiation process and how it can be utilized in the pursuit of interest.

Effective negotiators are not born; they are the product of focused training and application. This Guide serves as a handbook to convey an understanding of the negotiation process and the "think-negotiation" mindset, the essential elements of effective negotiation. The text includes many examples to broaden the experience base of the would-be negotiator. This permits clearer understanding of process and mindset; it allows the would-be negotiator to draw upon prior experience not formally associated with, but now understood to be relevant to, negotiation. Readers soon become believers because the Guide's approach is simple and it works. Doubters prefer to memorize a list of the basic rules and principles of negotiation rather than delve into, and understand, why negotiation is a mind game. This Guide exhorts a more analytical, reasoned approach: development of understanding and skills related to dialogue recognition, management, and control. It suggests, too, that reason usually prevails.

Selected Bibliography

Baer, Harold, and Broder, Aaron J. *How to Prepare and Negotiate Cases for Settlement.* Englewood Cliffs, N.J.: Prentice Hall, 1967.

Bailey, Thomas A. *The Art of Diplomacy.* New York: Appleton, Century and Crofts, 1968.

Bartos, Otomar J. *Process and Outcome of Negotiations.* New York: Columbia University Press, 1973.

Bastress, Robert M., and Harbaugh, Joseph D. *Interviewing, Counseling, and Negotiating Skills for Effective Representation.* Boston, Toronto, and London: Little, Brown and Co., 1990.

Bellow, Gary, and Moulton, Bea. *The Lawyering Process: Negotiation.* Mineola, N.Y.: Foundation Press, 1981.

Buckmann, Neal W. *Negotiations: Principles and Techniques.* Lexington, Mass.: Lexington Books, 1977.

Calero, Henry H. *Winning the Negotiation.* New York: Hawthorne Books, 1979.

Charell, Ralph. *How to Get the Upper Hand.* Briarcliff Manor, N.Y.: Stein and Day, 1979.

Coffin, Royce A. *The Negotiator: A Manual for Winners.* New York: AMACOM, 1973.

Cohen, Herb. *You Can Negotiate Anything.* Secaucus, N.J.: Lyle Stuart, 1981.

Colosi, Thomas R., and Berkeley, Arthur E. *The Negotiating Table: Bridging Troubled Waters.* Washington, D.C.: American Arbitration Association, 1982.

Dawson, Roger. *You Can Get Anything You Want, But You Have to Do More Than Ask.* New York: Simon and Schuster, 1989.

Druckman, Daniel, ed. *Negotiations: Social-Psychological Perspectives.* Beverly Hills: Sage Publications, 1977.

Edwards, Harry T., and White, James J. *Problems, Readings and Materials on the Lawyer as a Negotiator.* St. Paul, Minn.: West Publishing, 1977.

Fisher, Roger, and Ury, William. *Getting to Yes: Negotiating Agreement without Giving in.* Boston: Houghton Mifflin, 1981.

Gifford, Donald G. *Legal Negotiation: Theory and Applications.* St. Paul, Minn.: West Publishing, 1989.

Hoffman, Tony. *How to Negotiate Successfully in Real Estate.* New York: Simon and Schuster, 1984.

Ikle, Fred C. *How Nations Negotiate.* New York: Harper & Row, 1964.

Ilich, John. *Power Negotiating: Key Strategies and Techniques to Help You Get What You Want.* Reading, Mass.: Addison-Wesley, 1979.

Ilich, John, and Jones, Barbara Schindler. *Successful Negotiating Skills for Women.* Reading, Mass.: Addison-Wesley, 1980.

Jandt, Fred Edmund. *Win-Win Negotiating: Turning Conflict into Agreement.* New York: John Wiley, 1985.

Joy, C. Turner. *How Communists Negotiate.* New York: McMillan, 1955.

Karrass, Chester L. *The Negotiating Game.* New York: World Publishing, 1970.

———. *Give and Take: The Complete Guide to Negotiating Strategies and Tactics.* New York: Thomas Y. Crowell, 1974.

Kaufman, Johan. *Conference Diplomacy.* Dobbs Ferry, N.Y.: Oceana Publications, 1980.

Lall, Arthur. *Modern International Negotiation: Principles and Practices.* New York: Columbia University Press, 1966.

Leritz, Len. *No-Fault Negotiating—A Practical Guide to the New Dealmaking Strategy That Lets Both Sides Win.* New York: Warner Books, 1990.

Machiavelli, Niccolo. *The Prince,* Classic Ed. Toronto, New York, London, Sydney: Bantam Books, 1981.

Nelken, Melissa L., and Schoenfield, Mark K. *Problems and Cases in Interviewing, Counseling and Negotiation.* Minneapolis: National Institute for Trial Advocacy, 1983.

Nicholson, Harold. *Diplomacy.* New York: Oxford University Press, 1981.

Nierenberg, Gerald I. *Fundamentals of Negotiating.* New York: Hawthorne Books, 1973.

———. *The Art of Negotiating.* New York: Simon and Schuster, 1981.

———. *The Complete Negotiator.* New York: Nierenberg and Zeif Publishers, 1986.

Nierenberg, Juliet, and Ross, Irene S. *Women and the Art of Negotiating.* New York: Simon and Schuster, 1985.

Raiffa, Howard. *The Art and Science of Negotiation.* Cambridge, Mass.: Harvard University Press, 1983.

Rubin, Jeffrey Z., and Brown, Bert R. *The Social Psychology of Bargaining and Negotiation.* New York, San Francisco, London: Academic Press, 1975.

Schelling, Thomas. *The Strategy of Conflict.* Cambridge, Mass.: Harvard University Press, 1960.

Scott, W. P. *The Skills of Negotiating.* New York: John Wiley, 1981.

Senate Committee on Foreign Affairs. *Soviet Diplomacy and Negotiating Behavior.* Washington, D.C.: Government Printing Office, 1979.

Senate Committee on Government Operations. *Negotiation and Statecraft.* Washington, D.C.: Government Printing Office, 1970.

Warschaw, Tessa A. *Winning by Negotiation.* New York: McGraw-Hill, 1980.

Williams, Gerald R. *Legal Negotiation and Settlement.* St. Paul, Minn.: West Publishing, 1983.

Zartman, William I. *The 50% Solution: How to Bargain Successfully with . . . in This Modern World.* Garden City, N.Y.: Anchor Press, 1976.
Zartman, William I., and Berman, Maureen. *The Practical Negotiator.* New Haven: Yale University Press, 1982.

Index

About the Author

BERNARD A. RAMUNDO is a practitioner-specialist on negotiations and negotiation technique who offers a full range of negotiation services including training, consultation, and representation. During his more than 42 years of military and civil federal service, Dr. Ramundo represented the United States in international negotiations. From 1963 to 1990, he was a professorial lecturer at the National Law Center, George Washington University, where he pioneered and taught a course on negotiation concepts and techniques and one on Soviet law.

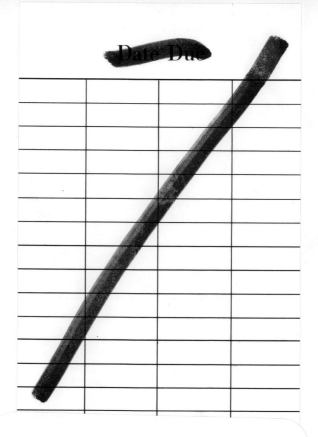